Cavendish
Publishing
Limited

CIVIL LITIGATION

J Clore

London Guildhall-Cavendish
Legal Practice Course Companion Series

LONDON GUILDHALL
UNITY
UNIVERSITY

First published in Great Britain 1993 by Cavendish Publishing Limited, 23A Countess Road, London NW5 2XH.

Telephone: 071-485 0303 Facsimile: 071-485 0304

British Library Cataloguing in Publication Data

Clore, J
Civil Litigation - (LPC Series)
I Title II Series
344.2075

ISBN 1-874241-96-1
Printed and bound in Great Britain

Outline contents

Contents

Table of cases

Table of statutes

Chapter 1

Introduction to civil litigation

The LPC Civil Litigation, Evidence and Advocacy course

1.1

This section of the Legal Practice Course deals with the process of a civil legal dispute.

If A has a civil dispute with B, how can A sue B? What are the procedures, skills, laws and principles involved in a court case? Alternatively, how can the dispute be settled without a court case? The LPC Civil Litigation, Evidence and Advocacy course deals with all of these matters.

This companion explains the main practice and procedures, laws and principles of a civil court case, and also how a dispute can be settled without a court case. The Evidence companion deals with the principles of evidence which are relevant to a civil case (as well as dealing with principles of evidence in criminal cases).

Authority for the rules on civil litigation

1.2

This companion explains the main procedures for fighting a case in the High Court and County Court. In fact, there are several hundred rules governing all aspects of High Court and county court procedure.

High Court procedure

1.2.1

High Court procedure is governed by the Rules of the Supreme Court which are set out in a huge two-volume work entitled the *Supreme Court Practice*. It is referred to by judges and practitioners as the *White Book*. The *White Book* is divided into (at present) 114 sections, referred to as 'orders' (because the rules are technically orders made by the court).

Each order sets out the rules for a particular aspect of litigation procedure. For example, O.6 sets out the rules on how to issue a writ commencing proceedings. There are several rules within each order; so the rules for issuing a writ, for example, are referred to as O.6 r.1, O.6 r.2 etc.

The orders are supplemented by notes in the *White Book* which explain the rules and summarise any case law interpreting the rules. (There is much case law on procedure.) Furthermore, the court occasionally issues 'practice directions' on how a particular aspect of procedure is to be carried out. These practice directions are printed in the notes to the relevant order. Litigators are not expected to know the rules off by heart, but continually refer to the *White Book* for instructions on how to carry out litigation procedure.

Note

The first volume of the *White Book* contains all the orders. The second volume contains various practice directions, examples of forms, special rules and many statutes relevant to procedure. A new edition of the *White Book* is published every two years. A regular supplement to the *White Book* is published, updating the material, ie. showing new rules, practice directions and cases which have appeared since the last edition was published.

1.2.2 County Court procedure

County Court procedure is governed by the County Court rules and the County Courts Act 1984. These are set out in the County Court practice, which is known as the *Green Book*. This is the County Court equivalent of the High Court's *White Book*.

The County Court rules are divided into orders containing the rules for each aspect of procedure, in the same way as the supreme court rules, and are supplemented by practice directions, case law and notes. The County Courts Act 1984 also contains important provisions on procedure.

The *Green Book* also contains examples of forms, tables summarising procedure, special rules, and statutes relevant to procedure.

The *Green Book* is published annually. There is no *regular* updating supplement but a supplement may be issued when important new rules are made.

1.3 Litigation forms and documents

There are many standard forms and documents used in civil litigation. Firms will have their own stock of standard forms (which are published by legal stationers) and will have their own system for producing certain standard documents, eg. pleadings and affidavits.

The *White Book* and *Green Book* contain examples (known as 'precedents') of most standard forms and affidavits. There are also many books available which show examples of standard forms and affidavits, and how to fill in/draft forms, affidavits and pleadings.

Civil litigation procedure outlined   1.4

The pre-action stage   1.4.1

The client comes to you with their problem. You should:

- First deal with and advise on the costs of the litigation. How will they pay? They may pay privately, by legal aid, through the financial support of some organisation, eg. their trade union, by having legal expenses insurance, or by contingency fees, ie. they only pay if they win (this is only permissible in certain limited cases, including personal injury).
- If the client is to apply for legal aid, fill in the relevant forms.
- Obtain the facts and evidence from the client.
- Advise on the merits, procedure and costs. (In particular, the loser of the case will pay much of the winner's costs.)
- Obtain and investigate evidence from various witnesses and third parties.
- Instruct an expert to prepare expert evidence, where relevant.
- Instruct counsel to advise, where appropriate.
- Correspond and negotiate with the other side.
- Consider various methods of solving the dispute other than by litigation.
- Fully investigate the evidence and the merits of the case and decide what course of action to pursue.

Pre-action court orders   1.4.2

In some cases, it may be relevant to apply to court, even before full proceedings are commenced, for one or more of the following:

- An emergency injunction to prevent certain action by the other party.
- An emergency injunction freezing the other party's assets so that they cannot dispose of their property and thereby render any judgment futile. (This is known as a *Mareva injunction*.)
- An emergency injunction allowing search of the other party's property and seizure of relevant goods. (This is known as an *Anton Piller* order.) It is often used in breach of copyright cases.
- An order allowing pre-action inspection of documents or property in the possession of the proposed defendant or a third party.

1.4.3   Commencing proceedings

Once you and the client have decided that the evidence and merits of the case justify commencing proceedings, and negotiations have not resolved the matter, civil proceedings should be commenced.

Before commencing proceedings, you should:

● Write a letter before action to the proposed defendant, threatening proceedings.

Note

Throughout this book, references to steps to be taken by and against the plaintiff and defendant really refer to their solicitor, where they have a solicitor acting for them. For example, the letter referred to here is written to the solicitor acting for the proposed defendant.

● Check that you are within the limitation period for commencing proceedings.

● Decide whether to commence proceedings in the High Court or County Court. There are rules governing the choice of court. Essentially, it depends on the value of the claim.

High Court proceedings are commenced by issuing a *writ* or *originating summons* (depending on the type of action).

County Court proceedings are commenced by issuing a *summons* or *originating application* (depending on the type of action).

The writ/summons/application is then *served* on the defendant within four months after being issued.

Note

In the High Court, the plaintiff serves the writ. In the County Court, the *court* usually serves the summons because, except in personal injury cases, only the court can serve *by post*, which is the usual method of service.

In the *High Court* only, the defendant must, within 14 days of being served with the writ/originating summons, send to the court an *acknowledgement of service* form, stating whether they intend to defend the proceedings. If they do not do so, or do not state that they intend to defend, the plaintiff can enter *judgment in default* and thereby win the case.

In the *County Court*, the defendant must, within 14 days of service of a summons, deliver to the court an *admission, defence or counterclaim*. If they do not do so, the plaintiff can enter *judgment in default*.

From commencement of proceedings to trial   1.4.4

The pleadings stage

Shortly after commencement of proceedings, the parties serve on each other documents setting out the details of their cases. The trial is then based upon the allegations made in these documents. These documents are known as 'pleadings'.

First, the *plaintiff* serves on the defendant the details of their claim. In the High Court, this is known as the *statement of claim*. In the County Court, it is known as the *particulars of claim*. The High Court statement of claim is served with the writ or separately, within 14 days after the defendant has acknowledged service of the writ.

The County Court particulars of claim is served *with the summons* commencing proceedings.

Within 14 days of being served with the statement or particulars of claim, the *defendant* then serves on the plaintiff their *defence*, giving details of their defence to the claim.

Note

There may be further pleadings; the defendant may serve a *counterclaim* with their defence, bringing their own claim against the plaintiff. The plaintiff may serve a *reply* to the defendant's defence, responding to the points in the defence. The plaintiff will also serve a defence to the defendant's counterclaim.

Shortly after the last pleading is served, pleadings are said to be 'closed'. The date of 'close of pleadings' is important because the subsequent litigation procedure takes its starting point from that date.

Note

The defendant may consider that someone else is to blame. For example, a defendant supplier being sued for supplying defective goods may consider that the manufacturer is to blame. In such a case, the defendant may turn round and sue the manufacturer by issuing a *third party notice* against the manufacturer. The action between the plaintiff and defendant, and between the defendant and third party, will then all be heard in the same proceedings.

From pleadings to trial

The directions stage There is a very long time gap (of months or years) between close of pleadings and trial. After the date of close of pleadings, the court gives *directions* for the future conduct of the case, ie. the court lays down what future procedural steps are to be taken in the action and a timetable for those steps.

The 'directions' or 'directions stage' therefore refers to the timetabled procedural steps which take place from close of pleadings until trial.

In *High Court personal injury cases* and in *most County Court cases* there are *automatic directions*, in other words, court rules lay down the steps, and their timetable, that are to take place in every case.

In all other cases the directions are not automatic but have to be laid down at a preliminary court hearing. This court hearing is known as a 'directions' hearing in the High Court, and a 'pre-trial review' in the County Court.

Whether the directions are automatic or ordered by the court, the following are the usual procedural steps that are ordered to take place from close of pleadings until trial.

1 *Discovery and inspection* Within 14 days after close of pleadings, the parties disclose to each other a list of all documents that they have that are relevant to the dispute. This process is known as 'discovery'.

Within seven days thereafter, the parties inspect each other's documents.

2 *Exchange of expert reports* Within a certain number of weeks after discovery and inspection, the parties exchange the reports written by their expert witnesses on any specialist matters in dispute.

Note

The directions also state how many expert witnesses are allowed on each side.

3 *Exchange of witness statements* Within a certain number of weeks after discovery and inspection, the parties exchange the written statements of their *factual* (as opposed to expert) witnesses, ie. the details of what those witnesses are going to say at trial.

4 *Setting down for trial (High Court) or requesting a date for trial (County Court)* 'Setting down for trial' is the High Court procedure by which the Court is informed that the case is ready for trial and can be inserted in the list of cases for trial.

In the County Court, 'setting down' does not apply, you merely request the court to fix a date for trial.

The directions normally provide that the case must be set down, or a trial date requested, within six months of close of pleadings (or of the directions hearing, if there is one). On setting down a case in the High Court, bundles of main documents must be given to the court.

5 *Other directions* There are other minor directions, eg. photos, plans and the police accident report (where relevant) are to be agreed and exchanged.

Interlocutory applications The gap between commencement of proceedings and trial is known as the *interlocutory* (interim) period.

During this period, the parties make various applications to the court for various orders. The applications may range from small procedural applications to more important ones. The applications are heard in short court hearings – they are usually heard not in open court by a judge but in private rooms by a *Master* (High Court) or *District Judge* (County Court). (A Master or District Judge is, in effect, a junior judge who hears these pre-trial applications. The private rooms are known as *chambers.*)

A party applies for an interlocutory hearing by issuing a *summons* (High Court) or *notice of application* (County Court). The summons or application is then served on the other side, notifying them of the hearing. The hearing then takes place within a few days or months, depending on the nature of the application.

At the hearing, evidence is not normally given orally but in the form of *affidavits*, ie. sworn written statements. The parties serve their affidavits on each other before the hearing.

The above procedure applies to an interlocutory application attended by both parties, which is normal. This is known as an '*inter partes*' application. However, in some urgent cases, due to the need for speed or surprise, the other side is not notified of the hearing; only one side attends to ask for a court order. This is known as an '*ex parte*' application.

There are a huge number of possible interlocutory applications that could be made, depending on the nature of the case, the particular problem and the decision of a party to make a particular application. However, the following are typical interlocutory applications that may be made during the proceedings:

An application for:

- Leave, ie. permission, to amend a writ or pleading.
- The other side to provide 'further and better particulars' of their pleading, ie. more details of their case.
- Disclosure by the other side of specific documents where it is believed they are being withheld.
- An order allowing an extension of time for carrying out a procedure.

- An order that unless the other side carries out a procedure within a certain time, eg. discloses a document, their case be struck out. This is known as an 'unless order'.

- The setting aside of a judgment entered in default of acknowledgement of service or in default of a defence.

- *Summary judgment* This is an important common application whereby the plaintiff can apply at an early stage of the proceedings for early judgment without a trial on the basis that the defendant has absolutely no defence to the claim.

- *An interlocutory injunction* This is another important common application, made by plaintiffs who are claiming an injunction. Due to the long time gap between commencement of proceedings and trial, a plaintiff obviously cannot wait until trial for an injunction to be granted. The plaintiff therefore applies for an interlocutory (interim) injunction to last from commencement of proceedings until trial.

- *Interim payments* In many cases, a plaintiff cannot wait until trial to receive damages. They need some compensation more quickly, eg. to pay for medical treatment. In such cases, the plaintiff can apply for early payment of some of the likely damages at a stage long before trial.

- *Security for costs* A defendant can apply at an early stage in the proceedings for the plaintiff to give some security to show that they will be able to pay the defendant's costs of the proceedings if the defendant finally wins. The plaintiff may be required to pay a proportion of the likely costs into court, pending the trial.

- *Striking out for want of prosecution* The defendant may apply to strike out the plaintiff's case on the grounds that the plaintiff has taken too long to proceed with the case after commencing proceedings. In the County Court, this procedure is rarely used, because *the court* automatically strikes out a case where a trial date is not requested within a certain time limit.

Negotiation and general case preparation
During this long time period between close of pleadings and trial, while the parties are complying with the directions, they will also usually try to negotiate a settlement and will be generally preparing their cases, investigating the evidence and investigating and trying to destroy the other side's case and evidence. There will be much correspondence between the parties and with witnesses.

There are in fact, two formal procedures that are used to attempt to force a settlement:

- *Payment into court* A common tactic is that a defendant will, under a formal procedure, pay into the court office the amount of damages for which they think they will be liable. If the plaintiff does not accept this amount in settlement of the case and is not awarded a greater amount at trial, the plaintiff will be ordered to pay the defendant's costs of the proceedings (and their own) from the date the money was paid in. This is despite the fact that the plaintiff has won the case.

- *A Calderbank letter* This is the equivalent of the payment into court procedure where the claim is for something other than money, eg. for an injunction. In such cases, the defendant can make an offer in settlement of the case by letter. If the plaintiff unreasonably rejects the offer, they may be ordered to pay the subsequent costs of the proceedings.

Throughout the case, you will continue to advise the client, investigate the evidence and take the advice of counsel. You may serve various documents, for example:

- Interrogatories (written questions about their case);

- Notice to admit facts (if they do not admit specified facts they will have to pay the costs of you successfully proving these facts);

- Notice of intention to adduce hearsay evidence at trial.

As the trial gets closer, you will have to:

- Prepare bundles of documents for trial;

- Notify all witnesses;

- Brief counsel to attend the trial.

Trial 1.4.5

At trial, witnesses are examined and cross-examined, and the parties make their submissions. Various principles of evidence apply.

At the end of the trial, the judge gives judgment (or may reserve judgment until a later date).

Costs orders 1.4.6

At the end of the trial, the judge will make orders as to who is to pay the costs of the case. Usually, the loser is ordered the pay the winner's costs.

However, the loser is not liable to pay *all* of the winner's costs, only a *reasonable* amount. What is a reasonable amount will be decided at a *taxation* hearing (*see* 1.4.9). The winner will have to pay the balance of their costs themselves.

Also, in the County Court the amount of costs the loser has to pay to the winner is governed not only by what is reasonable but also by *scales* of amounts of costs which are recoverable.

Note

At the end of each interlocutory application, the court will have made an order as to who is to pay the costs of *that* application, as opposed to the costs of the entire proceedings.

1.4.7   Appeal

A party may appeal against a judgment to the Court of Appeal.

1.4.8   Enforcement of judgments

Even if a judgment has been given in your favour, you still need to enforce it, ie. obtain the damages from the other side or to ensure they comply with an injunction.

A money judgment can be enforced against the defendant in various ways, for example by:

- Seizing and selling their goods;
- Taking money from their bank account;
- Imposing a charge on their land;
- Deducting money from their wages;
- Commencing insolvency proceedings.

All of these involve applications to the court.

If an injunction is breached, you can apply to have the defendant committed to prison for contempt of court.

1.4.9   Taxation

The loser is usually ordered to pay a reasonable amount of the winner's costs of the litigation. However, if the parties cannot agree on what is a reasonable amount, the matter will be decided by a Master (High Court) or District Judge (County Court) at a taxation hearing. (This has nothing to do with the ordinary meaning of the word 'taxation'.)

If a party is legally-aided, this taxation hearing will also decide how much the Legal Aid Board should pay to the legally-aided party's solicitor.

Pre-action stage

May be pre-action emergency injunction, *Mareva* injunction or search and seizure order (*Anton Piller*)

Obtain legal aid where relevant, interview, advise correspond, investigate case obtain evidence, pre-action inspection and discovery, instruct expert and obtain report, negotiate

Choice of court

Issue writ or County Court summons
(within limitation period)

Service of HCt writ or CC summons

(within 4 months)

In High Court acknowledgement of service within 14 days (Judgment in default if no acknowledgement.)

and particulars of claim in County Court

In County Court particulars of claim served with summons.

High Court statement of claim served

May be counterclaim and/or reply and defence to counterclaim and/or request for further and better particulars.

Defence

May be third party notice.

Close of pleadings

Directions stage

Discovery and inspection

Exchange of experts' reports

Exchange of witness statements

Other directions

May be interlocutory applications, eg. for:
- Summary judgment
- Interim payments
- Interlocutory injunction
- Security for costs
- Specific discovery.

Judgment in default if defence not served.

High Court Action set down for trial

There may also be procedures such as payment into court and service of interrogatories.

County Court Request to fix hearing date

Prepare trial bundles.

Trial

Appeal

Costs orders

Enforcement of judgment

Taxation

Main stages of civil procedure

Self-assessment questions

1 Prepare notes which you can use to describe the civil litigation process in outline to a colleague in your tutorial group.

2 What does RSC O.10 r.1 state? Where would you quickly find notes to this rule and a summary of cases interpreting this rule?

3 Which order in the *White Book* sets out the procedural rules on applications for judicial review?

4 What are practice directions and where will you find them set out in the *White Book*?

5 What matters are contained in volume 2, *White Book*?

6 Where will you find reference to High Court procedural rule changes and cases which have appeared since publication of the most recent edition of the *White Book*?

7 What does CCR O.7 r.1 say?

8 Which order in the County Court rules sets out the procedure for 'summary proceedings for the recovery of land or rent'?

9 Briefly outline the contents of the *Green Book*.

Chapter 2

Preliminary preparation

The first interview with the client

2.1

The pre-interview stage

2.1.1

The client may phone up or come into the office 'out of the blue'; or they may be introduced or write to you. Alternatively, they may be an established or previous client who contacts you or the office with their problem.

In most cases, a first meeting should be arranged. Although some clients may think a meeting is unnecessary, it is unwise not to begin with a face-to-face meeting.

Some cases may be urgent. For example, the client:

- May require an urgent injunction;
- May already have an injunction or judgment given against them which they want set aside; or
- May have an imminent court hearing.

Such cases will have to be dealt with at very short notice.

It is good practice – and standard procedure for many firms – to send a letter to the client before the interview confirming the interview and explaining certain matters, eg. explaining the very basic relevant law, asking the client to bring all relevant documents and explaining the firm's charges. Many firms, for example specialist personal injury firms, send a standard questionnaire on the case. The first letter must also explain the firm's complaints procedure.

If you know what the case is about before the interview, and/or have some documents relating to the case, you should prepare by researching the law in the area and reading the documents.

You should prepare for the interview by planning the length and structure of the interview and the questions you wish to ask. In many large firms, you will need to book a meeting room and refreshments.

Note

In practice, in many firms, the articled clerk's role will be to take notes at the interview.

The interview

2.1.2

You should begin by welcoming the client and making them feel comfortable and at ease, as far as is possible. Then proceed to the following.

Personal details
- Name;
- Address;
- Work and home phone number;
- Date of birth;
- Whether they live alone or with a partner (if relevant);
- Employment details (firms will have different standard procedures on this).

Costs
You must explain and deal with the question of how your costs will be paid. The client may:
- Pay privately;
- Pay by legal aid;
- Have their costs paid by a body to which they belong, eg. a trade union, or by some other interested body;
- Pay by having legal expenses insurance;
- Agree to pay a contingency fee (*see* below: this is not yet permitted).

Note

There is a system known as ALAS (Accident Legal Advice Service) under which certain personal injury firms give a free first interview.

If the client is to pay *privately*, under professional conduct rules, you must advise the client of certain cost matters at this stage. (These are explained in Chapter 3.) In particular you should give the best information possible about the likely cost of the matter and the hourly rate of the person(s) who will deal with the case. You can ask for an immediate payment 'on account'; this is an advance payment in respect of initial costs.

Advise the client at this stage:
- That they will be personally responsible for payment of your bill in full, regardless of any order for costs made against their opponent;
- Of the probability that if they lose they will have to pay their opponent's costs as well as their own;
- That even if they win, their opponent may not be ordered to pay the full amount of the client's own costs and may not be capable of paying what they have been ordered to pay.

Is the client eligible for *legal aid*? If they are, you will have to follow the *green form* and legal aid procedures set out in Chapter 4. The initial interview and initial work cannot exceed two hours' worth of work, although you can obtain an extension.

The green form is generally filled out at the interview as is the full legal aid application generally, although the client may take away the financial details part of the form (and the employment details form for their employer) to fill in and send back. (This is all explained in Chapter 4.)

If the client is legally aided, you should advise them at this stage:

- Of the effect of the statutory charge on their case;
- That if they lose the case they may still be ordered by the court to contribute to their opponent's costs even though their own costs are covered by legal aid;
- Of their obligation to pay any contribution assessed and of the consequences of any failure to do so.

What's the problem?
Ask the client to give full details of their problem. You should allow them to tell the full story, in their own way, rather than imposing your own structure or eliciting the story through questioning. This will allow the real and full situation and the client's worries to come across; also, you can begin to assess what sort of witness the client would be in court.

The client may go on at length, or the story may not be told coherently, and the client may give much irrelevant material. Nevertheless, you should allow the full story to be told at this stage. (You could tactfully remind the client of the time and cost restraints.)

During the telling of the story and afterwards, ask questions to clarify points or to elicit further relevant information.

When listening to the client, listen out for what the real problem is and what the client really wants. Also listen out for any problems which the client may be trying to hide.

In general, elicit the following specific information from the client:

- Details of the essential events, eg. the contract, the breach, the nuisance, the accident, as the case may be. In personal injury cases, it is useful to ask for a sketch plan or photographs of the situation;
- All relevant dates, names, times and places; (Check whether the limitation period is close or has expired.)
- Full and specific details of the financial and non-financial losses suffered by the client;
- Names and addresses of all witnesses, including any experts, eg. engineers, doctors involved;

- Look at documentation the client has with them;
- The remedy and course of action that the client wishes to pursue;
- Any points against the client's case.

Interview notes

Be sure to take a full note of the interview. This should, during the interview or afterwards, be written up into the form of a statement by the client. It should be given or sent to the client for approval and signing by them.

Note _____

Later on in the litigation, you will have to take an even fuller 'witness statement' from them. This is a formal statement served on the other side and used at trial (*see* Chapter 17).

Preliminary advice

This will necessarily be general and limited at this stage. Advise them in plain language on the law, the merits of their case, the possible remedies, the approximate amount of damages they might obtain (and compare this with the cost involved), the options open to the client, how long the proceedings will take and the procedures involved.

Note _____

You may particularly need to explain any of the following procedures: emergency, *Mareva* or interlocutory injunctions; third party proceedings; discovery and inspection; the need to obtain and prepare expert evidence: summary judgment; interim payments; and payment into court.

Discuss negotiation and settlement possibilities.

Explain and agree with the client the next steps to be taken. This may include agreeing a further meeting and confirming the further information that is needed from the client. Also, explain who in the office will have supervision of the case and who will have day-to-day conduct of the case and that the latter person is their contact and will keep them informed of events.

2.1.3   **After the interview**

You should:

- Put your notes into a coherent, comprehensible form;
- Write an attendance note of the meeting (*see* below);
- Draft a client statement to be sent to the client for approval and signing (if that was not done at the interview);
- Open a file, if not already opened (*see* below);

- Write to the client confirming
  - your advice
  - the decisions taken in the meeting
  - the next steps to be taken
  - an estimate of your likely costs and any costs limit or initial costs limit agreed, perhaps asking for money on account
  - the further information needed (and perhaps enclosing the client's statement for approval).

Personal injury cases   2.1.4

Specific initial advice and questioning is required in personal injury cases.

Advise the client on the benefits they may be entitled to. Advise them to enquire at and apply to their local DSS office.

Ask the client to fill in standard forms, consenting to disclosure of their medical records and disclosure of their employment details by their employer.

Ask them to give details of, and bring documentation relating to, the following (this is often done by giving them a standard questionnaire):

- Their gross and net earnings, including overtime – they should bring wage slips;
- Dates of periods off work, and details as to their future employment prospects;
- Details, plans and photos of the accident;
- Name and addresses of witnesses;
- Details of injuries (including medical reports), any relevant prior conditions, and details of activities they are now unable to carry out, and any effect on their mental condition;
- Name and address of GP and hospital where they were treated (and their hospital record number);
- National Insurance Number, tax office and reference number;
- Address of local DSS office;
- Details of welfare benefits and statutory sick pay received;
- Details of other expenses incurred, eg. prescription charges, travel expenses, lost clothing, help at home;
- If an accident *at work*, details of workplace; work process and equipment, other employees, managers, foreman, shop steward, safety representative, training and cloth-

ing given, details of previous accidents and complaints, reports and memoranda on the accident (entry in accident book or factory inspection after the accident?);

- If a *driving accident*, name and address of driver responsible and their insurers, details of owner, registration number and make of vehicles involved, your client's insurance details, were seat belts worn, damage to vehicle, cost of repair and other expenses, police station involved, prosecution(?);

- Future continuing expenses.

Note

There will be variations and additions to the above depending on the case and the firm's standard form of questioning.

2.2   Litigation file

2.2.1   Opening and structuring

At the beginning of the case, a file should be opened. The documents in the file should be maintained in a logical and efficient order.

Each firm will have its own standard filing system and layout but a litigation file will generally be structured as follows.

Cover

This will show the:

- Client's name;
- Address and phone number;
- Name of the case and reference number;
- Partner/fee earner dealing with the case; and
- Date of opening the file.

Inside the front cover

Here firms keep a standard form list of important events in the case with a space for their date to be inserted. For example:

- Expiry of limitation period;
- Date of legal aid and period for which it was granted (if applicable);
- Issue of proceedings;
- Service of proceedings;
- Acknowledgement of service (High Court only);
- Service of statement/particulars of claim;

- Service of defence;
- Close of pleadings;
- Discovery;
- Exchange of expert evidence;
- Exchange of witness statements;
- Setting case down (High Court) or requesting of date for hearing (County Court);
- Date when County Court will automatically strike out case if no hearing date requested;
- Trial date;
- Lodging of documents at court before trial;
- Payment into court;
- Case settled;
- File closed.

The list acts as a diary system so that important dates are not missed.

Costs and time
Records of costs and time spent on the case, bills and barristers' fee notes are often kept in a holder at the front of the file.

Sections
The file is then divided into sections:

- Correspondence between the parties (known as 'party and party' correspondence);
- Correspondence between solicitor and client, solicitor and third parties, memoranda within the firm and attendance notes (*see* below);

Note _____
Correspondence should be in strict chronological order and is usually filed from the bottom up, so that the most recent letters appear on top.
_____

- Pleadings;
- Summonses/applications and orders;
- Affidavits;
- Statements;
- Expert records and reports, eg. medical reports;
- Documents for discovery (*see* Chapter 23);
- Documents relating to losses, eg. in a personal injury case, documents relating to special damages;
- Instructions to counsel (which are sent at various stages

of the case); (This section often contains copies of documents already held in the file, these copies having been made for counsel.)

● Legal aid documents (if applicable).

The sections may be divided by binders within ring files or there may be a correspondence file with the other documents contained in folders or plastic holders.

2.2.2   Attendance notes

Every time you work on the case, including any telephone conversation, meeting, and reading and considering (known as 'perusing') of the file, you should make a full note of the work done/conversation/meeting and the date and time spent. This is known as an attendance note. It should be typed, but is often inserted in the file in handwriting.

The purpose of an attendance note is to:

● Keep a note of events, not only for your benefit but because others may work on or take over the file;

● Display evidence of the work so that its cost can be recovered at the end of the case from the other side, if they are ordered to pay your costs, or from your client. Attendance notes are important evidence in 'taxation' hearings at the end of the case (*see* Chapter 28) where the question of the costs recoverable is dealt with.

2.2.3   General case management

1 *Provide information* Keep the client informed of the progress of the case at every step and throughout. Send copies of all documents and letters to the client. Reply quickly to the client's letters.

2 *Take instructions* Always take instructions from the client before taking a step, particularly when negotiating, before making an offer of settlement and when considering an offer from the other side.

3 *Tactics* Whether to proceed quickly or slowly with the case is a question of tactics. Generally, a plaintiff will proceed quickly and a defendant will delay.

4 *Diary* Keep a diary of important dates in the case (*see* dates listed in 2.2.1). This diary is usually kept on computer, at the front of the file and in your personal diary. (Many negligence actions against solicitors are due to their having missed an important date, eg. the limitation period or date for acknowledging service (High Court) or serving a defence.)

5 *Standard forms* Many firms, particularly firms doing standard specialist work, eg. personal injury, use standard letters, precedents and questionnaires throughout the case.

The last two points are important because a litigator will be handling many cases at once. For this reason, you should also take care to put documents and letters in the file immediately and always quickly return the file to the cabinet after use, rather than allowing files to pile up on the desk or floor.

6   *Time recording* In most firms there is a time recording system. You must record your time spent each day on the case. The total time spent will eventually be multiplied by your hourly rate and added to a profit element and expenses in order to calculate the full bill. Throughout the case, you should ensure that the time spent on it is not disproportionate to the amount of the claim. For example, it is not wise to spend hours and hours preparing a claim for only £2,000 damages, so that the costs greatly exceed the claim.

Bills   2.2.4

In a private case the firm will be concerned that bills are regularly sent out and paid. This may be your responsibility or that of the accounts department, depending on the firm. (When you are qualified, you will be expected to bring in a certain amount of fees each month.)

Disbursements, eg. court fees, expert's and counsel's fees, should be paid promptly and recovered from the client as part of their bill.

In a legal aid case, you can apply to the Legal Aid Board for interim payment of your costs at various stages of the case. You can apply for payment of disbursements when the invoice is received, or when the disbursement is quantified.

Being 'on the record'   2.2.5

In the High Court, the solicitor acting for a party is said to be 'on the record'.

In both the High Court and County Court a party can change their solicitor by filing notice of change of solicitor on the old solicitor and the other party: *see* RSC O.67 and CCR O.90 r.9.

An important consequence of a solicitor acting for a party is that documents in the action can generally be served on that solicitor.

It is common practice for a solicitor on the record who is situated a long way from the court to use a solicitor's firm situated in the locality of the courts as an *agent* to conduct aspects of the litigation.

Self-assessment questions

1 List the main things you will deal with at the client interview.

2 What advice on the costs of the case will you give to your client?

3 What is meant by asking for money 'on account'?

4 Why will your advice be general and limited at this stage?

5 What is meant by 'party and party' correspondence?

6 Outline the course of an interview.

7 What is meant by an 'attendance note' and why is it important?

Chapter 3

Costs (RSC O.62; CCR O.38)

Costs payable by the client

Your client is liable to pay your fees for work carried out in the conduct of litigation. Such fees are known as *solicitor and own client costs*.

Calculating the fees

Fees for conducting litigation are usually calculated by adding together:

- The *hourly rate* of the person in the solicitor's office doing the work multiplied by the *number of hours* spent on the case;

  Note _____

  Hourly rates vary nationally from about £50 for an articled clerk to about £300 for a partner in a City firm.

- A percentage mark-up; and
- Expenses incurred by the solicitor in conducting the case, eg. payment of counsel's fees, fees of an expert, delivery and travel expenses, court fees.

The first two of these are known as *profit costs*. The last are known as *disbursements*.

Note _____

If the client's means are below a certain level, and a merits test is satisfied, the client will be eligible for legal aid, ie. their solicitor's fees will be paid by the State. In such a case, you must send your bill to the Legal Aid Board and not to the client. Furthermore, special legal aid rates, not your private rates, will apply. (Chapter 4 deals with legally-aided clients. This chapter deals with clients who are not legally-aided.)

Informing the client

It is not usual for the client and solicitor to agree a fee at the outset. Usually, the solicitor will give the client an *estimate* of the likely cost of the matter.

As a matter of professional conduct, at the outset you should:

- Give the client the best, most realistic information you can about the likely cost of the matter, including information on how the fee will be calculated, eg. you should inform your client of the hourly rate of the person doing the work;

- Confirm the estimate in writing – the final amount should not substantially vary from the estimate unless the client has been informed in writing of the changed circumstances;

- Inform the client that they may set a limit on the costs which may be incurred without further reference to the them;

- Discuss with the client how the fees are to be met – you should consider whether your client may be eligible for legal aid or whether the client's liability for their costs may be covered by insurance. (The liability of some clients may be met by a body to which they belong, eg. a trade union.)

You may ask the client, at the outset, for an advance payment on account of costs. (This is unlikely to cover all of the costs which will be incurred.) Further, you may present interim bills during the litigation. At the end of the litigation, you will present a final bill. (See ss, 64–9, Solicitors Act 1974 on solicitors' bills.)

3.1.3   Conditional fee agreements

Section 58 of the Courts and Legal Services Act 1990 provides for the Lord Chancellor to make regulations allowing conditional fee agreements. These are agreements where the solicitor is only paid in specified circumstances, eg. if the client wins the case. At present such agreements are not allowed under the Professional conduct Rules.

Note

At the time of writing, s.58 is not in force, and no regulations have been made. However, it is anticipated that such regulations will shortly be made.

3.1.4   Contentious business agreements

A solicitor and client may enter into a 'contentious business agreement', which is a written agreement fixing the amount of payment by reference to a gross sum, hourly rate or salary. Such an agreement is governed by ss.59–63, Solicitors Act 1974, as amended.

3.2   Challenging the bill

If the client is dissatisfied with your bill, the client may apply to have the bill taxed by the court: s.70, Solicitors Act 1974.

Taxation

3.2.1

By the process known as taxation (a technical term which has no relation to the usual meaning of the word) the High Court decides how much of the bill should be paid by the client.

The High Court will allow you to charge all costs except insofar as they are of an unreasonable amount or have been unreasonably incurred. Any doubts as to reasonableness are resolved in your favour. Technically, this is known as taxation of your costs on the *indemnity basis*.

Thus, your client must show that certain of your fees are unreasonable in nature or amount.

However, on a taxation, the court shall presume your costs to have been:

- Reasonably incurred if they were incurred with the express or implied approval of your client;
- Reasonable in amount if their amount was expressly or impliedly approved by your client;
- Unreasonably incurred if, in the circumstances of the case, they are of an *unusual nature*, unless you can satisfy the court that prior to their being incurred you informed your client that they might not be recovered from the other side. Generous fees paid to a barrister or expert might, for example, be costs of an unusual nature.

Costs recoverable from the other side

3.3

In litigation, one side will usually be ordered by the court to pay all or part of the other side's costs. This is known as the question of *inter partes* costs.

The general approach

3.3.1

Strictly, the question of liability for costs is at the discretion of the court. However, the *general rule* is that the court should order the loser of the case to pay the winner's costs, except when it appears to the court that in the circumstances of the case some other order should be made. The term for the order that the loser pays the winner's costs is the *costs follow the event*.

Unusually, the winner may be ordered to pay the loser's costs, perhaps where the winner has conducted the proceedings in a reprehensible and excessive manner. Alternatively, the judge may order that each side pays its own costs. This is also rare.

Even if the trial judge orders that costs should follow the event, the winner may be liable to pay the loser's costs in relation to certain *interim aspects* of the proceedings (*see* Chapter 18, *Interlocutory applications*). Furthermore, the winner may have to pay the loser's costs if there has been a *payment into court* by the loser. (*See* Chapter 24, *Payment into court.*)

3.3.2   The amount of costs

Even if the loser is ordered to pay the winner's costs, this does not mean that the loser is ordered to pay *all* of the costs that the winner is liable to pay to their solicitor. Usually, the loser is only liable to pay such of the winner's costs as are *reasonable*. This is because where one side is ordered to pay the other side's costs, they are only usually liable to pay that other side's costs on what is known as the *standard basis*, ie. they are only liable to pay such of the other side's costs as are reasonable in nature and amount. Any doubt as to questions of reasonableness will be resolved in favour of the paying party.

Unusually, the loser might be ordered to pay the winner's costs on the *indemnity basis*, as defined above (*see* 3.2), eg. if the loser has conducted the case in a morally reprehensible manner. If an order is made on this basis, the winner is likely to recover more of their costs than if the order had been made on the standard basis. This is because under the indemnity basis the burden is on the paying party to show that the other side's costs are unreasonable, whereas under the standard basis the burden is on the receiving party to show that their costs are reasonable.

In making an order that the loser pays the winner's costs on the standard or indemnity basis, the judge does not actually specify an amount in figures. The exact calculation of how much one side should pay to the other under a costs order is decided, in the event that the parties cannot agree it themselves, at a court hearing called a taxation, which takes place a few months after the trial.

Thus, if the judge has ordered the loser to pay the winner's costs on the standard basis, ie. so much of the winner's costs as are reasonable, and the parties cannot agree on a reasonable amount, there will be a taxation hearing at which a Taxing Master (High Court) or the District Judge (County Court) decides how much (in figures) of the winner's costs are reasonable (*see* Chapter 28 for details.)

Example

P sues D. P wins. In the usual way, D is ordered to pay P's costs on the standard basis. P's solicitor's bill is £50,000. The parties fail to agree on how much of that sum should be paid by D. They therefore apply for a taxation hearing. At the hearing, the Taxing Master (High Court) or District Judge (County Court) rules that only £30,000 of P's solicitor's bill is reasonable. Therefore, D only has to pay £30,000 to P's solicitor.

The £20,000 balance of the bill has to be paid by P, subject to P challenging the bill on the indemnity basis at the same hearing.

If P only obtained £20,000 damages or less in the action, it will not have been worthwhile suing (unless P was suing for a principle or for some other remedy as well as damages).

County Court scales

3.3.3

In the County Court, the amount of costs to be paid by one side to another is not just limited by the basis of taxation but also by the appropriate scale of costs. There is an ascending scale of maximum amounts of costs for items of work recoverable by one side from another under a costs order, depending on the amount of damages claimed in the action. There are three scales:

- Lower scale: £25–£100
- Scale 1:   £100–£3,000
- Scale 2:   Above £3,000.

The sums indicated are the amounts recovered, if the plaintiff wins, or the amount claimed, if the defendant wins.

Note

There are no maximum amounts prescribed for Scale 2 claims. The amount of costs recoverable in Scale 2 claims is in the district judge's discretion.

Example

If the plaintiff recovers £2,000 in damages, the costs recoverable are limited by Scale 1. Under Scale 1, using present figures, the plaintiff can only recover from the other side up to £31.50 in respect of the costs of preparing, issuing and serving proceedings. Other figures apply to other items of work.

Advising your client

3.3.4

As a result of all of the above, at the outset and at appropriate stages thereafter, you should inform the client:

- That in any event your client will be personally responsible for payment of your bill in full, regardless of any order for costs made against their opponent;
- Of the probability that if they lose they will have to pay their opponent's costs as well as their own;
- That even if they win, their opponent may not be ordered to pay the full amount of the client's own costs and

may not be capable of paying what they have been ordered to pay.

Further, you should:

- Consider whether it is worth suing and, at appropriate stages, worth making or accepting an offer of settlement, given the likely costs and damages recoverable or payable;

- Strive to keep costs reasonable in nature and amount, particularly in relation to the amount of damages being claimed, given that only a reasonable amount is likely to be recovered from the other side.

3.3.5 Keeping records

Throughout the conduct of the litigation, you should keep detailed records of all work carried out in order that the work and its reasonableness can be proved at taxation. Attendance notes of phone calls, meetings and other steps should be made throughout the litigation.

The attendance note will:

- Outline the work carried out;

- Summarise any conversation over the phone or at a meeting; and

- Make a note of time spent on the work.

These attendance notes should be kept carefully in the case file, as they may be needed in order to claim the cost of the work from the other side at taxation.

3.3.6 Fixed costs

In certain cases, where the plaintiff obtains early judgment (through, say, the defendant not delivering a defence or there being no defence) and the judgment is for a precise debt, the plaintiff is automatically entitled to recover a small, prescribed amount of costs from the other side, but no more. These are known as fixed costs. The actual amounts allowed are set out in the *Green Book*.

Example

On present figures, where in a claim for more than £3,000 damages the plaintiff obtains judgment because the defendant fails to deliver a defence, the plaintiff is only entitled to recover fixed costs of £18.25.

3.3.7 County court assessment

In the County Court, where the claim for damages does not exceed £3,000, instead of there being a taxation the judge may *assess* the amount of costs payable under a costs order. At the end of the trial the judge makes a 'rough and ready' decision on the amount of costs payable, although there are prescribed limits to the amount that can be awarded on an assessment (*see* Appendix C to O.38 in the *Green Book*).

Wasted costs 3.3.8

Assume that X is suing Y. If there is an improper, unreasonable or negligent act or omission by the solicitor (or barrister) acting for X, which causes X or Y to incur extra costs, the court may refuse to allow X to recover that cost from Y (even if Y is liable to pay the legal costs of X) *and may order the solicitor (or barrister) to personally pay to Y the extra costs incurred by Y.* This illustrates the 'wasted costs' provisions in s.51(6)–(9), Supreme Court Act 1981.

Note

The solicitor for X will, of course, be unable to recover the extra costs from X.

Other considerations 3.3.9

You should also advise your client at appropriate stages that, even if they win the case, they may not recover their costs from the other side:

- In respect of certain interim (interlocutory) applications to the court;
- Where your client is a plaintiff who *fails to beat a payment into court* or *Calderbank offer* made by the defendant;
- Where the other side is legally-aided;
- If the claim is a 'small claim' in the county court;
- If they fail to admit facts in response to a 'Notice to Admit Facts'.

Note

Different rules may apply generally if the client is legally aided.

Self-assessment questions

1 What is the difference between 'solicitor and own client costs' and '*inter partes* costs'?
2 What is the difference between 'profit costs' and 'disbursements'?
3 What is meant by a 'contingency fee' and when is it permissible?
4 What is meant by 'taxation'?

5   What is the difference between the 'standard basis' and the 'indemnity basis' of awarding costs and what is the relevance of these terms to the question of liability for costs?

6   P sues D for £100,000 damages in the High Court. P loses the case. P's solicitor's bill is £20,000. D's solicitor's bill is £25,000. Both are paying privately. Explain whether, and to what extent, P and D will have to pay:

(a) the legal costs of the other side;

(b) their own solicitor's bill.

How would your answer differ if this were a County Court case, and P were suing for £2,000 (in which case the bills would be much lower)?

7   What is meant by 'fixed costs'?

Chapter 4

Legal aid

Administration of the Legal Aid Scheme

4.1

If a person can satisfy certain means and/or merits tests, they are entitled to have their solicitor's fees paid by the State through the Legal Aid Board.

In respect of *civil cases*, the Legal Advice and Assistance and Legal Aid Schemes are administered by the Legal Aid Board under the guidance of the Lord Chancellor. The Board is based in London.

Each area has an area office, and an area committee, which deals with appeals against refusals of legal aid by the area office.

Franchising of legal aid

4.1.1

The Legal Aid Board is introducing, from October 1993, a new system – known as franchising – for the carrying out of legal aid work by firms. Under this system, any firm can apply for a franchise to carry out legal aid work in various branches of law.

'Franchise' does not have its ordinary meaning under this system: a firm does not have to have a franchise in order to carry out legal aid work. However, a franchise in a certain area of legal aid work means that the firm:

- Will have advantages in the way it is paid for the work (in essence, the firm will be paid more quickly by the Legal Aid Board than a firm without a franchise);

- Will have advantages in the way it can carry out the work. Most importantly the firm will be able to exceed the green form limit (*see* para. 4.2.7) and to carry out emergency legal aid work without needing the permission of the Legal Aid Board; (Under the old rules, which still apply to firms without a franchise, the Legal Aid Area office has to give a firm permission to carry out such work.)

- Must achieve substantial standards of quality and efficiency in its work and will work in close liaison with the Legal Aid Board towards achieving those standards.

The purpose of franchising is to improve the quality and efficiency (including cost efficiency) of legal aid work, whilst providing financial incentives for firms to work under a franchise.

Most of the fundamental procedures, rules and principles on legal aid in this chapter are not altered by franchising. Franchising mainly affects the way a firm carries out legal aid work and how the firm will be paid for the work. Further, franchising is not exclusive, and franchises will be granted gradually over a period of time.

Furthermore, you must first understand ordinary legal aid principles and procedures before seeing how these are affected by franchising. Therefore, this chapter will first set out the ordinary principles of legal aid but will highlight the differences, where relevant, for a firm with a franchise. At the end of the chapter there is a detailed section on franchising which shows how it affects the rules set out in the previous sections.

There are two separate legal aid schemes in respect of civil cases:

● The Legal Advice and Assistance Scheme; and

● Civil Legal Aid

Note

Legal aid for criminal cases is administered differently and has different rules.

4.2   The Legal Advice and Assistance Scheme

This applies to the payment of the client's legal fees by the State for initial advice and assistance given before court proceedings are commenced. Informally, the scheme is known as the 'Green Form Scheme', because application to the Legal Aid Board for payment under this scheme is made on a green form.

Note

The statutory framework for this scheme is contained in Parts I and II, ss.1, 2 and 8–13, Legal Aid Act 1988.

Details of the scheme, insofar as it affects civil proceedings, are set out in the Legal Advice and Assistance (Scope) Regulations 1989 and the Legal Advice and Assistance Regulations 1989.

Under this scheme, if a client's means are sufficiently low, the Legal Aid Board will pay your fees (at the appropriate legal aid rates) for two hours' worth (subject to extensions) of initial advice and assistance given to your client before proceedings are commenced.

4.2.1   What does it cover?

The initial advice and assistance for which you can be paid

under the scheme may include:

- Giving preliminary advice;
- Initial correspondence and negotiating;
- Interviewing witnesses;
- Obtaining evidence and inspecting property;
- Paying counsel for preliminary advice;
- The work involved in applying for Civil Legal Aid.

Subject to limited exceptions, the scheme does *not* cover:

- Taking or defending proceedings; and
- Advice and assistance consisting of conveyancing services and in the making of wills.

Note

Under this scheme, you can give informal advice and assistance to a person who is representing themselves in proceedings.

Eligibility   4.2.2

Eligibility for the scheme is subject to a *means test*. The client's capital must be below a certain limit (presently £1,000, if there are no dependants) and their weekly income must be below a certain limit (presently £61.00 a week).

Note

The income and capital limits are changed every year.

Social security entitlement

If the client is in receipt of income support, family credit or disability working allowance, they are entitled to free advice and assistance regardless of income, unless their capital exceeds the capital limit.

Calculating capital and income

In calculating the client's capital and income:

- Certain deductions are made, eg. in respect of the client's dependants;
- The income is calculated net of tax and National Insurance;
- The capital and income of the client's spouse is generally included in the calculation;
- The value of the client's house, furniture, clothes and tools of their trade are not included in calculating the client's capital;
- If the client is a child under 16, the calculation is based on the means of the parent or guardian, not those of the child.

Note

In certain cases you can advise and assist the child directly, in which case the calculation is likely to be based on the child's means.

4.2.3   What will be paid?

If your client is eligible for the scheme, the Legal Aid Board will pay you for up to two hours' worth of advice and assistance.

Payment is at a prescribed rate for each hour. The rate changes every year. You will also be paid a prescribed rate for every letter written and every telephone call made as part of the advice and assistance.

Strictly, therefore, you are not covered for two hours' work, but for work to the value of twice the hourly rate. This will constitute less than two hours' work if payment for letters and phone calls is included in that sum.

If the initial advice and assistance is likely to take more than two hours, you can apply for payment for further work under the scheme by applying to the area office for authority to exceed the prescribed limit, ie. for an extension. This is explained below.

4.2.4   Applying for payment

On first meeting the client, you should judge whether the client's means may be sufficiently low to qualify. You should then advise the client that they may qualify and should ascertain whether the client is indeed eligible by questioning the client in detail on their means. You use a 'key card' to ascertain eligibility. This sets out the details of the limits.

If the client is eligible, you then fill out a green form applying for payment for work under the scheme. If the client wants you to advise and assist, the client then signs the completed form.

If you think that the initial advice and assistance will take longer than two hours, you should, at the same time as filling in a green form, fill in and send off an application for an extension. (This is dealt with below.)

Once the green form has been completed and signed, you undertake the two hours' worth of work; you do not need the prior approval of the Legal Aid Board. You will then send off the green form to the area office. (In practice, legal aid practitioners send off batches of green forms relating to different cases, at regular intervals.) In due course, the Board will pay you for the work done at the prescribed rates.

Applying for an extension   4.2.5

> *Note* _____
>
> This will increasingly become unnecessary, since firms with a
> franchise will be able to exceed the two hour limit without
> setting the permission of the area office. (*See* next paragraph.)

If you estimate that more than two hours' worth of initial
advice and assistance will be necessary, you may apply for
authority to exceed the prescribed 'twice the hourly rate'
limit form using GF3.

In applying for an extension, you must provide the area
office with information as to:

- What work has already been done;
- What work needs to be done and why;
- The estimated cost of the work to be done; and
- Information as to previous extensions.

The area office will decide whether it is reasonable to grant
an extension, having regard to whether it is reasonable for
the extra advice and assistance to be given and whether the
estimate of extra costs is reasonable.

> *Note* _____
>
> Practice differs from area to area, but the basic criteria applied
> by the area offices are considered in the *Legal Aid Handbook*.

The office may require you to apply for full Civil Legal Aid
instead of granting an extension. The office may grant a
limited extension to enable you to do the work involved in
applying for legal aid. (Such work is usually carried out
under cover of the green form scheme.)

The green form charge   4.2.6

Under s.11, where money or property (this usually means
an offer of money in settlement) is recovered (or preserved)
from the other side during the Legal Advice and Assistance
stage, you must use this to pay your client's bill. The Legal
Aid Board only then pays the balance of the bill.

This of course reduces the compensation received from
the other side by the client. You should therefore warn the
client of this 'charge' at the outset. However, the area office
has power to authorise you not to enforce the charge in
cases of grave hardship or distress: Legal Advice and Assistance Regulations 1989, Regulation 33.

4.2.7 Green form powers given to firms with a franchise

One of the major changes brought in by franchising is that a franchisee will have power to exceed the two-hour limit without needing to apply to the Legal Aid Board for authority to do so. In effect, the Board devolves to a franchisee the power to grant green form extensions to the client. However, the franchisee must impose on itself a financial limit for each extension, as if it were the Legal Aid Board.

A franchisee is also given power to make any other decision relating to an application for green form advice and assistance (except power to waive the green form charge).

The board will monitor the exercise of powers by franchisees and has power to suspend the exercise of such powers.

When exercising a devolved power, the franchisee must note on the case file:

- The *date* the devolved powers were exercised;
- The *decision* made, including the financial limit imposed on an extension;
- The *reasons* for exercise of the power;
- A note of who *exercised* the powers.

A *financial incentive* for being a franchisee is given here. On exercising the devolved power, eg. granting a first extension, the franchisee can apply to the board for payment for two or three hours work, including disbursements. This will normally be paid within 28 days. (This is an advantage not given under the old rules.)

Note

Once all green form work, including all extensions, has been carried out, the franchisee then sends their final claim for payment to the board.

4.2.8 Other green form benefits given to franchisees

Payments

Franchisees may claim payment under the green form scheme for:

- Telephone advice given to a client before the client has signed the green form; and
- The cost of outward travel (but not travelling time) to meet a client away from the office before the client has signed the green form.

In both cases, the costs must have been reasonably incurred. These new benefits are meant to provide for the situation where the client cannot easily get the solicitor's office to sign the green form.

Note

The point is that, under the old rules which still apply to firms without a franchise, solicitors cannot claim payment for work done before the green form is signed.

Postal applications

Where justifiable, franchisees may accept postal applications from clients for green form advice.

Civil legal aid   4.3

Under the full Civil Legal Aid Scheme, the Legal Aid Board will pay the cost of representation in proceedings ('proceedings' here could refer to all steps from the beginning, not just the trial) of any person who can satisfy:

- A means test; and
- A merits test.

Note

The statutory framework for Civil Legal Aid is contained in Parts I and IV, ss.1, 2 and 14–18, the Civil Legal Aid (General) Regulations 1989 and Civil Legal Aid (Assessment of Resources) Regulations 1989. (All can be found in the *White Book* Vol. 2 and *Legal Aid Handbook*.)

Eligibility   4.3.1

Legal Aid is available to individuals who can satisfy the means and merits tests. It is not available to a company, or to an unincorporated body. However, it is available to partners or members of firms, where the firm or partnership is suing or being sued.

Legal Aid is available for all civil proceedings in the High Court and County Court, *except* for defamation, undefended divorce and (in practice) small claims, ie. claims for £1,000 or less. It is also available for cases in the Employment Appeal Tribunal and the Land's Tribunal but it is not available for proceedings in other tribunals.

Note

There are particular rules relating to legal aid in family proceedings. These are not dealt with in this course.

The means and merits tests   4.3.2

To be granted legal aid the applicant must:

- Fall within the financial eligibility limits; and
- Satisfy the area office that they have reasonable grounds for taking, defending or being a party to the proceedings.

Financial eligibility test

The applicant's income and capital must be below certain limits. If they are below the prescribed lower limits, the applicant is entitled to free legal aid. If they are between the lower and upper limits, the applicant will have to pay a contribution to the costs of the case. The area director assesses the amount of this contribution, which may be from either capital or income. A contribution from income is payable by monthly instalments throughout the case. A contribution from capital is payable immediately on the client accepting the offer of legal aid.

An applicant in receipt of *income support* is eligible for Civil Legal Aid without contribution, regardless of their capital.

In assessing an applicant's income and capital, the income and capital of a person living with the applicant as a husband or wife is taken into account. The income is calculated net and subject to deductions such as maintenance payments. The calculation of the applicant's capital is also subject to deductions, eg. the value of the applicant's house is not included.

If the applicant is a child under 16, the assessment is made on the child's own resources, not those of the parents.

Note

The eligibility limits together with full details on assessment of resources are set out in the Civil Legal Aid (Assessment of Resources) Regulations 1989.

The merits test

The applicant must satisfy the area office that they have reasonable grounds for taking, defending or being a party to the proceedings. The area office considers whether the applicant has a reasonable case and whether it is otherwise reasonable to grant legal aid. For example, legal aid may not be granted if the benefit to be achieved does not justify the cost, or the proposed defendant does not have the means to satisfy any judgment.

4.4   Applying for civil legal aid

4.4.1   The forms

You should complete form CLA 1 (relating to the merits) together with form CLA 4A, B, C or F (statement of applicant's financial circumstances). In addition, form L17 is completed by the employer where the applicant and/or their partner is in employment. Your work in making the application can be covered by the green form scheme.

The forms are then sent to the area office. The area director considers whether the case passes the merits test. The financial part of the form is sent to the Department of Social Security (DSS), who consider whether the applicant is financially eligible.

Applying for an emergency certificate 4.4.2

Note

The rules below do not apply to a firm with a franchise. A firm with a franchise can carry out emergency legal aid work without having to wait for an emergency certificate from the area office where the firm has a franchise. (*See* next section.)

Generally, the Legal Aid Board will not pay you for work carried out before the date of issue of a legal aid certificate to the client (see below).

However, it takes weeks or months for a certificate to be issued. In many cases, the nature of the case is such that you need to do the work immediately. Your client cannot wait for the issue of a certificate. Therefore, in such cases, you should apply for an emergency certificate. This can be issued very quickly allowing work to proceed while the full application for legal aid is considered.

The emergency certificate will last for a prescribed period, or until it is discharged or revoked or until a full certificate is granted.

You apply for an emergency certificate by completing form ClA 3. In a case of extreme urgency, the area office may accept an application made over the phone.

Your application should be accompanied by sufficient documents to enable the area director to determine the nature of the proposed proceedings and the circumstances in which it is required. The application should show that the applicant is likely to fulfil the conditions for a grant of full legal aid. Therefore, an application for full legal aid should be submitted at the same time.

Furthermore, the application must satisfy the area director that it is in the *interests of justice* that legal aid be granted as a matter of urgency. For example, an emergency certificate is likely to be granted where an immediate injunction is needed, or there is some forthcoming hearing which cannot be delayed while full legal aid is awaited.

In a case of the utmost urgency, eg. where work needs to be carried out overnight or at the weekend, the Legal Aid Board may pay for work done even before the grant of an emergency certificate where:

● It was not possible to apply for an emergency certificate because the area office was closed; and

● The emergency certificate is applied for at the first available opportunity and is granted.

If the conditions for an emergency certificate are satisfied, the area office will quickly issue an emergency certificate without the applicant's financial circumstances being considered by the DSS. The certificate will be for a specific period of time, which may be extended on application to the area director. It will be superseded by (shall merge in) a full certificate if that is issued.

Note

Your client will have to agree to pay the full costs of any steps taken under the emergency certificate if a full certificate is eventually not granted.

4.4.3   Emergency legal aid work by franchisees

The previous section does not apply to firms with a franchise. Firms with a franchise in the relevant area of work can carry out emergency work without needing to apply first for an emergency legal aid certificate. In effect, the Legal Aid Board devolves to franchisees the power to grant emergency legal aid to a client. The franchisee can then immediately carry out the emergency work. However, within seven days of exercising this power, the franchisee must send the area office an application for emergency legal aid (even though the work has already been carried out) and for full legal aid. An emergency certificate will be granted and retrospectively dated as at the date of the exercise of the power. At the same time, the franchisee can claim £250 on account, which will normally be paid within 28 days. (This is another financial advantage given to franchisees.)

However, if the power was exercised by the franchise outside the guidelines for the grant of emergency legal aid, the £250 will not be paid. An emergency certificate will still be issued but the Legal Aid Board will not pay for the emergency work done unless the costs are recovered from the other party.

Note

There is provision for the franchisee to challenge such a refusal of emergency legal aid.

The legal aid certificate 4.5

If full legal aid is granted, a legal aid certificate will be sent to the applicant's solicitor. This certifies that the applicant is entitled to legal aid from the date of the certificate for work covered by the terms of the certificate (*see* below). You will not be paid by the Legal Aid Board for work carried out before the date of the certificate unless the green form scheme or emergency legal aid applies.

A copy of the certificate must be left with (filed with) the court when proceedings are commenced. Furthermore, notice of issue of the certificate must be served on all other parties when proceedings are commenced, ie. you must notify the other parties that your client has legal aid. Doing so is important because this has cost consequences for the other side; they are unlikely to recover their legal costs from your client even if they win. This in turn will affect the way they fight the case. Therefore, the solicitor who fails to serve a notice on the other side may be penalised by having to pay a proportion of the other side's costs personally.

Scope of the certificate 4.5.1

The certificate will state the party and work covered by the certificate, ie. who is entitled to sue whom and for what. It may say that legal aid is granted to X for the purpose of suing Y for damages for negligence. The certificate will then cover all usual steps in such proceedings. However, the terms of the certificate may be more limited. For example, legal aid may only be granted for the purpose of obtaining counsel's opinion, or up until discovery (disclosure of documents) in the action, at which time the legal aid office can reconsider the merits of the case on an application for legal aid to continue.

Authorised expenditure 4.5.2

Generally, the Legal Aid Board will pay you, at legal aid rates, for all usual steps covered by the terms of the certificate. However, you should obtain prior authority from the area director before taking certain steps, otherwise you may not be paid for taking these steps. For example, you are required by the regulations to obtain prior authority before instructing a QC or more than one Counsel. You should also obtain prior authority before taking unusual steps or incurring large expenditure, such as use of a very expensive expert, otherwise the Legal Aid Board may not pay the costs of such steps or reimburse you for the expenditure.

4.5.3   Amendment

A legal aid certificate can be amended, for example, to add another party. The amendment must be within the categories set out in Regulation 51. The application is made on form CLA 30.

If the amendment is allowed, the amended certificate must be filed with the court and notice of the amendment must be served on all other parties.

4.5.4   Discharge and revocation

Legal Aid to the client can be terminated by the certificate being discharged or revoked.

The certificate is *discharged* (the Legal Aid Board will send a notice of discharge) on conclusion of proceedings but can also be discharged earlier where, for example, the:

- Assisted person's income or capital goes over the limit; or
- The assisted person no longer has reasonable grounds for the proceedings, or has required proceedings to be conducted unreasonably so as to incur unjustifiable expense to the Legal Aid Fund.

You have a duty to notify the area office of either of the above.

The certificate may be *revoked* where, for example, it is discovered that the assisted person obtained legal aid by making untrue statements, or has failed to attend the DSS for interview, or has not provided material information.

The distinction between discharge and revocation is that, if the certificate is *discharged*, legal aid terminates at that date. If the certificate is *revoked*, the client is treated as never having been legally aided. They will therefore be liable to reimburse the Fund for any costs already paid out on their behalf. They will also not be entitled to the benefit of the rule that the other side can only claim limited costs from a legally aided party in respect of the period during which the party was legally aided (*see* s.17).

4.5.5   Your duties

Although you must act in your client's best interests, you also have a duty to the legal aid office to keep them informed about the proceedings so that they can be satisfied public money is not being wasted. Therefore, you have a duty to report to the area director:

- If the assisted person requires the case to be conducted unreasonably;
- Reasons for you or counsel refusing to act, or giving up

a case, or having doubts about continuing to act;

- When the area office calls for information about the progress of proceedings;
- When an assisted person declines to accept a reasonable offer of settlement or payment into court (*see* Chapter 24);
- If a legal aid certificate is issued to another party in the proceedings (as this may mean the matter is not worth pursuing as costs or damages may not be recovered);
- If the assisted person dies or becomes bankrupt;
- If work authorised by the certificate has been completed;
- If you become aware that the client's means have changed – the client has a duty to inform you of this where this might affect the certificate – the office can then reassess the person's means.

The certificate may be discharged or revoked in the above cases.

Note

You are under a professional conduct duty to consider and advise a client on the availability of legal aid where the client might be entitled to legal aid or green form advice and assistance. This equally applies during the progress of a matter, where you become aware of a change in your client's means which might make the client eligible for legal aid.

Cost consequences   4.6

Payment of an assisted person's costs   4.6.1

At the conclusion of the proceedings you draw up a bill showing the work done, total hours spent (charged at legal aid, not private, hourly rates) and disbursements, ie. expenses, including expert's and counsel's fees at legal aid rates. There will be a legal aid taxation of this bill on the standard basis. In other words, a Taxing Master (High Court) or District Judge (County Court) will certify that the amount of the bill is reasonable.

Alternatively, in limited cases, you can ask for the amount of the bill to be assessed by the area office as an alternative to taxation, eg. where the your allowed costs are likely to be less than £1,000.

The Legal Aid Board will then pay you the amount of the bill which has been certified as allowed on taxation or assessment.

Note

You cannot bill the client privately for work covered by the certificate.

Although the Board will generally not pay you until the end of the case, you can claim interim payments on account in the circumstances set out in regulations 100 and 101. For example, a percentage of fees can be claimed after 12, 18 months and a further 12 or 24 months after the certificate; disbursements and 'hardship' payments can be claimed on account under regulation 101. (The claim is made on form CLA 28.)

However, an advantage of having a franchise is that a franchisee can claim 75% of profit costs outstanding nine months after the issue of a certificate and every nine months after that, as well as still being able to claim 'hardship' payments.

Any costs recovered or damages won from the other side are paid by the other side to you and you must then pay them over to the area office. The Legal Aid Board may then recoup the amount it has paid to the assisted person's solicitor from the costs or damages received from the other side (see the statutory charge below). The balance is paid over to the assisted person.

However, the area office has power to allow you to release all or part of the damages straight away to the assisted person: Regulation 90.

If the client obtained an order that the other side pay their costs, the legal aid taxation and the *inter partes* taxation will be conducted simultaneously.

4.6.2   The statutory charge

If the Legal Aid Board does not recover from the other side the whole amount of costs that the Board has had to pay to the assisted person's solicitor, the Board must recoup any shortfall from any money or property recovered by the assisted person in the action. This is known as the statutory charge: s.16.

Example

The plaintiff, an assisted person, wins £20,000 damages from the defendant. The plaintiff's solicitor's taxed bill of £5,000 is paid by the Legal Aid Board. However, it only recovers £3,000 of those costs from the defendant. The statutory charge entitles the Board to take the £2,000 balance out of the plaintiff's damages, leaving the plaintiff with £18,000 damages. Obviously, if the plaintiff had only won £2,000 damages, it will not have been worthwhile suing.

The Board will not recover the costs in full from the other side, and thus the charge will arise, where either:

- The other side is not ordered to pay the assisted party's costs; or
- The other side does not comply fully or at all with a costs order; or
- The amount of costs that the other side is ordered to pay to the assisted party is less than the amount that the Board is liable to pay to the assisted person's solicitor.

In an ordinary case, the last of these situations is rare. Since the legal aid taxation and the *inter partes* taxation are both conducted on the standard basis, ie. according to how much of the assisted person's solicitor's costs are reasonable, the amounts are likely to be equal. Therefore, the Board will usually recover from the other side all of the costs that the Board has had to pay to you (assuming the other side is ordered to pay the costs of the assisted person).

The charge is most likely to arise where the assisted plaintiff fails to beat a payment into court (*see* Chapter 24). This is because in such a case the assisted party recovers damages but does not recover all of their costs from the other side.

Note

You have a duty, at the outset and throughout, to explain the effect of the charge to a legally aided client.

Note that:

- The charge applies even to property or money recovered in a settlement achieved before proceedings are commenced;
- The Board has no power to waive the charge.

Note

There is a similar charge in respect of costs incurred under the green form scheme (*see* s.11), although the Board has power to waive this in cases of grave hardship or distress.

Cost orders against the assisted party   4.6.3

An order for costs against an unsuccessful assisted person cannot exceed the amount (if any) which is a reasonable one for them to pay having regard to all the circumstances, including the means of all the parties and their conduct in connection with the dispute: s.17.

Example

P is legally aided. D wins. Normally, P would be ordered to

pay D's costs. However, since P is legally aided, P will only be ordered to pay a reasonable amount of D's costs, having regard to P's means, among other things. Therefore, usually P will not be ordered to pay any of D's costs, or only a small amount equal to the amount of any contribution P has had to pay to legal aid. Alternatively, the court may make a 'football pools' order: P is ordered to pay D's costs, but the order is suspended until the judge orders otherwise, eg. when the assisted person wins the pools.

It is because of s.17 that non-legally aided parties are keen to settle cases against legally aided parties, as the former will not recover all of their costs even if they win.

In assessing the non-legally aided person's resources for the purposes of s.17, their house, its contents and the tools of their trade are not taken into account.

4.6.4 Costs recoverable by the non-legally aided party from the Legal Aid Board

Section 17 will often cause hardship to an unassisted party. Therefore, s.18 provides that the court can order payment of the unassisted party's costs by the Legal Aid Board where:

- The unassisted party is a defendant who has won the case against a legally aided plaintiff;

- The court has considered the application of s.17;

- It is just and equitable to make a s.18 order;

- In proceedings at first instance, the unassisted defendant will suffer *severe financial hardship* unless the order is made.

Note

This is very important. The case law shows that it is extremely unlikely that a defendant that is a company or other large body can recover their costs from the Board under s.18. To qualify, the costs would have to place a quite exceptional burden on their resources. *See R v Greenwich LBC* (1992).

4.6.5 Professional conduct

If your client is legally aided, you should inform them at the outset of the case and at appropriate stages thereafter:

- Of the effect of the statutory charge on their case;

- That if they lose the case they may still be ordered by the court to contribute to their opponent's costs even though their own costs are covered by legal aid;

- That even if they win, their opponent may not be ordered

to pay the full amount of their costs and may not be capable of paying what they have been ordered to pay; and

● Of their obligation to pay any contribution assessed and of the consequences of any failure to do so.

Appeals against legal aid decisions   4.7

An applicant has a right of appeal to the area committee against decisions of the area office. For example, there is a right of appeal against refusal of legal aid, refusal of amendment to the certificate and against revocation or discharge.

Franchising   4.8

Meaning and purpose   4.8.1

Franchising of legal aid work will significantly affect the way legal aid work is carried out, the purpose being to improve its quality and efficiency (including cost efficiency), while providing financial incentives for firms to work under a franchise.

Any solicitor's firm may apply for a franchise. Also eligible to apply are any law centre or independent advice agency employing a solicitor with a current practising certificate and complying with the solicitors' practice rules and other principles of conduct.

Franchising does not mean that a firm is granted a franchise to do all legal aid work. Rather, a firm is granted a franchise in one or more of nine categories of work:

● Matrimonial/family;
● Crime;
● Housing;
● Debt;
● Employment;
● Personal injury;
● Welfare benefits;
● Consumer/ general contract;
● Immigration/nationality.

So, for example, a firm may have a franchise in housing and personal injury but not in the other categories. It can still do legal aid work in the other categories, but it will not have the advantages and obligations of a franchisee in doing those areas of work.

If a firm has a franchise in a category of work, this has the following effects in *relation to that category of work:*

1   The firm has the *power to exceed the green form limit* and to take other green form decisions without needing the authority of the Legal Aid Board on exercising this power. The firm can claim early payment on account for the first two or three hours of green form work. Franchisees also receive certain other green form benefits (*see* para. 4.1.1).

2   The firm has the power to carry out emergency legal aid work before a certificate is issued, and to claim £250 on account for such work (*see* para. 4.4.3).

3   The firm can commence assistance by way of representation (ABWOR) proceedings without needing authority of the Legal Aid Board, and can claim £150 on account for such work. ABWOR is outside the scope of this book as it relates to family and mental health work.

4   The firm can claim from the Board interim payments of its costs on a more favourable basis than if they did not have a franchise (*see* para. 4.6.1).

5   The firm is expected to achieve substantial standards of quality and efficiency in its work and will work in close liaison with the Legal Aid Board towards achieving those standards. This is not just an obligation, it can also be seen as an advantage because the Board will help and force the franchisee to improve the quality and efficiency of its work.

4.8.2   Mandatory requirements

In order to obtain and maintain a franchise, firms must meet mandatory requirements:

● They must appoint a franchise representative;

● They must have at least one employee suitably qualified to recognise the need for welfare benefits advice and must ensure that all caseworkers/advisers in franchised categories are able to recognise the need for welfare benefits advice and refer clients to the appropriate source of advice;

● They must meet detailed standards of quality and organisation in relation to:

  – The giving of independent advice;

  – Equal opportunities, non-discrimination and professional indemnity insurance;

  – The strategy of their firm;

  – Planning of the service they provide;

  – Management structure;

  – Supervision and file review;

  – File management;

- Procedures for handling a case;
- Financial management;
- Personnel management;
- Client care and complaints.

The Legal Aid Board has published criteria, outlining the main steps that a competent franchisee should take in dealing with each category of work.

Example _____

The personal injury criteria set out the specific information that the lawyer should extract from the client, the advice the lawyer should give (eg. 'who the client may be able to claim against') and the action that a lawyer should take (eg. 'contact witnesses and interview them if possible').

_____

These criteria are known as 'transaction criteria' (*see* Sherr, Moorhead, Paterson *Transaction criteria*, HMSO 1992).

The Legal Aid Board will carry out pre-franchise and post-franchise audits, ie. full checks, of a firm's work, and will monitor the work of franchisees.

A firm may appeal against a decision to refuse, suspend or terminate a franchise.

Self-assessment questions

1 What is the difference between:

(a) the Legal Advice and Assistance ('Green Form') Scheme; and

(b) the Civil Legal Aid scheme?

2 How does a person qualify for Green Form Scheme? How much work can you carry out under it?

3 Why is it better for a firm to have a legal aid franchise when carrying out green form work?

4 How does a person qualify for civil legal aid?

5 What forms would you fill out on first meeting a client who qualifies for legal aid? What would you do if you wanted legal aid very quickly and why is it better to be a franchisee in such a case?

6 What is the disadvantage of having a limited legal aid certificate?

7 From your reading of this chapter, list the advantages, disadvantages and burdens of having a legally-aided client?

8 Explain the 'statutory charge'.

9 X, who is legally aided, is suing Y, who is not legally-aided.

   Explain whether, and to what extent:

   (a) the parties,

   (b) the Legal Aid Board will have to pay:

      (i) the legal costs of the other side,

      (ii) the legal costs of their own solicitor.

   Who decides the amount of costs payable by the Legal Aid Board to X's solicitor?

   What would be your answer if X is *not* legally aided and Y *is* legally aided?

10 What is meant by 'franchising' and what is its purpose?

   Does a firm have to have a franchise in order to carry out legal aid work?

11 What are the benefits and obligations of having a franchise?

Chapter 5

Initial steps

Initial investigations 5.1

1 *Information and documentation* Go through the client's statement and all relevant documentation that the client has. Ensure that the client has provided you with all you need.

2 *Witnesses* Investigate what possible witnesses there may be in addition to the known witnesses. Contact all witnesses and arrange to take statements from them.

> *Note* ————————————————————————
>
> Full witness statements will eventually have to be disclosed to the other side before trial (*see* Chapter 17); at this stage the statement may only be provisional, unless the case is small and straightforward.

3 *Information* Write to third parties who have or may have relevant information, eg. in a personal injury case, the police, the client's employer, the factory inspectorate (*see* further below); in a breach of contract or nuisance case, manufacturers, builders, the environmental health officer. These third parties may eventually appear as witnesses.

4 *The law* Research the law – including the measure of damages or other remedy – in the area if the case involves points of difficulty or points with which you are not familiar.

> *Note* ————————————————————————
>
> Your investigation into the facts, evidence and law should be as thorough as possible at this stage, so that you know your ground at an early stage.

5 *Experts* Instruct an expert(s) on the relevant expert matters in dispute, eg. a doctor, an engineer: *see* 5.2.

6 *Inspection* Inspect the relevant site, equipment, goods, photographs, working process, plan – as the case may be. You should do this with your own expert present.

You will often need to write to the proposed defendant asking them to allow you access, eg. to inspect equipment in their factory. If they will not cooperate, you can apply to court for an order allowing access (*see* Chapter 7).

7 *Defendant* Ask the proposed defendant if they will provide you with relevant documentation and any expert reports they have. It is not usually in their interest to do so

and they are not obliged to do so until later in the litigation (*see* Chapter 17). However, they may do so in an attempt to encourage a settlement or if they have documents or a report strongly adverse to your client's case.

8   *Instruct counsel* Instruct counsel to advise on the merits of the case or on a difficult point of law where necessary: *see* 5.2.

Note _____

In a legal aid case, ensure you are covered by green form or by full legal aid, before commencing this work.

5.2   Instructing an expert

5.2.1   General points

Instructions

In any litigation involving a matter of expert opinion, eg. the opinion of an engineer on defective equipment, or that of a doctor on the plaintiff's injuries, it is essential to obtain expert evidence.

Some cases may require experts on different matters, or more than one expert to give evidence on a complex matter. Your firm will have built up contacts with various experts or lists of experts in the particular field can be obtained from bodies representing that field or from the Law Society or the Association of Personal Injury Lawyers.

The expert should be formally instructed by letter. You should make clear the matters you would like them to cover in their report.

Fees

A fee will be payable. This forms part of the costs of the proceedings (it is part of the expenses known as 'disbursements') and is recoverable from the other side if you win. In a legal aid case, you have a general authority to incur expert expenditure but should obtain specific authority from the Legal Aid Board in an unusually expensive or complex case or where you use more than one expert.

Remember that if the expert's report is unfavourable to your client's case, you are not obliged to use that expert or to disclose that expert's report to the other side. You are entitled to suppress that report (technically it is 'privileged' evidence) and attempt to find more a favourable expert. You are only obliged to disclose to the other side the expert evidence you intend to use at trial.

Procedure
• Instruct the expert.

- The expert inspects/examines the relevant matter, eg. the equipment/property/injuries. You may need to ask the defendant for access or require a court order (*see* Chapter 7).

- The expert prepares a written report.

- Court rules (known as 'directions') provide that, at a certain stage in the case, both sides must disclose to each other, in the form of written reports, the expert evidence that they intend to rely on at trial.

- The other side may agree with the contents of your expert's report. This is known as reports being agreed. Usually, however, they do not accept its findings. In that case, the expert must attend at trial to give oral evidence, based on what they have said in their report. The other side then cross-examines them; this is an important part of the trial.

Note

The report itself is not put in as evidence at trial; the purpose of the pre-trial disclosure of the report is to give the other side advance warning of what the expert is going to say at trial.

- Court rules (the 'directions') also place a limit on the number of experts that can give evidence at trial (*see* Chapter 17).

- In practice, there may be a 'without prejudice' meeting, ie. the content of the discussions are not revealed to the court, between the experts for both sides, to attempt to settle the matter or to limit the areas of dispute. The court may order the holding of such a meeting.

Medical evidence in personal injury cases   5.2.2

In a simple case, the client's GP can be instructed (a fee is still payable). However, if the matter is more substantial, a consultant should be instructed. Alternatively, you could instruct the hospital where the client was treated. However, a hospital report is usually not written by a consultant, is not as full as an independent report and an independent consultant may be more experienced in writing reports for legal proceedings. It is therefore usual to instruct an independent consultant.

The consultant will arrange to examine the client, and will then write a report which should give details of:

- The accident;
- Its immediate effects;
- The subsequent history of injuries and treatment;
- Relevant pre-existing conditions and past history;

- Present complaints;
- Results of examination;
- Prognosis, ie. future prospects for the injuries and the effect of the injuries on the client's lifestyle and ability to carry out activities, and whether there is a risk of future serious deterioration or disease.

You should also ask for information relevant to a possible provisional damages claim.

You must have a report at an early stage:

- To commence settlement negotiations; and
- Because in personal injury cases, the plaintiff must formally serve their medical report on the other side with their statement/particulars of claim shortly after the commencement of proceedings. (In non-personal injury cases, the plaintiff does not need to serve their expert's report until later in the proceedings.)

It may be that at the time of commencing proceedings, the medical prognosis for the client is unclear. Nevertheless, a medical report should still be prepared and further, updated reports can be served during the course of the proceedings. Alternatively, the plaintiff can apply to court for an order allowing the statement/particulars of claim to be served without a medical report.

It is usual practice for the defendant's doctor to examine the plaintiff, in order to check the plaintiff's alleged injuries and to prepare a report for the defendant. The plaintiff is not entitled to refuse such an examination but may impose reasonable conditions, for example:

- That the defendant pay the plaintiff's travel expenses and loss of earnings for attending;
- If the plaintiff is a child, that their parent attends the examination;
- That only the plaintiff (and perhaps their parent) and the defendant's doctor is present;
- That discussion is limited to the injuries.

Note

If the plaintiff refuses to be examined by the defendant's doctor, the defendant can apply to court for a stay (suspension) of proceedings until they agree to be examined.

In practice, the parties may disclose their medical reports to the other at an earlier stage than that required by the rules in order to achieve a settlement.

Communicating with the other side before proceedings are commenced

Note _____

Despite all of the above investigations on your side, the full merits and circumstances of your client's case cannot be known until you see the information and evidence in the defendant's possession. Unless they choose to reveal things at an earlier stage, you will not receive this until much later on in the proceedings through such procedures as discovery (formal disclosure of documents), exchange of experts' reports and witness statements, and the giving of evidence at trial. The apparent merits of the case are likely to change during the proceedings as more evidence is revealed.

After your initial investigations into the case, you should write to the proposed defendant, introducing the claim. You should:

- State who you act for;
- State what the claim relates to
- Explain the basis of your claim and the remedy sought, and ask them to refer the matter to their solicitors or insurers.

The first letter may be a fairly tame letter, just introducing the claim. However, it is often a much stronger letter, asking for the remedy claimed, eg. damages, refraining from an act, and stating that if the defendant does not, for example, respond with proposals, pay up, desist within a certain number of days, you will commence proceedings.

This letter will be sent even if there has been earlier correspondence. It is known as the 'letter before action.' It may force the other side to pay up or to desist (as the case may be) and shows the court that you have given them the chance to comply before commencing litigation – this may affect costs liability.

Note _____

In personal injury cases, your first letter should also give the defendant certain information relating to the DSS compensation scheme (*see* 5.5.5).

You are likely to receive a response from the proposed defendant or their solicitors or insurers. (In practice, you will often be dealing with the defendant's insurers, although the defendant, not their insurers, is technically named as the other party.) They will usually deny liability.

Correspondence may now take place between the two sides which may be 'open' correspondence or 'without prejudice' correspondence. *Without prejudice* refers to correspondence which is never revealed to the court; it is conducted 'behind a curtain'. Negotiations for a settlement take place by virtue of this correspondence (*see* Chapter 6).

Open correspondence is revealed to the court. The parties argue their cases and correspond on procedural points. They may also attempt to obtain admissions in this correspondence. For example, the defendant may openly admit liability at an early stage, so that only the *amount* of damages is disputed, or they may admit that if there was negligence their client is vicariously liable.

The parties may also openly ask for the other side to disclose various documents or information, although the other side is not obliged to do so at this stage.

If negotiations do not seem to be getting anywhere and you feel that you have carried out sufficient investigations and the case has sufficient merit, you should, with the client's authority, commence proceedings. As explained above, a letter before action should be sent first.

Before commencing proceedings, you must ask the defendant's solicitors whether they have instructions to accept service of proceedings, otherwise service will be directly on the defendant. (The procedure for commencing proceedings is dealt with in later chapters.)

Note

In a *road accident case*, you must, by letter, give notice of intention to commence proceedings to the defendant's insurers (or the Motor Insurers Bureau if the defendant is not insured), before or within seven days of commencing proceedings: ss.151–2, Road Traffic Act 1988. This makes them liable even if they have cancelled the defendant's policy as a result of the accident.

5.4   Instructing counsel

5.4.1   When to instruct counsel

Counsel may be (and, in practice, usually is) instructed at any stage in the proceedings to:

● Advise on the *merits of the case* or on *quantum of damages*.

Note

It is common practice to instruct counsel to advise on the merits in the early stages of your investigations (in a legal aid case, the legal aid certificate may require this), and to advise on the whole case after discovery (when both sides disclose their documents) and before trial.

- Advise on specific points, particularly *difficult points of law*.
- Advise on *evidence* – this is usually done at a late stage in the proceedings, near to trial.
- Prepare *documents*. It is common practice to instruct counsel to draft the pleadings and they may also draft affidavits and witness statements.
- Attend *interlocutory hearings* and the *trial* to represent the client. This is known as briefing counsel to attend. It is common practice for counsel, rather than the solicitor, to attend a hearing of any complexity.

Note

At the time of writing, solicitors have no right of audience in the High Court. However, following the Courts and Legal Services Act 1990, solicitors are shortly expected to be granted rights of audience in the High Court. Further, with the increased emphasis on advocacy training in the solicitors' profession, it may be that advocacy will increasingly be carried out by solicitors. However, it is often *cheaper* to instruct a barrister to attend a hearing.

Who to instruct   5.4.2

Your firm will have built up contacts with specific barristers and will know those who specialise in different areas of the Law. Alternatively, an appropriate barrister can be recommended by word-of-mouth or by the clerk of a set of chambers used by your firm, or you can consult various guides and brochures (although there are strict limits on the manner in which barristers can advertise).

You will generally instruct a junior counsel. A Queen's Counsel (known as a 'silk') is only consulted or briefed to attend on very complicated or important matters. In a complicated case, a junior barrister will usually be instructed together with a QC. The junior will advise and draft documents before trial and do much of the preparation for the QC. The QC will then present the case in court, although the junior may present some of the case and do some of the cross-examination.

'Cab-rank' principle   5.4.3

By virtue of the 'cab-rank' principle, a barrister cannot refuse any instructions or brief, except for certain reasons set out in the Bar Code of Conduct. For example, they can refuse if they:

- Lack experience or competence in the area;
- Do not have time to do the work;
- Will not be available; or
- Have a conflict of interest.

(There are several reasons set out in the Code.)

5.4.4   Format of instructions

Instructions to counsel to advise or draft documents, and a brief to counsel to attend a hearing, are drafted in a certain form, enclosing all relevant documents. The drafting of instructions is dealt with below. (The drafting of a brief is dealt with in Chapter 25.) New written instructions must be sent for each advice, piece of drafting or attendance required.

5.4.5   Conferences

Counsel may advise in writing in a formal 'opinion' or at a 'conference'.

A conference is the name for a meeting at which counsel gives their advice. Conferences generally take place in counsel's chambers. Several conferences may take place during the course of the proceedings and the client and/or expert witnesses may attend. The solicitor may have a conference over the telephone with counsel on specific points or in urgent cases.

5.4.6   Contact with witnesses

Save in exceptional circumstances, counsel must not discuss the case with or in the presence of any potential witnesses other than witnesses as to character or expert witnesses; but even in these cases a solicitor or solicitor's representative must be present.

In a civil case counsel may, in the presence of the solicitor or solicitor's representative, discuss the case with a potential witness if counsel considers that the interests of the lay client so require and after counsel has been supplied with a proper proof of evidence (statement) of that potential witness.

Counsel must not when interviewing a witness out of court:

- Place a witness under any pressure to provide other than a truthful account of their evidence;
- Rehearse, practise or coach a witness in relation to their evidence or the way in which they should give it.

Direct professional access

Although counsel can generally only be instructed through

a solicitor, ie. a client cannot generally go directly to a barrister, certain professionals can instruct a barrister directly under the Direct Professional Access Rules.

Barristers who are registered to work under these rules can accept instructions from members of bodies designated by the Bar Council, for example, the Royal Institution of Chartered Surveyors and The Institute of Chartered Accountants. However, barristers can only accept instructions from these professionals to advise, draft documents and to appear at a tribunal, inquiry or arbitration. Counsel cannot accept direct professional access instructions to appear in court.

Fee   5.4.7

The fee for counsel's work will be negotiated and agreed with counsel's clerk once the instructions or brief is sent down. (A chambers is run by a team of clerks, headed by a senior clerk.) Solicitors and clerks come to know the level of fees payable for different work and different barristers. The actual fee will depend on the complexity and amount of work, and the experience of the barrister. You will need to be aware of the amount of the fee likely to be recovered from the other side at the end of the case; in personal injury cases, court rules lay down the amounts recoverable.

The fee is marked on the instructions or brief. However, in legal aid cases the fee is not agreed but is decided by the court at the end of the case by the process known as taxation (*see* Chapter 28). The instructions/brief is merely marked 'legal aid'.

The Bar council and the Law Society have agreed that fees should be paid within three months of a fee note being sent out by counsel's clerk.

Note _____

Counsel's fees form part of the 'disbursements' (expenses) when calculating the costs of the case.
_____

Drafting instructions   5.4.8

The instructions are headed with the title of the case as in a pleading, or, if proceedings have not been commenced, with 're ... (name of client or matter)'.

You should draft instructions:

- Giving an overview of the case, and/or the stage reached. You should not repeat what is in the enclosed documents if the relevant information appears clearly in them;

- Drawing attention to and explaining important and specific points;
- Explaining any important goings-on in the case, which do not appear clearly from the documents;
- Giving your own view on, for example, the law, the course of action to take, the merits of the case, in so far as that will help counsel;
- Instructing counsel clearly and specifically as to what you want counsel to do, eg. to advise on the merits, or on quantum, or on a particular point, or on evidence, or on whether to accept an offer that has been made.

The instructions will be covered by a 'backsheet', containing the title of the case and the name and address of counsel and the solicitor. The fee will be marked on this. When the work has been done, counsel will sign and date the backsheet to the effect that the work has been done and return the instructions/brief to the solicitor. In the case of a brief, counsel may record on the backsheet the terms of a settlement agreed at court.

5.4.9   Enclosing documents

You should list the documents sent and enclose copies, not originals, of all relevant documents, depending on the purpose of the instructions. Relevant documents will generally be:

- Writ or summons and pleadings;
- Client statement or completed questionnaire;
- Witness statements;
- Expert reports and third party reports, eg. police accident report in an accident case;
- All relevant documents, eg. the contract at issue;
- All relevant correspondence;
- Special damage calculations and evidence in a personal injury case;
- Legal aid certificate in a legal aid case (regulations provide that this *must* be enclosed);
- Previous instructions sent, with the documents then sent, to remind counsel about the case. (Counsel sends the instructions back once they have been dealt with, and may not recall the case in detail since they do not have the same day-to-day contact with the case as the solicitor.)

The documents should be set out in a clear and comprehensible order. You should not simply send your whole file or a mass of unstructured papers.

Investigating special and general damages in personal injury cases   5.5

In personal injury cases, it is important at an early stage to investigate and calculate the special and general damages suffered by the client in order to begin negotiations with the defendant's insurers and to prepare the statement of special damages which will accompany the statement/particulars of claim.

Loss of earnings from date of accident until trial   5.5.1

If the client was in regular employment, write to the employer asking for details of and documents relating to the following:

- The client's gross and net average wages for the past six months, including overtime.
- The wages, overtime, bonuses and any promotion the client would have received if they had not been off work, perhaps by showing evidence of a comparable employee in that period.
- Did the client receive statutory sick pay? They are likely to have done so for 28 weeks; after 28 weeks, they will not receive statutory sick pay but other benefits such as invalidity benefit and income support.
- Did the client receive extra sick pay beyond statutory sick pay, and was this only paid as a loan to be refunded to the employer from damages received (as is often the case)?
- Has the client lost a chance of promotion, will their job remain open for them and has the accident affected their future job prospects?

Note ──────────────────────────────

The client will have to give written consent to disclosure of their earnings. The written consent should be sent with the letter to their employers.

──────────────────────────────

- If the client was self-employed, an estimate of loss will have to be prepared from accounting records, past tax returns and projections of future profits. You may need to instruct an accountant.
- Write to the Inland Revenue asking for past tax returns, names and addresses of past employers and the client's code number. Again, signed authority from the client must be enclosed.

Note ──────────────────────────────

Preparation of past average earnings will obviously be a more complex task where the client has had several or changing jobs, or irregular employment.

5.5.2   Loss of future earnings

You must determine loss of future earnings beyond the date of trial, and loss of future earning capacity.

Note

Although this comes under *general* damages at common law, loss of future earnings is shown in the statement of *special* damages served with the claim. The confusion arises because the relatively new court rules on statements of special damages define special damages differently from the common law.

The letter to the employer (see 5.5.1) also applies to this head. However, where there is a long term inability to return to work, the client's full work history should be investigated.

- The client's medical report should express an opinion on the client's ability to work again.
- Write to the local Job Centre and also instruct an employment consultant to prepare a report on the client's future job prospects and how the accident has affected these.
- Obtain the relevant information from the client and employer, and possibly instruct an accountant, in order to include a claim for loss of pension rights.

5.5.3   Past and future expenses

Obtain from the client all relevant receipts and invoices.

Medical evidence may be needed to show the need for future expenses.

5.5.4   Pain and suffering and loss of amenity

These will be dealt with in the medical report.

5.5.5   Deductions

Calculate the tax and national insurance to be deducted from the loss of earnings claim, taking into account the client's personal allowances.

Write to the local DSS office, requesting details of all benefits paid to the client since the accident. Advise the client of their rights to apply for various benefits.

Do not forget the DSS Compensation Recovery Scheme (*see* Appendix). In your initial letter to the other side, give them the following details so that they can notify the DSS Compensation Recovery Unit (CRU) about the claim:

- Client's name;
- Address;
- Date of birth;
- National Insurance number;
- Date of accident and brief nature of illness or injuries;
- Employer's name and address;
- Client's department and works/payroll number.

The defendant will then notify the CRU of the claim on form CRU1. The CRU will set-up a record of all benefits claimed and paid to the plaintiff. Before the defendant pays compensation to the plaintiff, they will apply for (on form CRU 4) and obtain a certificate of total benefit from the CRU, and deduct this amount from the compensation paid to the plaintiff.

Interest 5.5.6

Calculate the interest due on the damages (*see* Appendix). It is important to serve the writ/summons as early as possible because interest on pain and suffering and loss of amenity only runs from date of service of the writ/summons.

Statement of special damages in personal injury cases 5.6

In personal injury cases, a statement of special damages (showing past and estimated future loss of earnings and expenses) must be served with the statement/particulars of claim. You should prepare the statement before the statement/particulars of claim is served. In a complex case, counsel will prepare the statement. The statement should:

- Show each item *of expense* incurred as a result of the accident, with brief explanation.
- Explain the plaintiff's *job and earnings* before the accident.
- Show dates of past *lost earnings and net earnings lost*. This may be broken down to show different losses during different periods.
- Give credit for *non-refundable sick pay received and earnings actually received*, eg. the plaintiff may have taken a less well-paid job since accident.
- Show *total past losses*.
- Show *future loss of earnings*. State the plaintiff's age and explain their present position and prospects, and their prospects and earnings if the accident had not happened.
- Show estimated future annual *loss of earnings* and explain the appropriate *multiplier* (*see* Appendix). Multiply future annual loss of earnings by multiplier.

- Explain and deduct any likely *future earnings* from the loss of earnings claim.
- Explain and show the amount of future *annual expenses* and multiply by the number of years for which they will be incurred, or by the appropriate multiplier if permanent.
- Show any *deductions* you must allow from total claim.
- Show total claim for *special damages*.
- Show *benefits paid to date*, which the defendant will have to pay to CRU.
- Show *interest* to date on special damages and the future continuing amount per day.

Note

The statement may have to be updated at times during the course of the proceedings. (The Appendix to this chapter shows how damages for personal injury are quantified.)

Self-assessment questions

1 What persons should you write to in investigating a case?

2 You act for P, who is suing D for personal injury. Before commencing proceedings, you obtain a medical report on your client's injuries from Doctor X but the report is unfavourable to your client, so you obtain a more favourable report from Doctor Y. Do you have to use the report of Doctor X in the proceedings? What will be the role of Doctor Y's report? Will Dr X or Dr Y have to give evidence at trial?

Can D's solicitor insist on P being medically examined by a doctor acting for D?

3 What is the difference between 'open' and 'without prejudice' correspondence. Is a 'letter before action' open or without prejudice?

4 What is the difference between 'instructions' to counsel and a 'brief' to counsel?

5 What is meant by:

(a) a conference

(b) a barrister's chambers

(c) a Queen's Counsel?

6 In what circumstances can a barrister talk directly to a witness without a solicitor being present?

7 In personal injury cases, what is the difference between special damages and general damages?

8 Distinguish between:

(a) damages for pain and suffering and damages for loss of amenity; and between

(b) loss of future earnings and loss of earning capacity.

9 Explain the DSS deduction from compensation scheme

10 Roughly calculate the likely amount of damages which, on a conventional, not structured basis, may be awarded in the following case and state what further details you need to know.

Miss X, aged 32 at the date of the accident in 1991, suffered a fractured skull, a compound fracture of the right radius and ulna, fractures of the left and right fibula and severe ligament injuries to the right and left knee; consequent severe headaches; 30% chance of osteoarthritis in the future.

She will never work again or play tennis (she was a well known county level player). She was earning £250 net per week before the accident and this would have risen over the next few years.

She has required a home-help and this may continue (and the cost may rise) for two years after the trial. She has incurred other expenses, eg. prescription charges, travel, damage to clothing, of £300 overall, and has lost pension rights amounting to £7,000.

She has received social security benefits of £60 per week for six months, rising to £80 a week for a further six months, and now continuing at £100 per week.

She received a redundancy payment of £10,000 as a result of the accident.

11 How could Miss X on the above facts be best compensated for the risk of future osteoarthritis?

Appendix: Calculation of damages for personal injury

The court calculates damages for personal injury by working through certain standard categories of damages, broadly divided into:

- Special damages; and
- General damages.

The plaintiff can, therefore, claim such of the following categories of damages as are appropriate. They are added together to give the total amount of compensation.

1 Special damages

These are items of actual quantifiable pecuniary loss from the date of accident until trial. They include:

- *Loss of earnings* (net of Income Tax and National Insurance) from the date of the accident until trial, due to the accident.
- *Cost of repairs* to the plaintiff's property which has been damaged in the accident, eg. clothes, car.
- *Travelling expenses* incurred as a result of the accident, ie. expenses of travelling to and from hospital or for travelling in respect of any other treatment.
- Any *other expenses* incurred as a result of the accident, eg. expenses of specially adapting the plaintiff's home, telephone calls, prescription charges.
- The cost of *private medical treatment.* The plaintiff is entitled to claim this by virtue of s.2(4), Law Reform (Personal Injuries) Act 1948. There is no duty to mitigate your loss by being treated on the NHS.
- The cost of *private nursing care* for the plaintiff.
- In some cases, *expenses incurred by close relatives* of the plaintiff in visiting or nursing the plaintiff.

2 General damages

These are items which are not capable of precise calculation and which, therefore, have to be assessed by the trial judge. They consist of the following non-pecuniary losses or future (post-trial) estimated pecuniary losses.

Pain and suffering

A sum is awarded for the injury, pain and suffering, scarring, shock and anguish suffered by the plaintiff. Conventional sums are awarded, from approximately £500 for minor bruising to approximately £100,000 for the worst cases of paralysis. There are no fixed sums or scales and no statutory guidelines – it all depends on the nature and seriousness of the injury, pain and suffering, and on looking at the amounts that judges have awarded for similar situations in the past.

The plaintiff's knowledge that their life expectancy has been reduced should be taken into account in assessing the amount for pain and suffering: Administration of Justice Act 1982.

Note

There is a massive body of precedents of the amounts awarded for particular injuries. Every month, *Current Law* and *Halsbury's Laws* publishes recent cases and awards, and there is a large reference work - 'Kemp and Kemp' - containing many precedents relating to all parts of the body.

Loss of amenity

A sum is also awarded for loss of ability to carry out activities, eg. sports and hobbies, as well as for the pain and suffering itself. However, a single lump sum is usually awarded to cover both pain and suffering and loss of amenity. Again, the sum to be awarded for loss of amenity depends on looking at precedents.

Loss of future earnings

The plaintiff is also compensated for estimated future loss of earnings after trial (loss of earnings before trial being part of special damages).

In order to quantify future loss of earnings, the judge calculates the likely average net annual sum that the plaintiff would have earned if they had continued working. (This sum is known technically as the 'multiplicand'.) The judge then multiplies that sum by the number of years for which the plaintiff will be off work. (This number of years is known as the 'multiplier'.)

However, if the plaintiff will never work again, the multiplier is not literally the number of years that the plaintiff will be off work; instead, conventional figures are used. If, for example, the plaintiff is 20 years old, the annual loss is not multiplied by 45. Instead, by convention, the maximum multiplier tends to be 18, decreasing the older the plaintiff is. There are no precise guidelines: the multiplier used again depends on looking at precedents.

The future loss of earnings is calculated according to the number of years the plaintiff would have worked if the accident had not happened, even if the accident has reduced the plaintiff's life expectancy.

Finally, if the plaintiff is being treated in a hospital, nursing home or other institution and is thereby saving money, eg. on heating and electricity normally used at home, this saving must be deducted from the amount awarded for loss of earnings: s.5, Administration of Justice Act 1982.

Loss of earning capacity

An amount may be awarded for this loss, usually where an award for loss of earnings is not appropriate. An award for loss of earning capacity may be made where the plaintiff is a young child, or changes jobs frequently, or is unemployed, or where the plaintiff has not as yet suffered any loss of earnings but the injuries will put them at a disadvantage in the job market if they are looking for a different job in the future. Conventional sums are awarded, in the low thousands. Again, precedents are used.

Future expenses

A sum is awarded for estimated future expenses which will be incurred after the trial (expenses incurred before the trial coming under special damages). These can include any expenses due to the accident, eg. medical and travelling expenses, cost of adapting the plaintiff's house.

As with 'future loss of earnings', the likely annual amount of expenses (the multiplicand) is multiplied by the number of years for which the expenses are likely to be incurred (the multiplier). Similarly, any saving on everyday living costs due to medical care must be deducted from the amount awarded for medical expenses. (This is known as the 'maintenance element' of those expenses.)

3 Deductions from the award

State benefits

It will often be the case that the plaintiff has received state benefits as a result of the accident. In order to avoid double compensation, s.22 and Schedule 4, Social Security Act 1989 provide for the defendant to deduct from the compensation payable to the plaintiff an amount equal to state benefits received by the plaintiff as a result of the accident. The defendant then pays that amount over to the Department of Social Security, who thereby recoups what it has paid to the plaintiff.

The procedure is that, when the defendant is about to make a final compensation payment, the defendant must obtain from the DSS Compensation Recovery Unit a 'certificate of total benefits' giving details of all benefit payments made to the plaintiff as a result of the accident, as well as an estimate of benefits to be paid in the next eight weeks.

The defendant deducts this amount from the compensation and pays the net compensation to the plaintiff accompanied by a certificate of deduction. Within 14 days the defendant must pay the deducted sum to the CRU.

This scheme only applies to benefits paid for five years after the accident or paid up to the date when final compensation is paid, whichever is earlier.

Where the compensation payment is £2,500 or less, a different scheme applies: the defendant deducts a sum equivalent to one half of state benefits paid or to be paid to the plaintiff for five years since the cause of action arose. The defendant does not have to pay this deducted sum over to the DSS.

Sick pay and redundancy payments

Sick pay is deducted from the loss of earnings claim because the earnings have not in that case been lost. Statutory sick pay is deducted under the Social Security Act Scheme described above; non-statutory sick pay is also deducted: *Hussain v New Taplow Paper Mills Ltd* (1988).

A *redundancy payment* is deducted if the redundancy is attributable to the accident: *Colledge v Bass Mitchells & Butlers Ltd* (1988).

Payments not deducted

The following are not deducted from compensation awards:

- A payout, as a result of the accident, from *private insurance* taken out by the plaintiff: *Bradburn v Great Western Railway Co* (1874);
- A *gift* to the plaintiff from a charity or a benevolent third party, as a result of the accident;
- *Pension payments* received by the plaintiff as a result of the accident: *Smoker v London Fire and Civil Defence Authority* (1991).

4 Interest

Where the damages awarded exceed £200, the court must award interest on the sum for which judgment is given unless the court is satisfied that there are special reasons why it should not: s.35A(2), Supreme Court Act 1981 (High Court); s.69, County Courts Act 1984 (County Court).

The court has a discretion as to the rate and period of interest: s.35A. However, the House of Lords has laid down the following guidelines, which are usually followed:

- *Special damages* carry interest at half the court's special investment account (a court bank account) rate from the date of accident until trial;
- Damages for *pain and suffering* and *loss of amenity* carry

interest from the date of service of court proceedings until trial at 2% per annum.

- There is no interest on damages for *future loss*. (*Birkett v Hayes* (1982) and *Wright v British Railways Board* (1983) are authorities for the above.)

5 Awards of provisional damages

The amount awarded for pain and suffering will take into account the future prospects for the injury, pain and suffering.

However, it may be more appropriate to apply for a provisional damages order under s.32A, Supreme Court Act 1981 when

'there is proved or admitted to be a chance that at some definite or indefinite time in the future the injured person will, as a result of the act or omission which gave rise to the cause of action, develop some serious disease or suffer some serious deterioration in (their) physical or mental condition'.

If there is such a chance, the plaintiff can both apply to the judge for an award based on the plaintiff's present condition only and also for an order that if a specified disease or deterioration occurs in the future, the plaintiff can come back to court and apply for further compensation.

However, the scope of s.32A appears to have been limited by the narrow interpretation given to it in *Willson v Ministry of Defence* (1991), where the judge said that further compensation under s.32A should only be awarded when there is a clear-cut future specific situation of deterioration, the section should not apply to a typical continuing deterioration.

6 Structured settlements

In cases of large compensation payments it is increasingly common for the parties to agree 'structured settlements' instead of relying on the payment of a lump sum or on provisional damages. Under a structured settlement, the plaintiff receives a reduced lump sum plus a guarantee of periodic payments for life which are obtained by the defendant investing a lump sum. These settlements have tax advantages and the guarantee of payments for life.

However, such settlements can only be agreed between the parties, the court has no power to order them (although it is a rule that any settlement on behalf of a child plaintiff must be approved by the court).

Chapter 6

Alternative dispute resolution

Introduction   6.1

Although this Companion deals mainly with the usual
procedure for fighting a case through to judgment in the
County Court and High Court, there are several other ways
of settling a dispute, these are set out below.

You should be aware of these other possibilities, and
should consider the most appropriate method of settling a
particular dispute.

Negotiation   6.2

Most cases do not go to trial. A settlement is usually negotiated.

Prior to and during litigation, the sides will usually
negotiate and make offers and counter-offers of settlement.
A negotiated settlement is usually preferable to going to
trial because a trial involves great expense, delay, stress and
the risk of losing. Also, a settlement could include provisions which would not be ordered by the court and may go
beyond the terms of the dispute, allowing for a more
satisfactory solution.

Often, steps in the litigation are only taken as a tactic in the
settlement negotiations. For example, the writ may be issued
to put pressure on the other side; the pleading is often as
detailed as possible, to show the strength of your case; and you
may apply for security for costs or request specific discovery
or interrogatories again mainly to put pressure on the other
side. (Other steps could equally be used.)

Before proceedings commence, you have no implied
authority to settle the dispute. After the proceedings have
commenced, you have implied authority in the absence of
express instructions to the contrary. However, you should
not negotiate, make or accept an offer of settlement without
the client's authority. Also, you should have thorough
knowledge of the case, its merits and the client's aims before
negotiating, making or accepting an offer. Counsel's opinion is often taken.

Chapter 24 explains the procedures for agreeing a settlement. Payment into court and Calderbank offers (*see* Chapter 24) are also formal methods of reaching a settlement.

6.3   Structured settlements in personal injury cases

Most negotiated settlements of money claims provide for payment of a lump sum, or perhaps of a sum payable by instalments. In large personal injury claims, the practice of agreeing a more sophisticated device known as a 'structured settlement' has developed, which generally provides for inflation-proofed payments for the rest of the plaintiff's life with tax advantages. The basic scheme of a structured settlement is as follows.

- The defendant's insurer pays to the plaintiff part of the sum agreed as a lump sum up front (although there may still be an instalment element here) to take account of the plaintiff's immediate needs and also to meet contingencies.
- The remainder is paid by way of future annual payments, usually index-linked, and calculated to last for the remainder of the plaintiff's life.
- The defendant's insurer provides for the future annual payments by purchasing an annuity which will produce the annual payments. This has tax advantages for the plaintiff.
- The scheme has advantages over the ordinary settlement procedure whereby a lump sum is paid to the plaintiff who is taxed on it and then has the cost and administration of investing the sum. Further, structured settlements are skilfully designed by accountants to last for the plaintiff's life, to be inflation-proofed, to produce an adequate annual income for the plaintiff's needs and to avoid tax.
- It is the practice for the plaintiff to agree that the amount the insurer pays to purchase an annuity should be less than the amount they would pay under a conventional lump sum settlement.

Note

The court does not have power to impose a structured settlement, or to order structured payment of a judgment. However, a structured settlement on behalf of a person under a disability (a child or mental patient) must be approved by the Court.

6.4   Specialist courts

Although this is not strictly a method of alternative dispute resolution, you should be aware that certain specialist matters are dealt with in specialist courts which have their own detailed procedures. These procedures are different from, but similar to, the ordinary litigation procedure described in this Companion.

The Commercial Court 6.4.1

This is part of the Queen's Bench Division but it has its own procedures and special expertise. Specialist commercial firms routinely use this court (and also the Admiralty Court *see* below). The commercial court is used mainly for disputes over shipping, insurance, banking, credit, international carriage of goods, aircraft, commodities, international markets and exchanges, mercantile contracts and arbitration. Commercial court procedure and jurisdiction is fully dealt with in RSC O.72 and the notes thereto.

The Admiralty Court 6.4.2

This is also part of the Queen's Bench Division and deals with shipping disputes. Its jurisdiction and procedure is dealt with in RSC O.75 and the *White Book*, volume 2, part 6.

The Patent's Court 6.4.3

This is part of the Chancery Division and deals with patent disputes. (*See* RSC O.104 for its procedure.)

The Official Referees' Court 6.4.4

Very complicated technical or scientific disputes, involving large amounts of paperwork and expert evidence, are generally tried in a special court within the High Court called the Official Referees' Court. An Official Referee is the name given to a judge designated to try these cases. Such cases are referred to in the rules as 'Official Referees' business'.

The Official Referees' Court deals mainly with construction disputes but also with, for example, technical disputes over land, claims between landlord and tenant for breach of repairing covenants, claims for defects in goods and environmental disputes.

Just as the Commercial Court is the specialist territory of the commercial litigator, the Official Referees' Court is the territory of the construction litigator. (*See* RSC O.36 for its procedure.)

Note _____

Cases in the Official Referees' Court, particularly construction cases, tend to involve massive amounts of documentation, schedules of dilapidations, expert reports and very long pleadings. A feature of litigation in this court is the *Scott Schedule* (named after a past Official Referee). A schedule is prepared listing the items in dispute and against each item are columns in which both parties put their comments and proposed price cost in respect of each item. There is then a final column for the Official Referee's decision in respect of each item.

6.4.5   The Court of Protection

This specialist court protects and administers the property and affairs of persons who are incapable by reason of mental disorder of managing and administering their own property and affairs. Its jurisdiction and procedure is laid down in the Mental Health Act 1983, Court of Protection Rules 1984 and *White Book*, volume 2, para 9.

6.4.6   The Restrictive Practices Court

This court considers 'restrictive agreements' and 'information agreements' in respect of goods and services under the Restrictive Trade Practices Act 1976 and Restrictive Practices Court Act 1976.

6.5   Tribunals and associations

Many specialist matters are not taken to litigation through the courts but to tribunals. There are many tribunals covering many aspects of the law, eg. industrial tribunals, the Employment Appeal Tribunal, the Lands Tribunal (which decides certain land valuation disputes), pensions appeal tribunals, the Rent Assessment Committee (which decides certain disputes over amounts of rent) and Social Security appeal tribunals. (The full list is set out in Schedule 1, Tribunals and Inquiries Act 1971.)

Further, a dispute over the provision of goods or services may be solved (or redress may be obtained) by going to the trade or professional association to which the provider belongs. Many of these associations have set up speedy, cheap, arbitration procedures for settling disputes between consumers/clients and providers. For example, the Association of British Travel Agents (ABTA) has a scheme for settling disputes between travellers and travel agents and the furniture and electrical industries have dispute settlement schemes.

Furthermore, the Solicitors' Arbitration Scheme, Legal Complaints Bureau and The Chartered Surveyors Arbitration Scheme have been set up to settle disputes between solicitors/surveyors and their clients.

6.6   Arbitration

6.6.1   Meaning and advantages of arbitration

Arbitration is where the parties submit their dispute to a private (usually professional) third party for a decision which is nevertheless *legally binding* and can be *enforced* in the same way as a court judgment.

It is a very important and commonly used alternative to litigation. In some specialist areas, eg. shipping disputes, construction disputes and commercial property rent disputes, arbitration is as common as litigation.

Litigation is a public system, decided by a publicly appointed judge according to a fixed procedure which applies (subject to variations) to all cases. The parties must submit to this usual procedure and are subject to the delay caused by being one of many cases. Arbitration is a *private procedure*. The parties are involved in the appointment of the arbitrator who is usually an expert in the particular area. The procedure is flexible and decided on by the parties and the arbitrator; the arbitrator is involved in the case throughout – unlike a judge, who may only see the case at trial.

Arbitration is generally quicker than litigation and is heard in private at any venue and at any time. Further, an arbitrator's decision is usually final (but *see* 6.6.4).

Despite being a flexible procedure in principle, arbitration rules have been devised in many areas where arbitration is commonly used, eg. the London Court of International Arbitration Rules, the London Maritime Arbitrators' Association terms, the Joint Contracts Tribunal rules for building contract arbitrations.

An arbitrator is paid privately by the parties, but the arbitrator's expertise and the speed and flexibility of the proceedings may offset this expense. (The arbitrator's fee is in addition to professional fees and legal aid is unavailable.)

Note

In many cases, eg. building disputes, arbitration may be as complex and expensive as litigation.

There are three main statutes governing arbitration: the Arbitration Acts 1950 and 1979, and the Arbitration Act 1975 (which deals only with international arbitrations). However, the Acts do not set detailed rules as to how arbitrations should be carried out, they lay down miscellaneous general matters, eg. appointment of arbitrators, court powers over arbitrations, costs and enforcement.

Some points on basic arbitration procedure　　6.6.2

Many contracts contain an arbitration agreement which means that any dispute between the parties over the contract will be submitted not to court litigation but to arbitration. Such an agreement is common in many standard specialist contracts, eg. building contracts.

If there is such an arbitration agreement and one of the parties commences litigation proceedings, the other party may apply to stay those proceedings under s.4, Arbitration Act 1950. The Court has a discretion as to whether to stay the litigation proceedings and will usually do so.

The arbitration agreement will state how many arbitrators there are to be and how they are to be appointed. It is common to provide that the appointment shall be by a professional body such as the Chartered Institute of Arbitrators or, for example, the Royal Institute of Chartered Surveyors.

The agreement may state that certain arbitration rules (*see* above) are to apply.

The procedure may be oral or by documents only, or by documents accompanied by written representations. Aspects of litigation procedure, eg. discovery, exchange of experts' reports, documents similar to pleadings, exchange of witness statements, meetings between experts are usually used. There is usually a preliminary hearing.

A decision by an arbitrator is known as an 'award' which in practice is given in writing. An award may, with leave of the High Court or County Court, be enforced in the same way as a court judgment: s.26, Arbitration Act 1950.

6.6.3   The main specialist arbitrations

Arbitration is common in the following main specialist areas.

Construction industry arbitration
Standard building contracts provide for resolution of disputes by arbitration, generally according to the Joint Contracts Tribunal Rules. The arbitrator is usually an expert appointed by the Royal Institute of British Architects, the Royal Institution of Chartered Surveyors, the Chartered Institute of Arbitrators or the Institution of Civil Engineers.

Arbitration is thus an alternative to litigation in the Official Referees Court (*see* 6.4.4).

Marine arbitration
Shipping disputes are commonly resolved by marine arbitration rather than by litigation in the Commercial or Admiralty Court. The arbitrator is usually a member of the London Maritime Arbitrators' Association, who will use the London Maritime Arbitrators' Association Terms.

International commercial arbitrations
These are carried out by the Court of Arbitration of the International Chamber of Commerce and the London Court of International Arbitration.

Rent review arbitrations

Most commercial leases have 'rent review' clauses which provide for the rent to be increased (or perhaps decreased) every few years. The clause usually provides that if the parties cannot agree on the new rent, it should be decided by an arbitrator, usually to be appointed by the Royal Institute of Chartered Surveyors.

Consumer arbitration

Many trades and professions have arbitration schemes to resolve disputes between their members and consumers/clients. Most of the schemes are administered by the Chartered Institute of Arbitrators and are by documents only. A National Small Claims Arbitration service is run by the Chartered Institute of Arbitrators.

Challenging an arbitration award in the courts　　6.6.4

The courts have limited powers to overturn an arbitration award.

- Under s.1, Arbitration Act 1950, the High Court can grant leave to revoke the authority of an arbitrator but this power is rarely exercised.

- Under s.22, the High Court may remit the matter for the arbitrator's reconsideration. Under s.23, the High Court may remove the arbitrator and/or set the award aside where the arbitrator is guilty of misconduct. However, these powers are only exercised in limited circumstances.

- Under s.1, Arbitration Act 1979, a party can appeal to the High Court against an award, *on a point of law.*

Resolution of a dispute by an expert　　6.7

Meaning　　6.7.1

Another alternative to litigation is expert determination. This is where the dispute is resolved by a third party expert looking at all the material and giving their own expert opinion, which the parties have agreed will be binding.

Expert determination differs from litigation and arbitration in that it is not a judicial inquiry as such. The expert does not sit as a third party 'referee' receiving evidence and submissions from both sides and then coming to a decision on the material submitted by both sides. Instead, the expert makes their own investigations and acts on their own expertise.

Basic points on expert procedure　　6.7.2

Expert determination is used as a method of dispute resolution in various contracts. The contract will provide that any dispute over value will be decided by the opinion of an expert. For example, agreements for the sale of a business may provide for any dispute over the value of the business to be referred to an expert; a rent review clause in a lease may provide for the new rent to be decided by an expert rather than an arbitrator.

The contract will provide for how the expert is to be appointed (usually, by a relevant professional body, eg. the Royal Institute of Chartered Surveyors, if the parties cannot agree). The contract may also set out the terms on and procedure under which the expert is to act.

There are no statutes or formal rules governing expert procedure and it is informal and relatively quick and cheap. However, the contract may provide for a procedure and the professional body may provide a code, eg. the guidance notes for surveyors acting as experts in rent review disputes published by the Royal Institute of Chartered Surveyors.

The Arbitration Acts do not apply to an expert and an expert's decision cannot be enforced as if it were a court judgment. It can only be challenged where the expert has acted outside their jurisdiction, or has been involved in fraud or collusion. An expert can, however, be sued for negligence in making their decision, unlike an arbitrator.

6.8   Mediation, conciliation and other methods

6.8.1   Meaning and advantages

There is increasing interest in the legal profession in alternative dispute resolution (ADR) methods. ADR refers to informal ways of solving a dispute as alternatives to litigation. ADR methods may have the following advantages over litigation:

- They are quicker and cheaper;
- The parties retain control of the situation, rather than being subject to an externally imposed, inflexible system;
- The parties can explore creative, comprehensive and commercial solutions to the problem and perhaps continue their relationship, instead of being forced into an adversarial win/lose situation and subject to limited court remedies;
- ADR methods are private and confidential.

On the other hand, ADR methods are not legally binding or enforceable.

Methods   6.8.2

There are many flexible and creative ways of solving a dispute other than by litigation or arbitration. *Negotiation* is obviously one way but there are many methods between negotiation at one end of the spectrum and litigation at the other. These methods generally involve a skilled or expert third party helping the parties to achieve a settlement. They include the following.

Mediation

This is the most commonly used method. A third party assists the disputing parties to reach a settlement. This can be done through a combination of, for example:

- Chairing meetings;
- Listening to both sides' cases;
- Sitting in on negotiations;
- Having separate meetings with both sides;
- Shuttling backwards and forwards between the sides;
- Suggesting terms and ways of settlement and/or appraising their cases.

Conciliation

This is similar to mediation, but the third party plays a less active role, not so much suggesting terms of settlement as helping the parties to communicate with each other and find terms of settlement themselves.

Executive tribunal

Representatives from companies in dispute present their cases to a neutral chairperson and a senior executive from each company. The executives then attempt to negotiate a settlement, with the assistance of the third party.

Assessment of the case by an expert, or non-binding adjudication by a third party

The parties may use these to assist further negotiations.

The Centre for Dispute Resolution (CEDR)   6.9

This is an independent, non-profit making organisation which exists to promote and encourage ADR and to provide ADR services, training and consultancy. Many companies and firms, including law firms, are members of CEDR.

CEDR can be used to suggest and/or set up an appropriate method of dispute resolution for a particular case.

Self-assessment questions

1   List the key points in a structured settlement.
2   What methods and forums exist for solving:
    (a) a shipping dispute
    (b) a construction industry dispute?
3   What is a *Scott Schedule*?
4   Explain the differences between:
    (a) courts
    (b) tribunals
    (c) arbitration
    (d) determination by an expert
    (e) mediation
    as forums for resolving disputes.
5   Your client has an arbitration agreement in a contract with P. P sues your client in the High Court for breach of that contract. What step would you take to prevent the litigation?
6   What statutes govern arbitration?
7   Name the main commercial and professional organisations that are commonly concerned in arbitration.
8   What is meant by alternative dispute resolution. How could you find out more about it?

Chapter 7

Formal pre-action procedures for obtaining information

Introduction 7.1

You may wish to obtain information or documents which are in the possession of someone other than your client in order to investigate your client's claim and to consider whether it is worth suing. Also, you may wish to inspect property in the possession of another, in order to investigate the client's claim and to consider whether it is worth suing.

> *Example*
>
> Your client may have been injured while using a machine at a factory. You will want to inspect the machine, obtain the records of the hospital where the client was treated and obtain information from any witnesses to the incident.

You should endeavour to obtain such documents, information and inspection informally, by writing to the relevant persons or places asking if they will allow such inspection or will disclose their documents or information. However, what if they refuse, as is probable where the relevant persons are likely to be the defendants to any action, or were involved in the wrongdoing, or have some other motive for refusing to cooperate?

This chapter covers the procedures under which you can obtain formal court orders forcing those persons to disclose documents or information or to allow inspection of their property.

The general rule 7.2

In general, there is not a lot you can do. In general, the court has no power to order X to disclose information to Y or to allow inspection by Y before any action has been commenced. In general, Y cannot bring an action against X purely requiring X to disclose information or allow inspection.

In general, your proper course of action is to commence an action based on a substantive cause of action, assuming you consider there is enough evidence and merit in the case even before the required further information has been obtained. In that substantive action there will then be various procedures under which substantial information can be obtained from the other party.

Note

Even if an action is commenced, the court still only has limited powers to order non-parties to the action to disclose information.

7.3   Exceptions

There are three exceptions to the general rule:

- Order for disclosure of documents by a likely party to a claim in respect of personal injuries or death;
- Order for pre-action inspection of property;
- Order for disclosure of identity of wrongdoers against innocent facilitator of wrongdoing – Norwich Pharmacal order.

7.3.1   Order for disclosure of documents

By virtue of s.33(2), Supreme Court Act 1981 (High Court) and s.52(2), County Courts Act 1984 (County Court), a person who is likely to be a party to a subsequent claim in respect of personal injuries or death may apply to the court for an order that another person likely to be a party, ie. usually, the probable defendant, should disclose relevant documents.

Thus, under this jurisdiction, your client in the example in 7.1.1 could apply for a pre-action court order that the factory employer (likely to be the defendant) should disclose maintenance records relating to the machine.

The Court of Appeal, however, has stated that before applying for such a pre-action order the solicitor for the potential plaintiff should write an open letter to the potential defendant setting out the nature of the proposed claim in order to make the potential defendant aware of the case against them: *Shaw v Vauxhall Motors Ltd* (1974).

Applying for the order

In the *High Court* the potential plaintiff should apply for the order by issuing an originating summons (*see* form 10, *White Book* vol. 2) applying for such an order. This is served on the potential defendant together with affidavit evidence showing how the case falls within s.33(2). (*See* RSC O.24 r.7A and the notes thereto for details of the procedure.)

In the *County Court* the potential plaintiff should apply for the order by issuing an originating application applying for such an order. This is served on the potential defendant together with affidavit evidence showing how the case falls within s.52. (*See* CCR O.13 r.7 for details of the procedure.)

The potential plaintiff's solicitor should ensure that, if the client qualifies for legal aid, the legal aid certificate covers this application. Alternatively, legal aid should be applied for to cover this application.

It will be a matter for the court as to whether the case falls within the Act and as to whether to exercise its discretion to allow pre-action disclosure.

The person against whom such an order is sought is generally entitled to an order that the other side pay their costs of the application and of complying with the order, unless the court otherwise directs.

Order for pre-action inspection of property   7.3.2

By virtue of s.33(1), Supreme Court Act 1981 (High Court) and s.55(1), County Courts Act 1984, (County Court), the court has power to make pre-action orders for:

- The inspection, photographing, preservation, custody and detention of property which appears to the court to be property which may become the subject matter of the subsequent proceedings, or as to which any question may arise in any such proceedings; and

- The taking of samples of any such property as is mentioned in the paragraph above and the carrying out of any experiment on or with any such property.

Therefore, under this jurisdiction, your client in the example at 7.1.1 could apply for a pre-action court order that the factory owner must allow your client to inspect the machine. The jurisdiction is not, as in the case of 7.3.1, limited to personal injury and death cases. Also, the rules do not say that the order can only be made against a likely party to the action.

As with 7.3.1 above, you should first write to the relevant person, asking if they will allow inspection etc. A court application will only be necessary if they refuse.

Applying for the order

In the *High Court* the potential plaintiff should apply for the order by issuing an originating summons (*see* form 8, *White Book* vol. 2) applying for such an order. This is served on the relevant person together with affidavit evidence showing how the case falls within s.33(1). (*See* RSC O.29 r.7A and the notes thereto for details of the procedure.)

In the *County Court* the potential plaintiff should apply for the order by issuing an originating application applying for such an order. This is served on the relevant person together with affidavit evidence showing how the case falls within s.52. (*See* CCR O.13 r.7 for details of the procedure.)

As in the case of pre-action discovery, the potential plaintiff's solicitor should ensure that if the client qualifies for legal aid there is legal aid cover for this application.

The person against whom the order is sought is generally entitled to an order that the other side pay their costs of the application and of complying with the order, unless the court otherwise directs.

Obviously, the potential plaintiff's solicitor should engage an expert to carry out the inspection etc on behalf of the potential plaintiff. The expert should then be asked to prepare a report.

7.3.3   Order for disclosure of identity of wrongdoers against an innocent facilitator of wrongdoing – Norwich Pharmacal Order

The court has no power to make an order for disclosure of documents or information against an innocent person who has no connection with the wrongdoing, even if that person knows the identity of the alleged wrongdoer. The innocent person cannot generally be compelled to disclose the identity of the wrongdoer. This is known as the 'mere witness' rule.

Example

A road accident victim cannot sue a witness who knows the identity of the other driver in order to compel the witness to disclose the driver's identity.

Where, however, the innocent person has facilitated the wrongdoing, even if innocently, that person can be compelled by the court to disclose the identity of the wrongdoer.

This jurisdiction derives from the Chancery Division of the High Court, rather than from the RSC. The basis of the modern jurisdiction is *Norwich Pharmacal Co v Customs and Excise Commissioners* (1974), where the owners of a patent for a chemical compound claimed that their patent was being infringed by illicit importations of the compound from abroad. The owners sued the Commissioners purely for discovery (disclosure) of documents which would show the identity of the importers. The House of Lords held that, since the Commissioner's had facilitated (albeit innocently) the wrongdoing, they were liable to disclose the identity of the wrongdoers.

Thus, where a client wishes to commence an action, but information is needed on the identity of the person to be sued, this information could be discovered by bringing an action for discovery against an innocent party who has facilitated the wrongdoing.

Applying for the order

In the *High Court*, the party seeking the information should issue a writ or originating summons seeking an order for disclosure of specified documents or categories of documents revealing the identity of the wrongdoer. This should then be followed by an interlocutory application by summons or notice of motion to a master seeking disclosure of the documents.

Alternatively, if the person with the information is themes a wrongdoer, the proper procedure is to bring proceedings against them in respect of the substantive wrong and, in that action, seek an order requiring the wrongdoer to disclose the identity of other persons involved.

Example

In *Loose v Williamson* (1978), the defendants were sighted removing shellfish from the plaintiff's fishery. The plaintiff was entitled to an order that the defendants disclose the identity of others involved. The order was sought by *ex parte* application on the same day that the writ was issued and the defendants were required to make the disclosure by affidavit within a short time.

By s.38, County Courts Act 1984, the *County Court* has power to make any order that the High Court could make. Application will be made by originating application and affidavit.

Note

For further details on this area, *see BSC v Granada Television Ltd* (1981); *RCA Corp v Reddingtons Rare Records* (1974); *Harrington v North London Polytechnic* (1984); and *X Ltd v Morgan-Grampian (Publishers) Ltd* (1990).

Order for discovery to help trace stolen assets   7.3.4

In commercial fraud/breach of trust cases, where the plaintiff is making a proprietary claim for the return of stolen assets, the court has power to order innocent third parties to disclose information and give discovery of documents which might lead to the location or preservation of the stolen assets.

Example 1

In *London and County Securities Ltd v Caplan* (1978), Mr Caplan was alleged to have embezzled £5 million of the plaintiff's money and transferred it to the Californian branch of a UK bank. The judge made an order requiring that bank to disclose whether it still had the money and, if not, where it had gone.

Example 2

In *Bankers Trust Co v Shapira* (1980), the Court of Appeal ordered the disclosure by a third party bank of all correspondence, debit vouchers, transfer applications, orders and internal memoranda relating to any account maintained by the alleged fraudster.

Conditions

The following conditions apply.

(a) The judge will not order disclosure by the third party unless there is a *real prospect* that the information may lead to the location or preservation of the assets.

Example

In *Arab Monetary Fund v Hashim (No 5)* (1992) (where these principles were fully explained), the plaintiff, who claimed that the defendant had stolen money from them, sought an order that a law firm that had acted for the defendant some years before should disclose documents relating to their work for the defendant.

The court refused to order disclosure since there was no real prospect that the documents would help to locate the plaintiff's stolen assets.

(b) Any order should be in narrow terms, requiring disclosure of *specific documents* and *specific information* as to the whereabouts of the assets.

(c) An order will not be made if the potential advantage of the order to the plaintiff is outweighed by the detriment to the third party in terms of cost, invasion of privacy and breach of confidence. (This was another ground for refusal of the order in *Hashim*.)

(d) As a condition of the order being made, the plaintiff will have to undertake to pay any damages wrongly suffered by the third party as a result of the disclosure, to pay the third party's expenses of making the disclosure, and to use the documents solely for tracing the money and not for any other purpose.

Note

In commercial fraud litigation where the plaintiff is tracing money, this power to order third parties to disclose information is an important weapon, which is used together with applications by the plaintiff for *Mareva* injunctions, *Anton*

Piller orders, discovery, and appointment of receivers to companies.

Procedure

Within the main action against the defendant claiming return of the asset, the plaintiff should apply by Notice of Motion (or *ex parte* in urgent cases) in the Chancery Division, requiring the third party to disclose documents, and/or to swear an affidavit as to what has happened to specified assets.

Self-assessment questions

1 P is hit by a car driven by D. W witnesses the accident. Can P bring an action against W, asking for a court order that W discloses what they saw?

2 In the example in question 1, could P, before suing D, sue the garage where D's car was recently repaired, in order to obtain a court order that the garage disclose the maintenance records?

   Alternatively, could P bring an action against D to force D to disclose the car maintenance records or to allow P to inspect the car before suing D for negligence?

3 D installed a machine in P's factory. The machine exploded causing P financial loss. Before commencing a substantive action, could P sue D to force D to disclose:

   (a) their documents relating to the machine

   (b) the identity of the manufacturers?

4 In the above questions, would it be easier for P to obtain the documents and information by commencing a substantive action against D and obtaining the documents and information during that action? (*See* Chapters 17 and 23.)

5 Explain the differences between the *Bankers Trust* case and the *Arab Monetary Fund* case. (It will be helpful to read the cases.)

Chapter 8

Emergency injunctions

Meaning of, and grounds for, injunctions   8.1

Note
_____

This section is not limited to emergency injunctions.
_____

What is an injunction?   8.1.1

An injunction is an equitable remedy whereby the court will order a party to refrain from doing an act or will order a party to do an act. (The principles governing the grant of an injunction are explained in the pre-knowledge primer on Civil Litigation.)

General procedure for obtaining an injunction   8.1.2

The plaintiff will issue a writ (High Court) or summons (County Court) claiming the injunction. In theory, at final trial, the court will decide whether to grant the injunction by reference to the principles explained in the Primer companion. However, in practice it will be months or years before there is a final trial and in most cases the plaintiff will not want to wait that long for an injunction. Therefore, the plaintiff usually applies for an *interim injunction* to last from commencement of proceedings until final trial.

This interim injunction is known as an *interlocutory injunction*. (The principles and procedures for obtaining an interlocutory injunction are explained in Chapter 20.)

The judge decides whether to grant an interlocutory injunction at an *inter partes* hearing, ie. a hearing of which the defendant is notified and which both parties attend, which takes place shortly after commencement of proceedings.

Meaning of *ex parte* injunction   8.1.3

However, in a case of real emergency, eg. where a tenant has been unlawfully thrown out of their property and wishes to get back in straight away, the plaintiff will not have time, or will not want to notify the defendant of the injunction application and will apply for the injunction immediately. Indeed, in many cases, the plaintiff will apply for an emergency injunction even *before* proceedings have been commenced.

An injunction application made urgently, and without

notifying the other side that the application is being made, is known as an *ex parte* application for an injunction.

8.2   When is an *ex parte* injunction application appropriate?

An *ex parte* application should only be made in cases of urgency (*see* RSC O.29 r.1(2) and *Bates v Lord Hailsham of St Marylebone* (1972). In such cases, the ex parte application can even be made before issue of the writ/summons commencing proceedings (RSC O.29 r.1(3); CCR O.13 r.6(4)).

In *Re First Express Ltd* (1991), Hoffmann J gave further guidance, stating that an application should only be made *ex parte* when:

(a) The applicant would otherwise suffer injustice due to delay, or because of action which the other party would be likely to take before an *inter partes* order could be made; and

(b) The other party can be later compensated in damages if it turns out that the injunction should not have been granted, or if the risk of uncompensatable loss is clearly outweighed by the risk of injustice to the applicant if the injunction is not granted.

As to (a) above, a tenant who has been thrown out of their property, for example, can apply *ex parte* for an immediate injunction. They would suffer injustice if they had to remain homeless while waiting for an *inter partes* hearing, due notice of which must be given to the landlord.

Further, if the tenant was required to give the landlord notice of the injunction hearing, the landlord could pre-empt the hearing by reletting the property, thereby making it difficult for an injunction to be ordered. This is an example of how a plaintiff can apply *ex parte* not only when speed is essential but also when surprise or secrecy is important in order to obtain an injunction before the other party can 'burn the evidence' or otherwise alter the situation in their favour.

The most common *ex parte* injunctions, for example, are the *Mareva* injunctions and *Anton Piller* orders. These are injunctions ordering the freezing of the other party's assets and the seizure of their documents respectively. Obviously, the injunction is applied for *ex parte* to ensure secrecy as well as speed. If the other party were given notice of the application, they might dissipate their assets or destroy their documents (as the case may be) before the hearing, thereby rendering any order ineffective.

Procedure for obtaining an *ex parte* injunction   8.3

Note _____

In most cases, only a judge, not a Master or District Judge, can grant an injunction.
_____

Documents to be drafted   8.3.1

The applicant should draft:

- An affidavit in support of the application; and
- The order that they wish the judge to make (using precedents of injunction orders, as adapted to the facts).

If the application is made before proceedings are commenced, the applicant should also draft:

- The proposed writ/County Court request for summons.

In this latter case, the documents are headed 'In the matter of an intended action'.

Details of the affidavit   8.3.2

The affidavit should contain a clear and concise statement of:

- The facts giving rise to the claim;
- The facts giving rise to the interlocutory claim;
- The justification for making the application *ex parte*;
- Details of any notice of the application given to the other party, or the reasons for giving none;
- Details of any response to the claim intimated by the defendant – including, for example, details contained in correspondence;
- Details of any facts which might lead the court not to grant the *ex parte* injunction;
- Details of the precise terms of the injunction required;
- In the County Court, how the court has jurisdiction to hear the matter.

Lodging documents with the court before the hearing   8.3.3

The point of an *ex parte* application is that no summons/notice of application is served on the other side notifying them of the hearing. The applicant merely lodges with the court the documents mentioned in 8.3.1 as explained below.

Queen's Bench

In the Queen's Bench Division, the documents are lodged with the clerk to the judge in chambers by 3.00pm on the day before the application (which is then heard at 10.00am on the following day). In a case of great urgency, the applicant can arrive with the documents at 9.50am for a 10.00 hearing, or lodge the documents by 12.30pm for a 2.00pm hearing (*see* Practice Direction 1983 1 WLR 433). Counsel (or solicitor, if counsel is not instructed) should prepare a certificate that the application is of extreme urgency.

Chancery Division

In the Chancery Division, the draft order sought is lodged with the clerk of the lists by 12pm on the day before the hearing.

Note

In the High Court, a fee of £15 is payable. The receipt of payment is stamped on the affidavit.

County Court

In the County Court the documents should be lodged the day before, or shortly before, the hearing – local practice varies.

All courts

In all courts, in cases of *extreme urgency*, where an injunction is needed straight away, an applicant can present themselves to the clerk to the judge and make their application at any time. A duty judge can be contacted to hear an application during the night or at weekends. In such cases, the applicant may not even have prepared any documents, and will have to undertake to prepare/issue/file/serve them straight after the hearing.

8.3.4   **The hearing of the application**

Usually, the other side will not be present – there are some 'opposed *ex parte*' applications where the other side is present, either because they have heard about the hearing or because the applicant is asking for the continuation of a previous *ex parte* injunction.

The judge will read the documents and listen to submissions by the applicant. The applicant should make full and frank disclosure of all points *against* their case.

If there is merit in the claim and the case is of sufficient urgency, the judge will grant an injunction for a short period, but usually only on condition that the applicant gives the following undertakings:

- To pay damages to the other party if it later turns out that an injunction should not have been granted;
- To notify the other party of the terms of the order forthwith;
- Where the injunction is granted before proceedings are commenced, to issue proceedings forthwith;

- Before the expiry of the *ex parte* injunction, to issue a summons/application for an interlocutory injunction in order to continue the injunction until trial (*see* 8.4 below and Chapter 20, *Interlocutory injunctions*);
- In an exceptional case where an affidavit has not been prepared or sworn in time for the hearing, to prepare and/or swear (as the case may be) the affidavit immediately.

The order granting the injunction   8.3.5

The judge will usually order that the costs of the application be 'reserved' (*see* Chapter 20).

If the judge agrees to grant the injunction, the judge will initial the draft order sought by the applicant (and perhaps amend it). In the Queen's Bench Division, the order is then formally drafted by the plaintiff's solicitor and sealed by the court. In the Chancery Division and County Court, the order is formally drafted by the court.

The order is then personally served on the other party, with a 'penal notice' warning them of the consequences of disobeying the order. (For details on all this, *see* Chapter 20.)

The order will contain provision for the other party to apply for discharge or variation of the order.

Continuation after the *ex parte* stage   8.4

The judge will only grant an emergency *ex parte* injunction for a very short period, eg. one week. The applicant will have to undertake to issue, within that week, a summons (High Court)/application (County Court) for a fuller *inter partes* hearing. At that hearing, which both sides will attend, the court will decide whether to grant an interlocutory injunction to continue from expiry of the *ex parte* injunction until trial.

The following is an example timetable:

(a) 5 June 1994 – applicant claims emergency *ex parte* injunction even before proceedings are commenced. As a condition of granting the injunction, the applicant undertakes to issue writ commencing proceedings and issue interlocutory summons claiming a further interlocutory injunction. *Ex parte* injunction is granted until 15 June.

(b) 6 June – applicant (now plaintiff) issues writ commencing proceedings and issues interlocutory summons for *inter partes* hearing, claiming interlocutory injunction to continue injunction until trial. Court gives hearing date for *inter partes* hearing of 1 October 1994. (This is a typical delay and is due to the court's workload.)

(c) In order to cover period between 15 June (expiry of *ex parte* injunction) and 1 October (application for further injunction), the plaintiff may apply *ex parte* (but the other party may well attend) for a further interim injunction until 1 October. Alternatively, the defendant may give an undertaking to refrain from the relevant act until the 1 October hearing. The plaintiff will give an undertaking in return (a 'cross-undertaking') to pay damages to the defendant if it later turns out that the plaintiff was not entitled to prevent the defendant from doing the act.

(d) At the 1 October hearing the judge will decide whether to grant an interlocutory injunction to continue the injunction until trial (which could be months or years ahead). (The principles and procedure governing interlocutory injunctions are explained in Chapter 22.)

(e) At trial, the judge will decide whether to grant a final injunction. Most cases do not reach trial, however, because the interlocutory injunction is often, in practice, the final decision on the dispute or the matter is settled in the light of the interlocutory injunction.

Self-assessment questions

1　What is the difference between a final injunction, an interlocutory injunction and an emergency *ex parte* injunction? Why does a plaintiff apply for an interlocutory injunction?

2　In what circumstances would you apply for an emergency *ex parte* injunction? Can you apply for one before commencing the main action?

3　What is the difference between an *inter partes* hearing and an *ex parte* hearing?

4　It is 3pm. Your client's landlord has unlawfully locked your client out of their factory. Your client needs access early tomorrow for their daily food distribution business. List the steps you would take to obtain access for your client.

5　What is an 'undertaking as to damages' in the context of an injunction?

6　What is an 'opposed *ex parte*' hearing and in what circumstances would it occur?

7　Who (a) drafts and (b) serves an injunction order?

8　After the first *ex parte* hearing asking for an emergency injunction, what is the next court hearing about?

Chapter 9

Mareva injunctions (RSC O.29)

What are they?   9.1

It could be that the defendant, or intended defendant, could frustrate a claim made against them by disposing of their assets, ie. spending, selling, or hiding them, or taking them out of the jurisdiction of the English courts, so that there are no assets which the plaintiff can take action against or trace to satisfy any judgment against the defendant.

To prevent the defendant doing this, the plaintiff can apply for a *Mareva* injunction – an injunction preventing the defendant/intended defendant from dealing with their assets. It takes its name from *Mareva Compania Naviera SA v International Bulk Carriers SA* (1980), the case in which such an injunction was first granted. (The case was actually tried in 1975 but was not reported in the All England Reports until 1980.)

Sections 37(1) and (3), Supreme Court Act 1981 statutorily recognises the *Mareva* injunction.

Form and effect   9.2

A *Mareva* injunction restrains the defendant from dealing with a certain amount of their assets within (or sometimes also outside) the English jurisdiction. The amount of assets frozen will be roughly equal to the amount of the plaintiff's claim, together with interest and costs.

However:

- The injunction will not cover sums needed by the defendant for reasonable living expenses, ordinary business dealings, legal fees, and payment of ordinary debts.
- The court will not grant a *Mareva* injunction which will substantially interfere with the business rights of a third party who is dealing with the defendant: *see*, for example, *Galaxia Maritime SA v Mineral Import-Export* (1982).
- A bank holding funds of the defendant frozen by a *Mareva* injunction is usually entitled to take funds from the account to satisfy debts owed by the defendant to the bank before the injunction was granted, eg. an overdraft.
- A plaintiff who has obtained a *Mareva* injunction does not rank as a secured creditor as against creditors with

prior claims to the funds: *see Cretanor Maratime Co Ltd v Irish Marine Management Ltd* (1978).

The injunction will be binding on third parties, most obviously the banks who hold the defendant's funds. They will be in contempt of court if they knowingly allow the defendant to dispose of funds so as to defeat any judgment.

Note

A *Mareva* injunction is an important tactic. It may force the defendant to settle the case.

9.3   Grounds

The plaintiff must show:

- That they have a *good arguable case*. This relates to the claim as a whole, not the claim for the injunction: *The Pertamina* (1978), and reiterated in *Aiglon Ltd v Gau Shan Co Ltd* (1992); and

- There are reasons to believe the *defendant has assets* within the English jurisdiction (or, in rare cases, elsewhere) to meet the judgment wholly or in part, but likely deal with them so that they are not available or traceable when judgment is given against the defendant.

9.4   Procedure

9.4.1   Which court?

Most applications for a *Mareva* injunction must be made to the High Court because, by virtue of the County Court Remedies Regulations 1991 (printed in the *Green Book* notes to s.40, County Courts Act 1984), a County Court can only grant a *Mareva* injunction in the following circumstances:

- In family proceedings within part v of the Matrimonial and Family Proceedings Act 1984;

- For the purpose of making an order for the preservation, custody or detention of property which forms or may form the subject matter of the proceedings;

- In order to help enforce a County Court judgment which has been made, ie. once a County Court judgment has been given, the successful party can then ask for the loser's assets to be frozen so that they can be seized to satisfy the judgment;

- In a patents County Court;

- A County Court can vary a *Mareva* injunction already

granted, where all parties are agreed on the terms of the variation.

Thus, if the plaintiff wishes to apply for a *Mareva* injunction in a County Court action, the plaintiff must apply to the High Court during the action. The High Court, having heard the application, will then transfer the proceedings back to the County Court.

Required documents

9.4.2

To apply for an injunction, the plaintiff must prepare:

* An affidavit; and
* A draft of the order required.

Further, if the application is made before proceedings are commenced, as is often the case, the plaintiff must draft:

* The proposed writ/County Court request for summons.

The plaintiff must then apply *ex parte* to the court with these documents.

The affidavit

In *Third Chandris Corp v Unimarine SA* (1979) it was stated that this must:

* Make *full and frank disclosure* of all material matters in the plaintiff's knowledge, including points against the plaintiff;
* Give *particulars of the plaintiff's claims*, including the grounds and the amount of the claim, and fairly stating the points made against the claim by the defendant;
* State grounds for thinking that the defendant has *assets* here;
* State grounds for believing there is a *risk* that the assets may be dealt with so that a *judgment cannot be satisfied*.

The draft order

This must:

* Give various *undertakings* to the court (*see* below);
* Specify the *amount to be frozen,* and the amount of living and business expenses or other amounts to be allowed to be used by the defendant;
* Specify named *amounts or assets* to be frozen;
* If required, ask for disclosure of the *identity and whereabouts of accounts and assets.* (This is known as asking for 'discovery', ie. disclosure of documents, and asking 'interrogatories', ie. formal written questions.)

Note _____

For a specimen Mareva injunction order, *see White Book* O.72, A.27.

9.4.3   The application

The plaintiff applies *ex parte* to the court, usually urgently on realising there is a risk that the defendant may dispose of their assets, and often before proceedings are commenced. The plaintiff should follow the procedure for making an *ex parte* injunction application (*see* Chapter 8).

At the hearing, the judge reads the affidavit and draft order. The plaintiff makes submissions on the points set out in the affidavit listed above, and as to the amount required to be frozen and the banks and third parties to whom notice needs to be given.

Plaintiff's undertakings
The plaintiff should also give the following *undertakings* to the court:

- If proceedings have not yet been commenced, to immediately issue a writ (High Court) or summons (County Court) commencing proceedings.
- In cases where the application is made so urgently that an affidavit has not yet been sworn, to swear and file at court an affidavit immediately.
- To immediately give notice of the order to the defendant and affected third parties, eg. banks, and to serve the order and affidavit(s) on them as soon as reasonably practicable.
- To pay damages to the defendant or third parties if they suffer loss due to the injunction and it later turns out that the injunction should not have been granted.
- To pay the reasonable costs and expenses incurred by any third party, eg. a bank, in complying with the order.
- To notify the defendant and third parties of their right to apply to the court to set aside or vary the order.

9.5   The order

If the grounds for granting the injunction are satisfied, the judge will make an order in the terms of the draft (by initialling the draft), amending it where relevant, eg. as to the amount to be frozen. The amount will usually cover the likely amount of the claim, together with interest and costs.

The order will specify for how long the injunction is to last, eg. for a few days, or until there is a further *inter partes* application or until trial or further order. The costs of the application will be 'reserved'.

The order is formally drawn up by the plaintiff in the Queen's Bench Division, and by the Court in the Chancery

Division. It is then served on the defendant and affected third parties, eg. the relevant banks.

Variation or discharge 9.6

The order will give the defendant or third parties liberty to apply to court, by summons to the plaintiff, for the variation or discharge of the order. They may apply if, for example:

● The defendant wishes to show there were no grounds for the injunction, or other security can be provided, or to vary the amount frozen, or on the ground that the plaintiff failed to disclose a material fact.

● A third party wishes to vary the order so as to free funds or assets owing to them.

Further *inter partes* hearing 9.7

After the initial *ex parte* application there is usually a further hearing, attended by both parties, to determine whether the *Mareva* injunction should be continued until trial or further order. This is because either the defendant will apply to discharge or vary the order; or the *ex parte* injunction may only have been given for a short time, on the plaintiff undertaking to issue an *inter partes* application for a continuation of the injunction.

Assets outside the court's jurisdiction 9.8

Usually, a *Mareva* injunction should only freeze, and require disclosure of, assets within the English jurisdiction: *Ashtiani v Kashi* (1987).

However, in rare cases, the injunction can extend to assets outside the jurisdiction, even worldwide. The conditions for this were discussed in *Babanaft International Co SA v Bassatne* (1988), *Derby and Co Ltd v Weldon (no 1)* (1989), *Derby and Co Ltd v Weldon (no 2)* (1989) and *Derby and Co Ltd v Weldon (no 6)* (1990).

The court may also grant a worldwide *Mareva* injunction in aid of *proceedings* in a foreign court, particularly in a tracing claim for the return of assets: *Republic of Haiti v Duvalier* (1989). The court will not, however, usually grant an injunction to *enforce the judgment* of a foreign court: *Rosseel NV v Oriental Commercial and Shipping (UK) Ltd* (1990).

Note _____

However, different rules apply in respect of EC, Lugano Convention countries and the UK. Under s.25, Civil Jurisdiction and Judgments Act 1982, an English court *can* grant a *Mareva* injunction before or after judgment to aid proceedings commenced in a Brussels or Lugano Convention country, or in the UK. The usual *Mareva* principles apply but the court may refuse the injunction if the fact that the English court has no jurisdiction apart from s.25 makes it inexpedient to grant the injunction: s.25(2).

Self-assessment questions

1   What is a *Mareva* injunction?

2   What documents would you draft in preparation for a *Mareva* injunction application? Which court would you apply to and what points would you make to the judge?

3   What usual extra undertakings are given on a *Mareva* injunction application in addition to the normal undertakings given on any emergency injunction application?

4   What is the next *Mareva* hearing about after the initial application? What points might the defendant argue about at that hearing?

5   Does a *Mareva* injunction make the plaintiff a secured creditor over the frozen assets? Can the injunction freeze assets outside the English jurisdiction? What useful purpose might be served by a *Mareva* application, in addition to freezing the defendant's assets?

Anton Piller orders
(RSC O.29)

Meaning

An *Anton Piller* order is a court order requiring the defendant to allow the plaintiff to enter the defendant's premises to search for and seize documents and articles. It is most often used in breach of copyright cases:

Example

P alleges D is selling pirate T-shirts, records and videos, in breach of P's copyright. Before suing D, P will seek an emergency *Anton Piller* order, allowing P to enter D's premises to search for and seize the goods. This will prevent D disposing of the evidence before trial. An *Anton Piller* order may also require D to disclose the identity and whereabouts of others involved, eg. their suppliers.

Note

It is called an *Anton Piller* order because it was recognised by the Court of Appeal in *Anton Piller KG v Manufacturing Processes Ltd* (1976).

Grounds for

The plaintiff, or intended plaintiff, may apply *ex parte*, even before proceedings are commenced, for an *Anton Piller* order where:

- The plaintiff can show an extremely *strong prima facie case*, ie. their substantive case, not their case for claiming an order.
- The *damage*, potential or actual, due to the defendant's conduct, is very serious for the plaintiff.
- There is clear evidence that the defendant has in their possession *incriminating documents or things*.
- There is a real possibility that the defendant may *destroy* such material before an *inter partes* application can be made.

Therefore, the typical *Anton Piller* case is where the defendant is infringing the plaintiff's copyright, causing serious damage to the plaintiff. On discovering this, as a matter of urgency, the plaintiff will seek a pre-action order allowing them to seize the infringing material before the defendant can dispose of it. In this way, the plaintiff preserves the evidence for the proceedings which are then commenced.

The plaintiff applies *ex parte* so as to act quickly and to take the defendant by surprise.

10.3   Procedure

10.3.1   Which court?

By virtue of the County Court Remedies Regulations 1991 (printed in *Green Book* notes to s.40, County Courts Act 1984), a County Court (unless it is sitting as a patents County Court) has no power to grant an *Anton Piller* order. However, a County Court can *vary* an order already granted, where all parties are agreed on the terms of the variation.

Therefore, if the plaintiff wishes to apply for an *Anton Piller* order in a County Court action, they must apply to the High Court during the action. The High Court, having heard the application, will then transfer the proceedings back to the County Court.

10.3.2   The application

In order to apply for an *Anton Piller* order, the plaintiff must prepare:

● An affidavit; and

● A draft of the order required (*see* below).

Further, if the application is made before proceedings are commenced, as is often the case, the plaintiff must draft:

● The proposed writ.

The affidavit must show how the grounds for obtaining an order (*see* 10.2 above) are satisfied. The affidavit must be very full and frank, and must disclose all relevant points, including points against the plaintiff's case.

The plaintiff (or intended plaintiff) then applies, with the above documents, *ex parte* to the court (usually urgently and often before proceedings are commenced) on realising there is a risk that the defendant may dispose of evidence. (The plaintiff must follow the procedure for making an *ex parte* injunction application, set out in Chapter 8.)

At the hearing, the judge reads the affidavit and draft order. The plaintiff makes submissions on the points in the affidavit and on the terms of the draft order.

Required undertakings

Plaintiff

An *Anton Piller* order is a draconian order, one which could be abused. The plaintiff must therefore give the following undertakings to the court before an order will be granted:

- If proceedings have not yet been commenced, to *issue a writ immediately* after the *ex parte* application.
- If the application for an order has been made so urgently that the plaintiff has not even sworn/filed an affidavit in support, to *swear and/or file an affidavit immediately* after the application.
- To *serve the order by a solicitor*, together with the writ, copies of the order, the plaintiff's affidavit and exhibits attached to the affidavit.
- To *pay damages* to the defendant and third parties if they suffer loss as a result of the order and it later turns out that the order should not have been made.

Plaintiff's solicitor

The plaintiff's solicitor must give the following further undertakings to the court:

- That the order will be *served by a solicitor*.
- To offer to *explain to the defendant*, fairly and in everyday language, the meaning of the order, and to advise the defendant of their right to obtain *legal advice* – the defendant is entitled to take a reasonable time to obtain legal advice before the order is carried out.
- To retain in *safe custody* until further order all articles and documents taken under the order.
- Prior to removal, to make a *list* of all articles and documents taken, and to give a copy of the list to the defendant.
- To *return the originals* (having made copies) of all documents taken, within a specified short time.
- Where ownership of an article is in dispute, to *immediately deliver such article* to the defendant's solicitor, who will undertake to keep it in safe custody immediately after taking it and as soon as the defendant has a solicitor acting for them. (There may be a delay before the latter condition is satisfied.)

Terms of an order

Standard terms

If the grounds for obtaining an order are satisfied, the judge will grant an order in the following terms:

- Setting out the undertakings given by the plaintiff or their solicitor.
- Ordering that a closely defined class of articles or documents (and their whereabouts) be disclosed and delivered by the defendant to the plaintiff.
- Ordering that the defendant permits the plaintiff to enter specified premises at a specified time to look for, inspect, copy and take specified documents and articles.
- Ordering the defendant to serve on the plaintiff an affidavit disclosing the required information.
- In some cases, restraining the defendant from disposing of the material and from warning others involved.
- In some cases, requiring the defendant to serve an affidavit identifying others involved, eg. their suppliers.

The order will give the defendant and any affected third party permission (the technical term is 'liberty') to apply to vary or discharge the order.

The order will reserve the question of costs.

Note

For a specimen order, *see White Book* O.27 A.27.

10.4.2 Safeguards

As an *Anton Piller* order could be abused by the plaintiff, the courts have laid down the following safeguards: *see* particularly *Columbia Picture Industries v Robinson* (1986), and *Universal Thermosensors Ltd v Hibben* (1992).

- Generally, the *undertakings* listed in 10.3.3 that the plaintiff and their solicitor must give.
- The order must extend no further than the *minimum extent* necessary to preserve materials which may otherwise be destroyed or concealed. No material should be taken unless it is clearly covered by the order.
- The order should be permitted to be executed only on *working days in office hours*, when a solicitor can be expected to be available so that the defendant may obtain legal advice.
- In general, the order should expressly provide that, unless it is seriously impracticable, a *detailed list of the items being removed* should be prepared at the premises before they are removed, and that the defendant should be given an opportunity to check that list at the time.
- An *injunction* in the order restraining those on whom it

is served from informing others of the existence of the order should be for a limited period, which should be less than a week.

- The order should provide that, unless there is good reason for doing otherwise, it should not be executed at *business premises* except in the presence of a responsible officer or representative of the company or trader in question.

- Consideration should be given to devising some means, appropriate to the facts of the case, by which the plaintiff is prevented from carrying out a thorough *search of all of the competitor's documents* when the order is executed at a competitor's premises.

- Judges should seriously consider providing that:

  – the order should be served, and its execution supervised by, an *experienced solicitor* familiar with the workings of *Anton Piller* orders, other than a member of the firm of solicitors acting for the plaintiff;

  – the solicitor should prepare a written report on the execution, with a copy served on the defendant;

  – the report should be put before the court within a few days at an *inter partes* hearing, preferably before the judge who made the order.

Duration   **10.4.3**

The order will only be made to last for a short time.

Within that time, the plaintiff must issue a summons for an *inter partes* hearing at which the court will decide whether to continue the order, eg. until trial (this is insofar as the order provides for continuing actions or restraints, rather than a one-off search and seizure).

Thus, the order will usually be expressed to last until the hearing of the further *inter partes* hearing or until further order.

Setting aside or varying the order   **10.5**

The defendant may apply to have the order set aside or varied, eg. on the ground that the order should not have been made or that the plaintiff did not make full disclosure of the facts to the court (the order will automatically be set aside on this latter ground).

The defendant's application to set aside or vary the order should be heard at the same time as the plaintiff's *inter partes* application order (*see* 10.4.3).

10.6   The privilege against self-incrimination

The general rule is that an *Anton Piller* order will not be made if the search and seizure might incriminate the defendant, ie. expose them to criminal proceedings (*see* Evidence Companion).

However, the defendant cannot rely on this privilege to prevent an *Anton Piller* order in cases of infringement of intellectual property rights or cases of passing-off (s.72, Supreme Court Act 1981) or in cases of possible offences under the Theft Act 1968 (s.31, Theft Act 1968).

Self-assessment questions

1   What is an *Anton Piller* order?

2   What documents would you draft in preparation for an *Anton Piller* application? Which court would you apply to and what points would you make to the judge?

3   Why are there so many undertakings and safeguards in an *Anton Piller* order in comparison to other injunctions?

4   After the initial application, what is the next hearing about? What points might the defendant argue about at that hearing?

Chapter 11

Limitation and choice of court

Time limits for commencing proceedings: limitation
11.1

General rule
11.1.1

By virtue of various provisions of the Limitation Act 1980, various types of action must be commenced within certain time periods, ie. the writ or originating summons in the High Court, or summons or originating application in the County Court, must be *issued* within the relevant time period.

Contract and tort
11.1.2

An action founded on tort or contract must be brought within *six years* from the date on which the *cause of action accrued*, eg. in a contract case, proceedings must be commenced within six years from the date of the breach.

Personal injury and death
11.1.3

By virtue of s.11, Limitation Act 1980, however, a claim for damages for negligence, nuisance or breach of duty (including a contractual duty) causing personal injuries or death must be commenced within three years from the:

- Date on which the cause of action accrued, eg. within three years of a road accident; or

- *Date of knowledge* of the person injured (or of a deceased's personal representatives).

The date of knowledge
11.1.4

The relevance of the 'date of knowledge' is that it may be that the client does not become aware of their injuries, or that they are significant, until more than three years after the act of negligence. (For example, the symptoms of diseases suffered by miners as a result of their working conditions may not appear for many years.) It would be unfair if it were too late for the client to bring an action. Accordingly, the client in such a case has three years from 'the date of knowledge', ie. basically the date they know of their injuries, in which to bring an action, *see* s.14 , Limitation Act 1980.

Section 33 discretion
11.1.5

In cases of *personal injury* or *death* the court, by virtue of s.33, has a discretion to allow an action to be brought *after* the statutory time limits, having regard in particular to certain criteria laid down in s.33 (broadly based on the justice of the case).

11.1.6 Fraud, concealment or mistake

By virtue of s.32, special time rules apply to an action based on the fraud of the defendant or an action for relief from the consequences of a mistake, or where the defendant has deliberately concealed any fact relevant to the plaintiff's action.

11.1.7 Plaintiff under a disability

Where the plaintiff is under a disability, ie. is under 18 years of age or of 'unsound mind', the limitation period commences from the date the plaintiff ceases to be under a disability, not from the date of the cause of action. For example, a 14 year old child who is injured in an accident has three years from the date they become 18 in which to bring an action.

11.1.8 Other types of action

The 1980 Act also specifies periods for the commencement of certain other categories of action, eg. in respect of land, trusts and defective consumer products.

11.2 Choice of court

The civil courts are the High Court and the County Court. In deciding in which court to commence proceedings, the following considerations apply:

- *Jurisdiction* – the County Court does not have jurisdiction, ie. does not have power, to hear certain types of cases. Therefore, these cases must be commenced in the High Court and they will be tried in the High Court unless the case is transferred to the County Court either by the High Court under s.40(2), CCA 1984 or by agreement between the parties under s.18.
- *Remedies* – the County Court does not have power to grant certain remedies.
- The *High Court and County Courts Jurisdiction Order 1991* – even if the County Court has jurisdiction to hear a case, the 1991 order provides rules governing:
  - The court in which the action should be commenced;
  - The court in which the actions should be tried.
- *Transfer* – there are rules and procedures providing for transfer of the action from the High Court to the County Court and vice versa.

11.2.1 Jurisdiction

By virtue of Article 2 of the High Court and County Courts

Jurisdiction Order 1991, the County Court has power to hear any of the types of cases listed in that Article, regardless of the amount involved in the proceedings. For example, the County Court has power to hear any action founded on contract or tort, whatever the amount involved: s.15, CCA.

In contrast, the County Court hs no jurisdiction to hear an action for libel or slander: s.15(2)(6), CCA; or a case of judicial review (*see* s.1(10), Courts and Legal Services Act 1990).

By virtue of Article 2 of paragraphs (2)–(7) of the 1991 order and various statutory provisions, the County Court has power to hear certain types of cases where the amount involved does not exceed a certain limit. For example, the County Court has jurisdiction in relation to various equity matters where the amount involved does not exceed 'the County Court limit' (currently £30,000).

Remedies   11.2.2

The County Court does not have power to give the following remedies:

- *Mandamus, certiorari* or prohibition: s.38(3)(a), CCA 1984; or
- An order requiring a party to admit any other party to premises for the purpose of inspecting or removing documents or articles which may provide evidence in any proceedings, whether or not the proceedings have been commenced; or
- An interlocutory injunction:
  - Restraining a party from removing from the jurisdiction of the High Court assets located within that jurisdiction; or
  - Restraining a party from dealing with assets whether located within the jurisdiction of the High Court or not.

Thus, under the second and third points above, a County Court has no power to make an *Anton Piller* (*see* Chapter 10) or inspection order, or to grant an interlocutory *Mareva* injunction (*see* Chapter 9): County Court Remedies Regulations 1991 made under s.38, CCA 1984.

If a party to an action proceeding in the County Court requires one of these remedies, that party must apply to the High Court, although the action as a whole continues in the County Court. (*See* County Court Remedies Regulations 1991, regs 4 and 5, for the procedure.)

High Court and County Court Jurisdiction Order 1991   11.2.3

Where the High Court and the County Court both have

jurisdiction in relation to a case, the 1991 jurisdiction order contains provisions as to:

- Where the action may or should be commenced; and
- Where the action should be tried.

Commencement

Proceedings in which both the County Court and the High Court have jurisdiction may be commenced in either court.

However, personal injury cases must be commenced in the County Court unless the value of the action is £50,000 or more. (The 'value of the action' is the amount the plaintiff reasonably expects to recover – *see* fuller definition later.)

However, although *non*-personal injury cases can be commenced in either court, it is advisable to commence proceedings in the court in which the case is likely to be tried. The 1991 order contains the following provisions on where cases should be tried.

Trial

If the value of the action is *less than £25,000* the action must be tried in a County Court unless:

- A County Court, having regard to the criteria set out in 12.5.1 below, considers it ought to transfer the action to the High Court for trial and the High Court considers that it ought to try the action; or
- The action is commenced in the High Court and the High Court, having regard to the same criteria, considers that it ought to try the action.

If the value of the action is *£50,000 or more*, it must be tried in the High Court unless:

- It is commenced in a County Court and the County Court does not, having regard to the criteria set out in 12.5.1, consider that the action ought to be transferred to the High Court for trial; or
- The High Court, having regard to the same criteria, considers that it ought to transfer the case to a County Court for trial.

If the value of the action is between £25,000 and £50,000, the case can be tried in either court. In practice, however, where the case is likely to be tried will depend on the criteria set out in 12.5.1 below.

11.2.4   Transfer

Criteria

The High Court has power to transfer cases to the County Court: s.40, CCA 1984. The County Court has power to transfer cases to the High Court: s.42, CCA 1984. In deciding whether to exercise their powers of transfer, the courts must have regard to the following criteria:

- The *financial substance* of the action, including the value of any counterclaim;
- Whether the action is otherwise *important* and, in particular, whether it raises questions of importance to persons who are not parties or questions of general public interest;
- The *complexity* of the facts, legal issues, remedies or procedures involved; and
- Whether transfer is likely to result in a *more speedy trial* of the action. However, no transfer should be made on this ground alone.

Note

Straightforward cases are likely to be tried in the county court and therefore should be commenced there.

Practice direction

By a practice Direction at 1991 1 WLR 643, the Lord Chief Justice has stated that the following types of case may be considered 'important' and therefore suitable for trial in the High Court:

- Professional negligence;
- Fatal accidents;
- Fraud or undue influence;
- Defamation;
- Malicious prosecution or false imprisonment;
- Claims against the police.

In practice

The effect of the rules is that where the action will be tried really depends on the above criteria. Thus, these criteria also govern the decision as to where to commence the proceedings, because the action should be commenced where the action is likely to be tried for the following reasons:

- If the action is commenced in the wrong court, it will only be transferred to the other court;
- A party who brings an action in the wrong court may be penalised by having to meet the legal costs of the other side which have been thereby wasted. Alternatively, the amount of costs they can recover from the other side in the action may be reduced accordingly. Furthermore, the solicitor or barrister for that party may be made personally liable for

such wasted costs, or may suffer a reduction in the costs they can recover: s.51(6)–(9), SCA 1981;

- Both courts will strike out proceedings where the plaintiff knew, or ought to have known, that the proceedings should have been brought in the other court.

Where the case is a borderline one, however, there are some practical advantages in bringing proceedings in the High Court: it is considered to be more efficient than the County Court and the process quicker in the early stages of proceedings. It may carry greater psychological impact and the judges are alleged to be of greater quality. Furthermore, it may be advisable to commence proceedings in the High Court where a remedy is required which cannot be granted by the County Court.

On the other hand, the trial date may come up more quickly in the County Court and the County Court may be geographically more convenient.

Procedure for transfer
A court may transfer the case to the other court either 'of its own motion' or as a result of an application for transfer by a party to the action.

Proceedings transferred by the High Court should be transferred to such County Court as the High Court considers appropriate, having taken into account the convenience of the parties and that of any other persons likely to be affected and the state of business in the courts concerned.

High Court cases will be automatically transferred to a County Court unless the plaintiff files at court a 'statement of value', ie. that the value of the action (as defined in the next section) exceeds £25,000 or the action is suitable for determination in the High Court, at each of the following stages of the action:

- Before the hearing of a summons for directions;
- On the setting down of the action; and
- On an application for summary judgment, if leave to defend is given.

The detailed procedures for transfer can be found at Practice Direction 1991 1 WLR 643, Practice Direction 1988 1 WLR 653 (modified by the 1991 Direction) and CCR O.16 rr.6, 9 and 10.

Statement of value
In calculating the value of an action for the purposes of the High Court and County Court Jurisdiction Order 1991, the following rules apply:

- The value of an action for a sum of money, whether specified or not, is the amount which the plaintiff or applicant reasonably expects to recover.

- An action for specified relief other than a sum of money, eg. a claim for an injunction, has a value equal to the amount of money which the plaintiff or applicant could reasonably state to be the financial worth of the claim to them. Where there is no such amount, it has no quantifiable value and therefore the claim could be brought in either court depending on non-financial criteria, eg. the complexity of the case.

Example

X obtains an injunction to prevent disruption of their business. X can state this injunction to be worth £100,000 in terms of preserving profits. Alternatively the financial benefit to the business is not precisely quantifiable so the claim could be brought in either court.

Self-assessment questions

1   Sally, who is 17, is beginning to suffer symptoms from exposure to chemicals at school over the last two years. How much time does she have to commence a negligence action against the local education authority?

What would be your answer if Sally were now 19?

2   D, a well known supplier of specialist dog food to breeders of racing greyhounds, supplied the food to P, a famous breeder P. One of P's dogs died after eating the food and P has therefore lost profits of £35,000. P claims the food is defective. D claims it was fed to the dog in the wrong quantity.

In which court should P commence an action for breach of contract?

3   What is the most important reason for ensuring that you commence proceedings in the correct court?

4   What is meant by:

(a) a wasted costs order

(b) a statement of value?

5   In which court will a personal injury action be tried?

Chapter 12

Organisation of the High Court and County Court

High Court Divisions 12.1

The High Court is based centrally at the Royal Courts of Justice, Strand, London, but it has district registries in large centres, eg. Manchester.

The High Court is divided into three divisions:

- Queen's Bench;
- Chancery; and
- Family.

Note _____

The Family Division is covered in the Family Law option.

Queen's Bench Division 12.1.1

This deals with:

- Common law actions (contract and tort);
- Judicial review; and
- Other general actions which are not, as a result of various rules and practices, dealt with in the Chancery Division (*see* below).

The Queen's Bench Division contains two specialist courts: the Commercial Court and the Admiralty Court. Both have their own specialist jurisdiction and procedures.

The *Commercial Court* deals with commercial disputes, eg. in relation to insurance, banking, arbitration and mercantile contracts. The Admiralty Court deals with shipping disputes.

Chancery Division 12.1.2

The Chancery Division, by virtue of rules and accepted practice, deals with disputes relating to, for example:

- The sale of land;
- Mortgages;
- Trusts;
- Administration of estates;
- Insolvency;
- Partnerships;
- Companies;

- Probate;
- Patents – there is a specialist patents court.

Note

Practitioners come to know the rules and practice governing the appropriate division in which to bring a case. In the absence of rules governing the choice in a particular case, the choice may depend on practical factors such as the speed and expertise of the division.

12.2 Personnel

Trials are heard by High Court Judges or Deputy High Court Judges. These judges also hear some interlocutory (interim) applications.

Interlocutory hearings, that is, preliminary hearings in respect of procedural matters or small substantive hearings, eg. for early judgment on the basis that there is no defence to the action, are heard by 'Masters'. (Masters are, in effect, junior judges.)

Note

Masters are known as District Judges in the High Court district registries outside London.

12.3 Administration and procedures

Judges hear trials in open court in London or at a district registry. Masters and District Judges have their own private rooms called 'chambers' where they hear applications (though High Court Judges hear some applications in 'chambers'). There are complicated timetabling and listing systems for the hearing of trials and interlocutory applications.

Note

There are several rooms in the High Court, well known to practitioners, where the administration of cases is carried out, eg. the Central Office in London, where Queen's Bench actions are commenced.

Most of the procedural rules for High Court actions are contained in the *Rules of the Supreme Court* (RSC) and in 'Practice Directions' issued by the Judges and Masters.

These rules and directions can be found in the Supreme Court Practice – known as the *White Book* – which is the practitioners reference book on High Court Procedure.

Organisation of the County Court   12.4

The County Courts Act 1984 divides England and Wales into about 300 districts and there is a county court for each district. Its jurisdiction is limited by the rules outlined in Chapter 11: *Limitation and choice of court*. There are no separate divisions in the county court.

Trials, and some interlocutory applications, are heard by Circuit Judges. A circuit judge has jurisdiction to try cases at any county court in a particular geographical circuit, eg. the South-Eastern Circuit.

Each county court has its own administration office and staff headed by the Chief Clerk.

The rules of county court procedure are contained in the County Courts Act 1984, the County Court Rules 1981 and Practice Directions. These can be found in the County Court Practice –known as the *Green Book* – which is equivalent to the High Court *White Book*.

Computation of time in both courts   12.5

Many of the court rules provide that procedures must be carried out within certain time periods. For how these time periods are calculated, eg. what days are included in 'seven days' and on what day that period ends, *see* RSC O.3 and CCR O.1 r.9 and O.2 r.2.

Self-assessment questions

1 Explain the difference between the following:

(a) a master

(b) a High Court district judge

(c) a County Court district judge

(d) a circuit judge

(e) a High Court judge.

2 How many High Courts are there?

3 Look in the *White Book*. How many specialist courts are there within the High Court?

Chapter 13

Commencing proceedings in the High Court

Introduction

High Court proceedings can be commenced by:

- Writ;
- Originating summons;
- Petition;
- Originating motion.

> *Note* _____
>
> The last two methods are very rarely used. Election and certain trade mark disputes would be examples.

Most High Court proceedings are commenced by *writ* and this is the form of commencement on which your course will concentrate.

However, many types of proceedings are commenced by originating summons. Such proceedings are those required or permitted by rule or statute to be commenced by originating summons, eg. an application for a new business tenancy under the Landlord and Tenant Act 1954 or proceedings mainly involving a question of law and construction rather than a question of fact (*see* further 13.8).

Commencing proceedings by writ (RSC O.6)

> *Note* _____
>
> In High Court proceedings, a limited company must have a solicitor acting for it, although service of the writ may be acknowledged (*see* below) by an officer of the company.

Drafting the writ

Once the client has decided, on advice, to commence proceedings in the High Court, their solicitor must draft a writ.

A writ is formally a 'writ of summons', a document summoning the defendant to court to contest the action. The solicitor will have a stock of standard printed forms of writ (All such legal forms are obtainable from legal stationers.) The solicitor must fill in the gaps on the standard writ form.

Note

The drafting of the writ, ie. filling in the gaps, will be dealt with in lectures.

13.2.2   **Issuing the writ**

Proceedings are commenced by the issue of the writ, ie. by the court placing the court seal on it.

Note

It is at that moment that proceedings are commenced for purposes of the limitation period.

The writ is issued by the plaintiff's solicitor (or, in practice, their clerk) posting the necessary documents to, or attending personally at, the Central Office (Queen's Bench Division), Chancery Chambers (Chancery), or District Registry (outside London) of the High Court.

The documents to be taken or posted are:

- One copy of the writ for the court, one copy for the plaintiff, and one copy for each defendant.
- The court fee for issue of the writ – this fee changes every so often. (Cheques should be made payable to HM Paymaster General.)
- The legal aid certificate, if applicable.
- If the plaintiff is under a disability, the next friend's consent to act and the solicitor's certificate that there is no conflict of interest.
- A stamped addressed envelope for their return if the documents are sent by post for issue.

On receipt of these documents, a court officer will seal each copy of the writ in red ink and seal one copy with the word original – that copy will be treated as the original writ. The officer will assign an action number to the action and insert the number on the writ. The officer will retain in a file the court copy of the writ and return all other documents to the plaintiff's solicitor.

13.3   **Service of the writ (RSC O.10)**

The plaintiff's solicitor must then serve the writ on the defendant within *four months* of the date of issue.

Note

The plaintiff may apply to the court for an order extending the time for service.

The defendant must be served with:

- A sealed copy of the writ;
- A standard 'acknowledgement of service' form, by which the defendant acknowledges service of the writ;
- A notice of issue of legal aid, if applicable.

In practice, the original writ is also posted to the defendant's solicitor so that the defendant's solicitor can endorse their acceptance of service on the original and return it (as proof of service).

Methods of service   13.4

Postal service   13.4.1

The document may be sent by ordinary first class post to the defendant at their usual or last known address, or it may be inserted through the letter box at that address in a sealed envelope addressed to the defendant. An accompanying letter should be sent, saying 'We enclose herewith by way of service ...', and then referring to the documents.

Service is then presumed to be effected on the *seventh* day after the date on which the documents were posted or inserted through the letter box, unless the contrary is shown. Thus, the time limits for acknowledgement will run from this date and not the date of actual posting.

Service on defendant's solicitor   13.4.2

If the proposed defendant has a solicitor acting for them, it is common practice before commencing proceedings to write asking the solicitor if they have instructions to accept service of proceedings. If the solicitor writes back saying they do, proceedings can then be served on the solicitor, enclosing the original writ for acceptance of service as outlined in 14.3 above.

Personal service   13.4.3

This is effected by giving the documents to the defendant personally. If the defendant will not take them, they can be left as nearly in their possession or control as possible. For example, the documents can be thrown on the floor next to the defendant – as long as the defendant is aware of their nature.

Service on limited companies   13.4.4

Service on a limited company is effected by leaving the documents at or by posting them to its registered office: s.725, Companies Act 1985.

Note

Care must be taken to ascertain the correct registered office, eg. by carrying out a company search.

If the documents are posted, they are deemed to arrive in the ordinary course of post, ie. the second working day after posting if by first class post. This is a special rule for service on companies.

Special rules apply to service on partnerships and on people under a disability: RSC O.80 and 81.

13.4.5   Other methods of service

If the plaintiff is unable to effect service in accordance with the above rules, application may be made to a Master for an order allowing 'substituted service', ie. that service be by some other means. Examples would be service on an agent or by newspaper advertisement.

13.4.6   Service out of the jurisdiction

A writ can be served outside the UK *without leave* of the court:

- Where the UK courts have jurisdiction to hear the claim under the Civil Jurisdiction and Judgments Act 1982 and, generally, the defendant is domiciled in an EC country; (The rules are very detailed and can be found in that act and RSC O.11.)

- Where a statute gives the court jurisdiction to entertain a claim even though the defendant is not within the jurisdiction;

and *with leave*:

- Under the conditions in RSC O.11.

13.5   Acknowledgement of service (RSC O.12)

The defendant must complete the 'acknowledgement of service' form – sent with the writ – and return it to the court office within *14 days* of service (counting the day of service); therefore, 21 days from the date of actual posting of the writ, if it was served by post.

Before sending the form, the title of the case, the action number and the name and address of the plaintiff's solicitor must be entered on it.

Note

The most important action for the defendant is to tick the box saying whether they intend to defend the action.

When the completed form is received by the court office, it will be stamped with the date of its receipt by the court office and a photocopy will be sent to the plaintiff.

Judgment in default (RSC O.13)   **13.6**

Acknowledgement of service entitles the plaintiff to enter judgment in default, ie. the plaintiff wins the case there and then by default, if the defendant:

- Fails to return the form within 14 days of service of the writ (in the case of service by post, 21 days from the date of posting); or
- Returns the form but does not state that they intend to contest the proceedings.

If either of the above apply, the plaintiff can enter judgment purely by administrative procedure, generally without leave of the court, by taking or sending to the court:

- The original writ;
- Two copies of a completed standard form of judgment; and
- Evidence that the writ has been served. (Such evidence may be, for example, the acceptance of service from the defendant's solicitor or an affidavit of service by the server.)

A court officer will check that all this is in order and enter judgment in the records.

Judgment in default *cannot* be entered if:

- The defendant applied for a stay of execution;
- The defendant is a minor and no guardian *ad litem* has been appointed;
- If the plaintiff is claiming provisional damages in a personal injury case.

Liquidated claims   **13.6.1**

If the claim is for a fixed specified sum, ie. a liquidated claim, the plaintiff can enter judgment for that sum, for interest if the precise amount of interest owing has been properly shown on the writ, and for a fixed prescribed amount of costs allowable under court rules in the case of judgment in default.

For these reasons, a plaintiff claiming a precise debt, to which there is no defence, issues a 'liquidated demand' writ, showing 'fixed costs' and the precise interest recoverable in anticipation of obtaining the judgment in default.

13.6.2   Unliquidated claims

If the claim is for damages rather than a specific sum, ie. an unliquidated claim, the judgment in default will be as to liability only. The plaintiff will then have to apply for a hearing in front of a Master (or District Judge), at which the amount of damages for which the defendant is liable will be assessed, ie. both parties will attend and argue over the amount of damages. Costs will then be taxed rather than fixed (*see* Chapter 3).

13.6.3   Setting aside default judgments (RSC O.13 r.9)

Grounds for setting aside default judgment

The defendant can apply to have a judgment in default set aside and to be given leave to defend on one of two grounds:

- If the defendant can show that there was some irregularity in the judgment, eg. it was entered too early, or the writ was not properly served, the judgment will be set aside as of right, ie. automatically, and the plaintiff *may* be ordered to pay the defendant's costs. A relevant factor as to costs is whether the plaintiff was at fault in causing the irregularities.

- If the judgment was 'regular', ie. there was no breach of procedure, the court has a *discretion* to set aside the judgment.

  It is an almost inflexible rule, however, that the judgment will only be set aside if the defendant shows a meritorious defence: *Alpine Bulk Transport Company Inc v Saudi Eagle Shipping Company Inc, The Saudi Eagle* (1986). The court will also take into account the defendant's explanation as to why service was not acknowledged in time.

If the court is unsure of the bona fides of the defendant, or the defendant is impecunious, the court may only set aside the judgment on terms that the defendant *pays a sum of money into court*, although the court will not impose a financial condition that the defendant will be unable to meet: *City Construction Contracts (London) Ltd v Adam* (1988).

Procedure

The defendant should apply by summons to a master. If the judgment was *regular*, the application should be supported by an affidavit showing a meritorious defence and explaining the delay.

If the judgment was *irregular*, the defendant's affidavit should state the nature of the irregularity and explain the delay.

Note

It may be prudent for the defendant to also show a meritorious defence in case the argument that the judgment was irregular fails.

If the regular judgment is set aside and the defendant was at fault in not acknowledging service, the court will usually award costs to the plaintiff 'in any event'.

Amending the writ (RSC O.20)   13.7

The writ can be amended, eg. to change or add some wording, to amend a date or fact etc, or to add a party or cause of action.

Leave of the court   13.7.1

The leave of the court is needed in order to add or substitute a party or cause of action *after service of the writ*.

Any other amendments, ie. other than alteration of a party or cause of action, may be made without leave *once* before 'close of pleadings', otherwise, leave is required.

Procedure   13.7.2

The writ should be *retyped*. The superseded words should be shown crossed out in red and the new words should be added in red. If the writ is later amended a second time, the amendments are made in green. Further colours apply to further amendments.

If leave is needed, application is made to a Master. The Master will usually grant leave on condition that the amending party pay the costs incurred by the other side due to the amendment.

If *leave* is needed, the title of the amended writ should be endorsed in the appropriate colour with the words 'amended pursuant to the order of Master ..., dated the ... day of ..., 19....

If *leave is not needed*, the endorsement should read 'amended the ... day of ..., 19..., under RSC O.20, r.3.

The amended writ must then be served on the defendant.

Originating summons procedure   13.8

Where required or permitted by rule of statute, or where the case mainly involves a question of law or construction rather then fact, eg. an application to the Chancery Division for a decision on the effect of a will, proceedings are commenced by an originating summons.

An originating summons is very different from a writ and it has its own form. It not only commences proceedings but includes full details of the application, whereas a writ is commonly followed by a statement of claim. The summons should include a statement of the question on which the plaintiff seeks the court's direction, or a concise statement of the relief or remedy claimed.

The originating summons is issued and served in a similar way to a writ. However, there are no pleadings (no statement of claim and defence) in this procedure. Instead, the sides must serve affidavits on each other, and then a 'Directions' hearing usually follows. The procedure is set out in RSC O.28.

13.9   Commercial Court proceedings

Proceedings in the Commercial Court have their own special, detailed procedure, with many differences from normal procedure. For example, writs in the commercial court may be issued by fax to the Commercial Registry (RSC O.2 r.7A).

Note

The details on procedure in commercial actions are contained in RSC O.72.

13.10   Persons under a disability

In both the High court and County Court, special procedural rules apply throughout to 'persons under a disability', ie. parties under 18 years of age and parties who, by reason of mental disorder within the meaning of the Mental Health Act 1983, are incapable of managing or administering their property and affairs.

Such persons must sue by an adult called a 'next friend' and must defend by a 'guardian *ad litem*'. Although the name of the person under the disability appears as a party to the proceedings, the next friend or guardian in practice conducts the proceedings on the person's behalf (usually through a solicitor, which is compulsory in the High Court). The next friend is primarily liable for the costs of the action. A guardian is only liable if the costs are incurred due to the guardian's negligence or misconduct.

The next friend or guardian has powers to carry out various procedures and their special rules apply, eg. as to service of documents on the next friend or guardian.

Any settlement on behalf of a person under a disability must be approved by the court.

Note _____

For the rules on persons under a disability, *see* RSC O.80.

Partnerships   13.11

For the special procedural rules relating to actions by and against partnerships, *see* RSC O.81.

Self-assessment questions

1 How do you commence High Court proceedings?

2 What documents must be taken or posted to court on commencing proceedings?

3 How much time does the plaintiff have to serve the writ after issuing it?

4 P serves a writ by post on D on 14 September claiming damages. By what date must D acknowledge service? What can P do if D does not acknowledge service by that date?

5 Your client rushes in and shows you a 'judgment in default' for a debt that has been entered against her. Your client tells you she was on holiday throughout the time of service of the writ and entry of the judgment. She says that the plaintiff had previously orally promised to waive the debt.

   What would you do to protect your client's position?

6 Shortly after D has acknowledged service of the writ, you (as P's solicitor) decide to amend a date alleged in the writ. Do you need the leave of the court to do this? How would you effect the amendment?

7 Explain the difference between a writ and an originating summons.

Chapter 14

Commencing proceedings in the County Court

Types of action   14.1

There are two types of action in the Country Court:

- A *fixed date action*

  This is an action in which a claim is made for any relief other than the payment of money, eg. where the claim is or includes a claim for possession of land or for an injunction or declaration.

- A *default action*

  This is an action in which the claim is only for money, ie. for damages or a debt.

Historically, the differences between the two types of action were that:

- On commencement of a fixed date action, the parties were given a fixed date for the preliminary hearing (pre-trial review) of the action, unlike in a default action. However, this is now not usually the case, since there is usually no longer a pre-trial review; usually, no fixed date is given for any hearing on commencement of the action.

- In a default action, judgment in default could be entered if the defendant did not reply to the summons commencing proceedings. This could not be done in a fixed date action. Today, judgment in default can now be entered in many fixed date actions.

Choice of county court   14.2

There are approximately 300 county courts, one for each geographical district. In which court should proceedings commence?

A *fixed date action* may be commenced in the court for the district in which the defendant, or one of the defendants, resides or carries on business, or in the district in which the cause of action wholly or partly arose.

Note _____

Proceedings for the recovery of land or for enforcing any charge on land may be commenced only in the court for the district in which the land is situated.

A *default action* may be commenced in any county court. Where a defence is served in an action for a liquidated sum, the proceedings will be automatically transferred to the defendant's home court unless the defence states that the sum has been paid, in which case the transfer will only take place if the plaintiff states in writing that they wish the proceedings to continue.

14.3   Types of originating process

County court proceedings can be commenced by:

- A *summons* (fixed date or default).

  This is used in most cases, but it should not be confused with a high court interlocutory summons.

- An *originating application*.

  This is used in all cases where no other method is prescribed, eg. an application for approval of a settlement made on behalf of a child before proceedings are issued, and in cases where an Act or the rules provide that this procedure should be used, eg. an application for a new business tenancy under Landlord and Tenant Act 1954.

- A *petition*.

  This is only used in special cases, eg. divorce or bankruptcy proceedings.

  Note _____

  The course will only be concerned with proceeding by summons.

14.4   Commencing proceedings by summons (CCR O.3 & 4)

The County Court summons is the equivalent to the High Court writ. In effect, it is a document summoning the defendant to contest the plaintiff's claim.

In contrast to the High Court, the County Court fills in the summons. Usually the plaintiff sends to the court a completed request for a summons, and the court then prepares it by filling in a standard form of summons. The summons may be prepared by the plaintiff if the court officer allows this.

14.4.1   Request for a summons

The standard request forms are:

- N201: Request for issue of *default summons*.

- N201: Request for issue of *fixed date summons*.
- N204: Request for issue of *summons for possession of land*.

The plaintiff must then take or post to the court:

- The *request* for a summons or, if prepared by the plaintiff, a summons itself plus copy.
- One copy of the *particulars of claim* plus one copy for each defendant.
- If the plaintiff is under a disability, the next friend's *undertaking as to costs*.
- If the plaintiff is legally aided, the *legal aid certificate* (and notice of issue of legal aid if the court is to serve the summons).
- In a personal injuries case, a *medical report* and a 'statement of special damages', plus a copy of each document.
- The *court fee* for issue, made payable to HM Paymaster General.
- A *stamped addressed envelope*, if the court is to return the documents to the plaintiff for service.

The court will then, unless already done by the plaintiff, prepare the summons.

Standard forms of summons 14.4.2

There are different standard forms of summons according to the type of case, eg:

- N1: Default summons for fixed amount.
- N2: Default summons for unliquidated amount.
- N3: Fixed date summons where pre-trial review.
- N4: Fixed date summons where no pre-trial review.
- N5: Summons for possession of land.

Issue of the summons 14.4.3

The court will issue the summons by sealing it, and will attach to the summons the particulars of claim (and the medical report and statement of special damages in a personal injury case), and a form for admission, defence and counterclaim by the defendant.

It will also send the plaintiff a 'plaint note'. This is a document notifying the plaintiff of the issue and service of the summons and, in a fixed date action, of the date of the pre-trial review or hearing.

Note _____

There is not usually a pre-trial review and the plaintiff often asks that a hearing date is not set at this stage.

14.5 Service of the summons (CCR O.7)

The summons must be served on the defendant within *four months* after issue. In contrast to the High Court, the County Court itself, not the plaintiff, usually serves the summons because the plaintiff has no power to serve *by post*, except in personal injury cases.

The court serves the summons by first-class post, including with it the documents listed above under 'Issue of the summons' and notice of issue of legal aid in a legal aid case. Service is deemed to take place *seven days* after posting, unless the contrary is shown.

Alternatively, in a *personal injury* action only, the plaintiff's solicitor may serve the summons by post, where they have prepared a summons. (Obviously, the documents are returned to them for service after issue.)

In all other cases, the plaintiff's solicitor can only effect service by personal service on the defendant.

A defendant company is generally served at its registered office: CCR O.7 r.14. CCR O.7 r.13 deals with service on partnerships.

Note

If the above methods fail, there is a provision for service by the County Court bailiff or substituted service, ie. an order for service by some other means (as in the High Court): *see* 14.4.4.

14.6 Amending the summons

The court has power to allow amendment of a summons, including the addition or substitution of a party, on the same principles as those applicable to amendment of a High Court writ: CCR O.15 r.1.

14.7 Admission, defence and counterclaim (CCR O.9)

In response to the summons, the defendant can do the following:

- Pay the whole sum claimed;
- Admit the whole or part of the claim;
- Serve a defence and/or counterclaim.

The following alternative procedures will then apply.

Note

A defence can be combined with part admission.

Payment of the whole sum claimed (CCR O.11 r.2)

14.7.1

The action is stayed, ie. stops.

Where the claim is for a *debt* or *liquidated* demand, ie. for a precisely known sum, and the defendant pays:

- Whole sum; plus
- Interest; plus
- Fixed costs stated on the summons

within *14 days* of the service of the summons plus the *fixed costs* stated on the summons, the defendant will not be liable for any other costs of the plaintiff unless the court otherwise orders.

Note

'Fixed costs' are a fixed amount of costs prescribed by court rules which can be automatically claimed back from the other side when obtaining early payment or judgment in the case.

In other cases, eg. where the claim is for unliquidated damages or a liquidated claim is not paid within 14 days, the plaintiff is not limited to claiming 'fixed costs' but can have their costs *taxed*, that is, decided on by the district judge.

Liability admitted for the *whole* of a liquidated sum but time to pay requested (CCR O.9 rr.2 & 3)

14.7.2

The *defendant* must, within *14 days* after service of the summons, deliver to the plaintiff (*not* the court) a *standard form of admission* which includes details of the defendant's means and a request/proposal for time for payment, eg. at a later date or by instalments. This is Form N9A which the defendant can obtain from the court, if it has not been sent with the summons.

The *plaintiff* may then either apply for judgment (including interest) and costs on the admission – using Form N205A – or may, on the same form, reject the defendant's proposals for payment.

The court officer must then make a decision on how the money should be paid, ie. by what date and/or by what instalments, and enter judgment in the records accordingly.

Note

Either party may apply for the district judge to reconsider the question of how the money should be paid. The procedural details for this are at O.9 r.3 (4) and (5).

14.7.3 Liability admitted for the *part* of a liquidated sum but ime to pay requested (CCR O.9 rr.2 & 3)

A similar procedure applies to that in 15.7.2 above, except that the defendant delivers the admission to the *court* rather than to the plaintiff and also delivers to the court a *defence* and any *counterclaim* to the part of the claim which is denied. (Forms for admission, defence and counterclaim are sent with the summons.)

14.7.4 Liability for an unliquidated claim admitted but the amount of damages claimed disputed (CCR O.9 r.3(7))

If the *defendant* offers to pay a specific sum, which offer is *accepted* by the plaintiff, the above rules on admission of liability for part of a liquidated sum apply (including dispute over time for payment). Form N9 – sent with the summons to the defendant – is used.

In other cases, the *plaintiff* may apply for judgment using Form N205A, which will usually be for judgment on liability with the amount of damages to be assessed by the district judge at a later hearing.

14.7.5 All or part of the action is to be defended and/or a counterclaim brought

The defendant must deliver the defence and/or counterclaim to the court within *14 days* of service of the summons – Form N9 in an unliquidated case, Form N9B in a liquidated case.

If the sum claimed or amount involved does not exceed £1,000, the proceedings will be automatically referred to the small claims procedure, known as 'Arbitration' (*see* 15.9).

Note _____

County Court arbitration must be distinguished from forms of non-judicial arbitration.

In cases where a pre-trial review applies, after service of the defence in a default action the court fixes a date for the pre-trial review.

14.8 Judgment in default

14.8.1 In a default action (CCR O.9 r.6)

If the defendant does not respond in any way to the summons within 14 days, the plaintiff can enter judgment in default against the defendant.

This is done by:

- Delivering at court a *request for judgment* – Form 205A for a liquidated claim, Form N234 for an unliquidated claim;
- In the case of a liquidated claim, certifying that the defendant has not sent any *reply* to the summons;
- Stating what (if any) *payment* has been made;
- In the case of a summons served by post by the plaintiff's solicitor, delivering with the request an *affidavit* verifying that service was effected and the summons was not returned undelivered.

The court will then, without any hearing, enter judgment.

Judgment in a *liquidated claim* will be for the debt, interest and fixed costs. Judgment in an *unliquidated claim* will be judgment on liability (interlocutory judgment) with the amount of damages to be assessed by the district judge at a later hearing. Costs will then be taxed rather than fixed.

Note _____

Where the defendant is a minor, the plaintiff cannot generally get judgment in default without first applying to the court for a guardian *ad litem* to be appointed to represent the minor.

In a fixed date action   14.8.2

Where the defendant fails to deliver a defence within 14 days, the court has power to order judgment in default in fixed date actions to which the automatic directions apply: CCR O.9 r.4A (*see* Chapter 19). However, this rule is more flexible than that in default actions; the court may give directions for service of the defence within a certain time rather than allow default judgment.

Setting aside a default judgment (CCR O.37 rr.3 & 4)   14.8.3

The defendant can apply to have a default judgment set aside on similar principles and procedures to those in the High Court (*see* Chapter 13), except that the defendant applies by notice of application to the District Judge rather than by summons to the Master.

Further, there is a particular rule that judgment may be set aside if the service of the summons did not come to the notice of the defendant: CCR O.37 r.3.

Arbitration: 'small claims' procedure   14.9
(CCR O.19)

Reference to arbitration

Any proceedings in which the sum claimed or amount involved does not exceed £1,000 will, upon receipt by the court of a defence, be automatically referred to the much more informal small claims procedure known as 'Arbitration'.

However, the District Judge may order that the case be heard by ordinary trial proceedings if:

- A difficult question of law or a question of fact of exceptional complexity is involved; or
- Fraud is alleged; or
- The parties agree that the case should be heard by ordinary trial; or
- It would be unreasonable for the small claims procedure to be used having regard to:
  - the subject matter of the case
  - the size of any counterclaim
  - the circumstances of the parties, or
  - the interests of any non-party likely to be affected.

14.9.2 Procedure

The automatic procedural directions which apply to most cases do not apply and there is usually no pre-trial review.

Instead, the following standard 'directions', ie. procedural rules, apply:

- Not less than *14 days* before the hearing of the case, each party shall send to the other copies of all documents in their possession which they intend to rely on at the hearing.
- Not less than *7 days* before the hearing, each party shall send to the other and to the court a copy of any expert report on which that party intends to rely and a list of the witnesses they intend to call.

The hearing is held in private and evidence is not given on oath, unless the District Judge orders otherwise. It is informal and the strict rules of evidence do not apply. The District Judge adopts any method of procedure considered fair.

Usually, an arbitration is short, with the parties sitting in front of the District Judge and putting their cases, the judge helps them by explaining the law and asking questions.

Some parties use lay representatives as they are now allowed to under s.11, Courts and Legal Services Act 1990.

14.9.3 Recovery of costs

Parties are not usually represented by solicitors in arbitration proceedings because, even if they win, a party cannot usually recover their legal costs from the other side other than:

- The costs stated on the summons (the issue fee and a small amount of fixed costs);
- The costs of enforcing the judgment;
- Costs incurred as a result of unreasonable conduct by the other side;
- Witness travelling expenses;
- Up to £29.00 in respect of a party's or witness's loss of earnings when attending a hearing;
- Up to £112.50 in respect of fees of an expert.

Originating application procedure   14.10

Most county court cases are required to be commenced by summons. However, in some special cases where so required by a statute, eg. a tenant's application for a new business tenancy under the Landlord and Tenant Act 1954, the proceedings are commenced by originating application. This is a document similar to an originating summons in the High Court.

The procedure for commencement by this method is set out at CCR O.3 r.4.

In some cases, eg. under the Landlord and Tenant Act 1954, the other side has to serve a document known as an 'answer' in reply to the application: *see* CCR O.9 r.18.

Persons under a disability and partnerships   14.11

See CCR O.1 for the special procedural rules on persons under a disability, ie. parties under 18 years of age and those suffering from a mental disorder, and CCR O.5 r.9 for the rules on suing and being sued by partnerships.

Self-assessment questions

1   Is a claim for an injunction together with damages a 'fixed date' or a 'default' action?
2   What is the difference between a County Court summons and a High Court interlocutory summons?
3   You have been instructed to commence County Court proceedings to recover a debt.

(a) In which court would you commence proceedings?

(b) How would you commence proceedings and which numbered forms would you use?

(c) Who serves the summons on the defendant?

(d) What steps would take place if the defendant admits the debt but wants time to pay?

How would your answers to (a)–(d) differ if the claim was for damages for personal injury and the claim is denied by the defendant.

4   What is a 'plaint note'?

5   When is the small claims procedure used? How does this procedure differ from ordinary proceedings?

Chapter 15

Pleadings: RSC O.18; CCR O.6 and O.9

What are pleadings? 15.1

Pleadings are formal documents in which the parties set out the details of their cases. In the first pleading (the statement or particulars of claim) the plaintiff, in numbered paragraphs, states the factual allegations which make up their cause of action and which, if proved at trial, would entitle the plaintiff to the remedy claimed in the proceedings, eg. damages or an injunction. The defendant in response sets out, in numbered paragraphs, the details of their defence to the claim.

The parties serve these documents on each other shortly after the commencement of proceedings. Further pleadings, eg. counterclaim, defence to counterclaim and reply, may follow.

Pleadings are a very important part of litigation. In essence, the trial is all about whether the plaintiff can prove each allegation in their pleading and whether the defendant can successfully rely on the defences stated in their pleadings. The trial is in fact *limited to the issues raised in the pleadings.*

Also, the pleadings serve the purpose of explaining your case to the other party and to the judge. A party's pleading is one of the first things read by the trial judge in order to see what the case is about.

The pleading process 15.2

The statement/particulars of claim 15.2.1

The first pleading that is served is the plaintiff's 'statement of claim' (High Court) or 'particulars of claim' (County Court). This is the formal document prepared on behalf of the plaintiff, setting out the details of the plaintiff's claim. (The drafting of a statement/particulars of claim is explained in 15.3.1.)

High Court
In the High Court, the statement of claim can be either:

- Set out (endorsed) on the back of the writ; or
- Served on the defendant with the writ; or
- Served on the defendant *after* service of the writ at any time before the expiration of 14 days after the defendant gives notice of their intention to defend.

Note

In most cases, the statement of claim is served within the 14 day period allowed after the defendant has acknowledged service of the writ, or within an extended time period allowed by the court or the other side.

The statement of claim is generally only set out on the back of the writ in simple debt claims where the form of statement of claim is short.

The statement of claim is served on the defendant, or on their solicitor, if the defendant is represented, by ordinary post.

In *personal injury cases*, the plaintiff must serve with the statement of claim:

- A medical report; and
- A statement of special damages (*see* Chapter 5).

Note

The medical report is prepared by the appropriate doctor.

The plaintiff can apply by summons to a master for an order allowing them to dispense with service of the report and statement, or for an extension of time for their service. Alternatively, if they are not served with the statement of claim, the defendant can apply for an order that they be served and that the action be stayed until they are served.

The County Court
The County Court equivalent of the statement of claim is the particulars of claim. This is drafted in a similar way to the High Court statement of claim but, in contrast to the High Court, the *court* serves the particulars of claim on the defendant *with the summons*.

When requesting the court to serve the summons commencing proceedings in the County Court, the plaintiff must file at court the particulars of claim and one copy for each defendant. The court then serves a copy on the defendant together with service of the summons commencing proceedings.

On commencing proceedings in *personal injury cases*, the plaintiff must file at court with the particulars of claim a medical report and statement of special damages and a copy for each defendant. These are served on the defendant by the court with the summons and particulars of claim. Alternatively, *in personal injury cases only*, the *plaintiff's solicitor* can elect to serve the proceedings by post (including particulars, medical report and statement of special damages) instead of the court serving the proceedings; (CCR O.7 r.10A).

As in the High Court, the County Court may make orders dispensing with the service of report and statement, or extending the time for their service or staying the action until they are served.

The defence   15.2.2

The defence is a formal document in which the defendant, in numbered paragraphs, denies or admits the allegations in the statement/particulars of claim, and asserts defences to the claim. The drafting of a defence is explained below.

In the *High Court* the defendant must serve their defence on the plaintiff within 14 days after service of the statement of claim, or within 14 days after the time allowed for acknowledgement of service of the writ by the defendant. Thus, if the statement of claim is endorsed on the writ or served with the writ, the defendant has 28 days from service of the writ to serve their defence (remembering that service of a writ by post is deemed to take on the seventh day after posting unless the contrary is shown).

In the County Court the defendant must deliver their defence *at the court office* within 14 days after service of the summons (remembering that service of a summons by post is deemed to take place on the seventh day after posting, unless the contrary is shown).

Note

In some cases, an unrepresented defendant serves a very basic 'home-made' defence before instructing a solicitor. The solicitor should apply to amend the defence so as to serve a more detailed defence in formal, legal style.

In some cases, the defendant does not have the time to prepare and serve a full defence within the time limit. In such cases, the defendant may serve a holding defence, which is a simple defence denying the claim but without the detail needed to defend the case at trial. The defendant later applies to amend their defence so as to serve a more detailed defence. Alternatively, the defendant may ask the plaintiff, or apply to court, for an extension of time for the service of their defence (*see* 15.2.6).

Note

In the High Court only, where the plaintiff serves a summons on the defendant claiming summary judgment before the defendant serves their defence (*see* Chapter 19), the usual time limit for service of the defence does not apply. Instead, if the defendant is given leave to defend at the summary judgment hearing, the defendant has 14 days (or such other time as is ordered) after the hearing to serve their defence.

15.2.3   Judgment in default of defence

High Court (RSC O.19)

If the defendant fails to serve a defence within the time limit, the plaintiff can enter judgment in default by taking or sending to the court office:

- The original *writ*;
- Two completed copies of the form of judgment (one being endorsed with a certificate that the time limit has expired without a defence being served); and
- A copy of the statement of claim, unless it was endorsed on the writ.

County Court (CCR O.9 r.6)

If the defendant does not respond to the claim within 14 days after service of the summons, the plaintiff may enter judgment by:

- Filing a request for judgment (Form N205A or N234);
- Stating what payments (if any) have been made;
- If the action is for a liquidated sum, certifying that the defendant has not sent any reply to the summons;
- If the summons was served by post by the plaintiff's solicitor, filing an affidavit verifying that service was effected and that the summons was not returned undelivered.

In both courts, in the case of a liquidated claim, the judgment will be for the sum claimed and fixed costs. In the case of an unliquidated claim, the judgment will be an interlocutory judgment for an amount of damages to be assessed at a later hearing by a master.

Setting aside a default judgment

In both courts, the defendant may apply to have a default judgment set aside (*see* Chapters 13 and 14).

15.2.4   Counterclaim

In addition to their defence to the plaintiff's claim, the defendant may have their own claim against the plaintiff.

Example

P sues D for payment for goods delivered by P to D. D may have a counterclaim for damages for defects in the goods or, for example, D may have a counterclaim for damages for personal injuries caused by P to D on an unconnected occasion – the counterclaim need not be connected to the plaintiff's claim.

The defendant is entitled to raise a counterclaim in response to the plaintiff's statement/particulars of claim. The counterclaim is not strictly a defence to the plaintiff's claim unless it amounts to a 'set-off' (*see* below). However, the point is that the counterclaim can be pleaded in response to the claim and is dealt with in the same proceedings, in practice reducing or extinguishing the eventual amount of damages owed by the defendant to the plaintiff.

The counterclaim is effectively written in the form of a statement/particulars of claim by the defendant against the plaintiff. The counterclaim is written in the same document as the defence, underneath the defence.

If the plaintiff wishes to defend the counterclaim, the plaintiff must serve a defence to the counterclaim within 14 days. The defence is written in the same form as a defendant's defence.

Note

The following are important examples of counterclaims which amount to a 'set-off'.

● Mutual debts between the plaintiff and defendant.

● A buyer's claim for damages for breach of warranty in relation to the goods against the seller's claim for the price: s.53(1)(a), Sale of Goods Act 1979.

● A tenant's claim for damages for defects in the premises against the landlord's claim for rent.

● Generally, a defendant's own claim against the plaintiff's claim where the two claims arise out of the same transaction and are closely connected: *Hanak v Green* (1958).

If the counterclaim does amount to a defence of set-off, this has advantages for the defendant in terms of costs, avoiding summary judgment and procedurally in various ways.

The reply   15.2.5

The plaintiff may serve a 'reply' in response to the defendant's defence. They will do this where they wish to meet points raised in the defence which have not already been dealt with in the statement/particulars of claim.

Example

The defendant may state in the defence that there was an oral agreement negating the plaintiff's claim. The plaintiff may

> serve a reply denying there was an agreement or stating why it does not negate the plaintiff's claim.

It is unnecessary to serve a reply if the plaintiff simply wishes to deny the allegations in the defence, rather than to make positive assertions in answer to the points in the defence. This is because the plaintiff is automatically taken to deny ('to join issue with') the defence.

In the High Court, the reply must be served within 14 days after the defence. The County Court rules do not appear to provide for a reply but it is used in practice in the County Court.

15.2.6 Extension of time for service of a pleading

Despite the above rules on the time in which each pleading must be served, parties often need an extension of time for the service of their pleading. For example, the defendant's solicitor will often want more than 14 days to draft and serve the defence because they will need time to investigate the claim.

In such cases, the first step is to write a letter to the other side asking for an extension of time for a certain period. If the other side do not agree to this (they usually do agree but may refuse in order to exert pressure), an application must be made to the court for an order allowing an extension of time.

In the County Court, application is made to the district judge (CCR O.13 r.4). Notice of the application is served on the other side, who may attend and argue against an extension.

In the High Court, a 'time summons' is issued applying to a master for an extension. In the Queen's Bench Division in London, the application will generally be heard two days after the summons is issued. The summons may be served on the other side only the day before the hearing (see RSC O.3 r.5 and notes thereto).

A time summons should obviously be issued urgently.

15.2.7 Close of pleadings

At a certain date after the last pleading is served, pleadings are said to be 'closed'. The actual date is important because the timetable for the future procedural steps in the case begins from the date of close of pleadings. The rules on this future timetable are known as 'directions' (*see* Chapter 17). These directions are timed as from close of pleadings.

Example

In the County Court, the directions provide that within 28 days of close of pleadings the parties must disclose to each other all documents that they have relating to the case.

In the High Court, the date of close of pleadings is:

- 14 days after service of the reply or, if there is no reply but only a defence to counterclaim, 14 days after service of the defence to counterclaim; or

- If neither a reply nor a defence to counterclaim is served, 14 days after service of the defence.

In the *County Court*, the date of close of pleadings is 14 days after delivery of the defence or, where a counterclaim is served with the defence, 28 days after delivery of the defence.

Drafting pleadings   15.3

Drafting a statement/particulars of claim   15.3.1

Heading

There should first be a heading stating the:

- Court division (if it is a High Court Case);

- Year;

- Action number and date the writ was issued (if High Court) or case number (if County Court);

- Parties; and

- Description of the pleading, eg. statement/particulars of claim.

Paragraphs

Then, in separate numbered paragraphs, the pleadings should concisely set out the essential facts which, taken together, show a cause of action and entitle the plaintiff, if those facts are proved at trial, to the remedy claimed.

Example

In a straightforward breach of contract claim, in order to claim damages for a breach of contract, a plaintiff must show that there has been:

- A contract;

- Certain express or implied terms of the contract;

- A breach of one or more of those terms;

- Consequent loss.

Thus, a basic statement/particulars of claim for damages for breach of contract must assert, in separate numbered paragraphs, that the above elements have taken place, thereby entitling the plaintiff to the damages claimed at the end of the pleading.

As far as possible each allegation should be in a separate paragraph. Only *material* facts should be asserted, and each assertion of fact should be in a summary form and as brief as the nature of the case allows.

Technically, a trial is about whether the plaintiff can prove each factual assertion in their statement/particulars of claim. So for example, in a basic breach of contract statement/particulars of claim:

- Paragraph 1 is often used to describe the *parties* where this is relevant so as to explain the context of the dispute. ('At all material times, the defendants carried on business as manufacturers of ... and the plaintiff carried on business as ...'.)

- Paragraph 2 asserts there was a contract, how it was made, its date and parties and what it was essentially for.

- Paragraphs 3 and 4 assert the relevant express and implied terms of the contract which have allegedly been breached.

- Paragraph 5 may then tell some necessary part of the story, eg. that the goods were delivered and installed.

- Paragraph 6 asserts there was a breach and sets out the details (known as 'particulars') of the breach.

- Paragraph 7 may then explain the consequence of the breach, eg. the details of the damage that ensued. (This paragraph is necessary to tell the story and to explain the damages being claimed.)

- Paragraph 8 sets out in figures the details ('particulars') of the amount of damages claimed showing the breakdown of the amount claimed and what it relates to.

- In the final numbered paragraph, the pleading must always claim interest in a standard form.

Note

Numbers in a pleading must be expressed in figures, not words.

The above is purely an example of one of the most basic forms of pleading. There are few strict rules on format and certainly no rules on how many paragraphs there should be, what should be in each paragraph or the form of wording to use. What is important is that the numbered paragraphs should separately assert the essential facts which go to make up the plaintiff's cause of action and their right to the remedy claimed. Also, there will be some paragraphs which are there to tell the story of the case to the judge and to put the material facts in context. This will all depend on the nature of the case and the branch of law involved.

Prayer

After the numbered paragraphs comes the prayer. In this the plaintiff states the remedy claimed, eg. damages or an injunction, and interest. This has a standard format.

The pleading ends with the name and business address of the plaintiff's solicitor and the date it was served (High Court) or the date that the pleading was drafted and the plaintiff's address for service of documents (County Court). It must be signed by the plaintiff's solicitor (in the firm name) unless it was drafted by counsel (which it often is), in which case counsel signs it.

Note

This chapter merely sets out the basic outline and rules. The main precedent books on pleadings are Atkin's Court Forms, which comes in 42 volumes, showing many examples of pleadings for each branch of law, and Bullen, Leake and Jacob's *Precedents of Pleadings*. There are also several textbooks which explain and illustrate pleadings.

Further basic rules on drafting statements/particulars of claim

1 *Assert facts only* The pleading should plead facts, *not law, arguments or evidence.*

Example

A pleading merely has to assert that goods were defective, it does not set out the law, nor should it set out its evidence, ie. how the defects will be proved.

2 *Defence not dealt with* The statement/particulars of claim need not deal in advance with any defence that might be raised.

Example

If the defendant to a claim for defective goods is expected to raise the existence of an exclusion clause in their defence, it is neither necessary nor usual for the plaintiff, in anticipation of this, to deny the efficacy of the exclusion clause in their statement of claim. It is for the defendant to raise the matter.

3 *Reference to the parties* All pleadings refer to the parties as 'plaintiff' or 'defendant' rather than by their actual names, except in the heading.

4 *Essential inclusions* Although the content of a statement of claim is generally a matter of practice, in the High Court the following matters *must* be included in the statement of

claim (and a County Court particulars of claim includes them in practice):

- If intending to adduce evidence of a previous conviction under s.11, Civil Evidence Act 1968, details of the conviction and its date, the court which made the conviction and the issue in the civil proceedings to which the conviction is relevant.
- A claim for exemplary or provisional damages.
- A claim for interest. (In the High Court, interest is claimed under s.35A, Supreme Court Act 1981; in the County Court under s.69, County Courts Act 1984.)
- Full particulars (details) of any alleged misrepresentation, fraud, breach of trust, wilful default or undue influence.

5 *'Exceeding three folios'* In complex cases, where the details of the damages 'exceed three folios' (an ancient rule, a folio being 72 words), those details must be set out in a separate document referred to in the pleading and either served with the pleading or later.

6 *Claims above £5,000 in the County Court* In a county court particulars of claim, the prayer must state whether the claim exceeds £5,000. If it does, the case can only be heard by a circuit judge. Claims for less than £5,000 can be heard either by a district judge or by a circuit judge.

7 *Joining causes of action* Separate or alternative causes of action may be joined together in the same pleading.

Example

A statement/particulars of claim can include a contract claim and a tort claim or, for example, the plaintiff can claim negligence and/or breach of statutory duty in the same pleading.

15.3.2 Examples of the elements to be included in some basic contract and tort statements/particulars of claim

Short form of statement/particulars of claim for a debt
Where a straight forward debt is being claimed, eg. for the non-delivery of goods, the plaintiff will simply prepare a short form of statement/particulars of claim (which will be included on the back of the writ in a High Court case rather than being served separately). This short form should:

- State the amount of the claim and briefly what the debt relates to (there is a standard form of words);
- Give details, in similar form to an invoice;
- In the prayer, show the amount and rate of interest due

on the debt from the date the debt became due to the date the pleading is drafted;

- Show the continuing future daily amount of interest which will become due until judgment or payment before judgment.

Claim for damages for breach of contract

- Contract: date, how made, parties, what the contract is essentially for, amount of consideration;
- Express and/or implied terms;
- Breach of terms;
- Loss (including amount of loss).

Claim for rescission and/or damages for misrepresentation

- Details of representations made;
- Reliance;
- Details of contract;
- Details of how representations were false;
- Loss, including amounts of loss;
- Prayer may include claim for rescission.

Claim for negative injunction to restrain breach of contract or to restrain the defendant from committing a tort

- Contract and terms as above.
- Breach or intention to breach by defendant; or in case of tort
- Facts giving rise to the tort, eg. the nuisance alleged.
- In the case of an intention to breach or to commit the tort, the following standard form of words is used 'The defendant threatens and intends, unless restrained by this court, to ...' (specify precisely the intended breach).
- Loss, if loss has occurred at date of pleading.
- In the prayer, specify the injunction required in precise terms using the following standard wording 'An injunction to prevent the defendants by themselves, their servants, agents or otherwise from ...' (indicate precisely what you want the injunction to restrain them from doing).

Claim for damages for negligence

- Explain the context and who the parties are, eg. their business, or what cars they were driving.
- Explain how accident took place.
- Assert that the accident was caused by the defendant's negligence.

- Give details (particulars) of how the defendant was negligent.
- At the bottom of the particulars of negligence paragraph the plaintiff may state that they will rely on the principle *res ipsa loquitur,* and may plead a criminal conviction, in which case they must plead the conviction, date, convicting court and the issue in the proceedings to which the conviction is relevant.
- Explain the plaintiff's injuries – the pleading may simply refer to the medical report served with the pleading.
- Explain the special damages – the pleading may simply refer to the statement of special damages which is served with the pleading.

Note

The drafting of the statement of special damages is important. This is dealt with in Chapter 5, para.5.6.

- In some cases, the pleading may include a claim for provisional damages.

Claim for damages for negligence and breach of statutory duty

The pleading will be similar to a claim for damages for negligence but it should:

- Show how the case falls within the statute.

Example

In a case of breaches of the Factories Act 1960, it must show that the plaintiff was employed in the defendant's factory, and in a case under the Occupiers' Liability Act 1957, it must show that the defendant was owner and occupier of the premises and that the plaintiff entered as a lawful visitor.

- Give particulars of the breach of statutory duty, specifying the breach and the statute and section breached.

15.3.3 Drafting a defence

The basic structure of a defence consists of the defendant, in numbered paragraphs, responding to each allegation in the statement/particulars of claim. The defence will deny, admit or not admit each allegation.

A non-admission (as opposed to a positive denial) is appropriate where the facts are not within the defendant's knowledge and the defendant wishes to put the plaintiff to proof of the allegation. For example, the losses claimed by the plaintiff are generally 'not admitted' by the defendant. It is for the plaintiff to prove them.

The defence should respond to *every* allegation in the claim, making it clear whether each allegation is denied, admitted or not admitted. A general denial of all the allegations is not good practice and, in the High Court, is not allowed. Further, in the High Court an allegation of fact is deemed to be admitted unless it is specifically denied or not admitted.

A paragraph in a statement/particulars of claim may contain different express or implied allegations, some of which the defendant may deny and some of which may be admitted. The defendant should read the paragraphs of the claim carefully and the defence should distinguish between those parts admitted and those denied, eg. '... save that it is denied that ... paragraph 1 of the statement of claim is admitted.'

The defence may, and often does, raise positive allegations of its own, as well as just denying, admitting or not admitting the allegations in the claim. The defence will raise positive defences, eg. the existence of an exclusion clause, which obviously are not raised in the claim. The wording often used to raise defences is 'the defendant avers that ...' (although you should try to avoid such language). In many cases, the positive aspects of the defence are substantial, eg. where the defence pleads defects in goods in response to a claim for their payment.

In the *High Court*, the rules provide that certain matters *must* be specifically pleaded in the defence (and they are also specifically pleaded in the County Court, in practice). These matters include:

- An allegation of negligence against the plaintiff or a third party. A defence to a negligence action will often allege that the accident was caused or contributed to by the negligence of the plaintiff and/or a third party. The defence will give particulars of how the plaintiff and/or third party were negligent.
- Details of any facts relied on in support of a defence of mitigation of damages.

Drafting a counterclaim 15.3.4

A counterclaim is written in the same document as the defence, below the defence.

The document is headed 'Defence and Counterclaim'. Then the defence is pleaded. If the defendant wishes to raise the counterclaim as a defence or set-off to the plaintiff's claim (*see* 15.2.4), the last paragraph of the defence should state 'Further or alternatively, the defendant will rely upon their counterclaim herein by way of set-off, in extinction or diminution of the plaintiff's claim.'

Then, after the heading 'Counterclaim' the counterclaim is pleaded. Where the counterclaim is related to the claim and defence, its first paragraph should state 'The defendant repeats paragraphs 1–(however many paragraphs there are in the defence) hereof'.

The counterclaim is then drafted in the same way as a statement/particulars of claim, except that the prayer states '... and the defendant counterclaims'.

Note

The plaintiff's defence to a counterclaim is drafted in the same way as a defendant's defence.

15.3.5   Drafting a reply

The standard form of the first paragraph of a reply is:

Save and in so far as the defence consists of admissions and save as hereinafter appears, the plaintiff joins issue with the defendant on the defence.

This means that the plaintiff disputes ('joins issue with') the defence.

Then, in numbered paragraphs, the plaintiff sets out their assertions in response to the defence (remembering that a reply is only appropriate where the defence raises points which the plaintiff has not already dealt with in the statement/particulars of claim).

15.3.6   General points of style

Structure
The structure should be logical, should set out all the material elements of the claim/defence and should tell the story clearly to the reader. In general, each main point should be in a separate paragraph.

Conciseness
The pleading and paragraphs should be as concise as the case allows and should not include irrelevant material. However, it should also be thorough and accurate.

Language
The language used should be as plain and clear as possible. However, it should also be as precise as possible. Further, you will come across traditional phrases, such as:

- 'By reason of the matters aforesaid ...';
- 'In the premises ...', which means 'therefore, as a result of the foregoing ...';

- 'At all material times', which means, 'at all times relevant to the dispute';
- 'It is averred that ...', which means 'it is positively asserted that ...';
- 'The said ...' (it is doubtful whether 'said' is really necessary in most situations).

Claims and allegations

A pleading can include several claims and allegations, even if they contradict one another. The theory behind pleadings is that a party is quite entitled to state that for example:

1   I did not drive negligently.

2   If I did, that did not cause the accident.

3   If it did, the plaintiff did not suffer any loss anyway.

In introducing a further or alternative allegation in a pleading, the practice is to use the words 'Further or alternatively ...'.

Further and better particulars: RSC O.18 r.12;   15.4
CCR O.6 r.7

It may be that part of a pleading does not give sufficient details of what is being alleged. For example, the statement of claim may state that a contract exists but does not say when and how it was made, or the plaintiff may not give any details of the alleged financial losses suffered. In such cases, the other party may ask for further details of what is being alleged. This is known as requesting 'further and better particulars' of a pleading.

The request is drafted in a formal standard form and sent with a covering letter to the other party asking for further particulars to be given. No time limit is given.

If the other side does not give the particulars, or does not give sufficient particulars, the requesting party may apply to a master/district judge for an order that the particulars, or sufficient particulars, be given. At this stage, or sometimes later if a first order is not complied with, the master/district judge may make an 'unless order', ie. unless the particulars are given within a specified time, the party failing to comply will have their case struck out.

Particulars are not generally ordered before service of the defence. Further, the court will only order particulars of facts to be given, not particulars of evidence or arguments. Furthermore, particulars will only be ordered to be given where the information given is insufficient to allow the other side a reasonable opportunity to respond to the allegation.

The particulars are given in a formal standard form. The request and particulars given then become part of, and are read together with, the pleadings.

Note

A request for further and better particulars is a very useful tactic for putting pressure on the other side, for preventing them from presenting a vague pleading and for discovering further information as well as gaps in their case.

15.5   Amending pleadings (RSC O.20; CCR O.15)

15.5.1   In the High Court

A pleading can be amended, eg. to change or add some fact or wording, once before close of pleadings, without the leave of the court being needed.

A party needs leave of the court to amend a pleading after close of pleadings, or after it has already been amended on one occasion.

The pleading should be retyped. The superseded words should be shown crossed out in red and the new words should be added in red. If the pleading is later amended a second time, the amendments are made in green. Further colours apply to further amendments.

If leave is needed, application is made to a master. The master will usually grant leave on condition that the amending party pay the costs incurred by the other side as a result of the amendment.

If leave is needed, the heading of the amended pleading should be endorsed in the appropriate colour with the words 'amended pursuant to the order of master ... dated the ... day of 19 ...'.

If leave is not needed, the endorsement should read 'amended the ... day of ... 19 ..., under RSC O.20, Rule 3.'

The amended pleading is then served on the other party.

15.5.2   In the County Court

A pleading may be amended at any time before 'the return day', without the leave of the court being needed. The 'return day' means:

- In a default action, the day of the trial;
- In an action where there is a pre-trial review, the day of the pre-trial review;
- In a fixed date action where automatic directions apply, the date of close of pleadings.

If leave is needed, application is made by notice of application to a district judge.

Similar principles and procedure apply as in the High Court.

Self-assessment questions

1 Outline the order of pleadings and their time limits.

2 What differences are there between a statement of claim and particulars of claim in terms of drafting and procedure?

3 When is the statement of claim served?

4 Who serves the particulars of claim on the defendant?

5 What must be served on the defendant with the statement/particulars of claim in personal injury cases?

6 What would you do if you needed extra time to serve your defence? What will happen if you fail to serve your defence in time?

7 What is the difference between a counterclaim and a set-off?

8 In what circumstances will a plaintiff serve a reply?

9 Explain the date and importance of 'close of pleadings'.

10 When would you insert the statement of claim on the back of the writ?

11 What is meant by the following:

(a) the 'particulars' paragraph;

(b) the prayer;

(c) a non-admission, as opposed to a denial;

(d) 'in the premises ...';

(e) 'at all material times';

(f) 'the defendant avers that ...';

(g) 'the plaintiff joins issue with the defendant ...'.

12 As the defendant's solicitor, what would you do if the particulars of claim does not give any details of the loss alleged but merely says 'full details will be provided on discovery'?

13 Just before trial, you wish to amend your defence to add a further point in defence. Do you need the leave of the Court? How will you effect the amendment? Answer for both High Court and County Court.

Chapter 16

Procedure where further parties are involved

Joinder (RSC O.15, CCR O.5)   16.1

Joinder of causes of action   16.1.1

A plaintiff can claim relief for several causes of action in the same proceedings without leave of the court if the plaintiff claims and the defendant is liable in the same capacity for all the causes of action.

Example

If P has a breach of contract claim and a personal injury claim against D, P can sue D in respect of both matters in the same action and the claims would appear in the same statement/ particulars of claim. Conversely, joinder would not be possible, for example, if the defendant is liable in one action personally and in another as a trustee.

Joinder of parties   16.1.2

Two or more persons may be joined together in one action as plaintiffs or defendants without leave of the court where, if separate actions were brought, a common question of law or fact would arise in all the actions and the claims arise out of the same transaction or series of transactions.

Example

If, in a road accident case, P thinks drivers X and Y were both responsible, P may sue X and Y in the same proceedings. Similarly, in a defective goods case, the plaintiff may sue the supplier and manufacturer in the same proceedings. Equally, co-plaintiffs may sue in respect of the same matter in the same action.

In cases falling outside the above rules, *leave of the court* is needed to join parties or causes of action together in the same action.

The court has power to consolidate similar actions, ie. deal with them together, under RSC O.4 r.9 and CCR O.13 r.9. Conversely, the court has power to order separate trials of joined actions where that would be more convenient (RSC O.15 r.5 and CCR O.5 r.3).

16.2   Third party proceedings (RSC O.16 and CCR O.12)

16.2.1   What are third party proceedings?

A *defendant* may claim a remedy against someone who is not already a party to the action by bringing third party proceedings. In other words, the defendant, having been sued by the plaintiff, may turn round and sue some other person who the defendant claims is responsible, bringing that other person into the action as a third party. There is then, in effect, a separate action between the defendant and the third party but, for convenience, the third party proceedings are heard in the same proceedings as the main action between the plaintiff and the defendant.

Although there is no action between the plaintiff and the third party, the plaintiff may wish to join the third party into the main action as a second defendant. If this is so, the principles on 'joinder' apply and the plaintiff will need to amend the writ/summons, pleadings and, where applicable, the legal aid certificate.

16.2.2   When can they be brought?

A defendant may bring third party proceedings against a person where they claim against a person not already a party:

- A contribution or indemnity;
- Any relief or remedy relating to or connected with the original subject matter of the action and substantially the same as some relief or remedy claimed by the plaintiff;
- That any issue relating to the original subject matter of the action should be determined not only as between the plaintiff and the defendant but also as between either or both of them and the non-party.

Example

P is a passenger in a car driven by T which is involved in a collision with a lorry driven by D. P sues D. D can issue third party proceedings against T claiming a contribution to or indemnity for the damages if D is found liable to pay damages to P, on the ground that the accident was caused wholly or partly by T's negligence. There is, therefore, a main action between P and D, and a third party action in the same proceedings between D and T. The pleadings will indicate all three parties in their headings.

16.2.3   Procedure

The defendant brings third party proceedings by issuing

(having filled in) a 'Third Party Notice', to the third party. This notice is a standard form (similar to a writ in the High Court, and Form N15 in the County Court) which contains a statement of the nature of the claim made against the third party and the grounds of the claim or the question or issue to be determined.

In the *High Court*, the defendant cannot issue a third party notice until *after* they have given notice of intention to defend to the plaintiff. *Leave* of the court to issue a notice is required after the defence has been served.

In the *County Court*, *leave* to issue is required in:

● A fixed date action;
● Most default actions, after close of proceedings;
● Default actions listed in CCR O.17 r.11, where a hearing or pre-trial review date has been fixed.

Where leave is required, the defendant must apply for leave to issue by *ex parte* application to a master/district judge, with an affidavit setting out the:

● Nature of the claim made by the plaintiff;
● Stage the proceedings have reached;
● Nature of the third party claim;
● Name and address of the proposed third party.

If a *prima facie* case is made out which would bring the matter within the grounds for bringing a third party notice, leave will be granted.

The notice is issued on being sealed by the court office. A signed copy should be left with the court. The notice is then served on the third party in the same way as a writ or county court summons. The notice is served together with writ/pleadings/form for acknowledgement of service (High Court) or summons/pleadings (County Court). A copy of the notice is sent to the plaintiff.

In the High Court, the third party should acknowledge service within 14 days. In the County Court, the third party should file a defence within 14 days.

Third party directions   16.2.4

High Court
Once the third party has given notice of intention to defend the third party proceedings, the defendant must fill in and issue a standard form of Summons for Directions, which is then served on all other parties. This is an application to a master/district judge for directions as to the timetable and procedure to be followed in the third party proceedings.

At the hearing of this application, various orders will be made, for example:

- A timetable for the service of pleadings between defendant and third party;
- Orders for disclosure of documents between them; and
- Directions as to the involvement of the third party in the trial of the main action.

County Court

On an application for leave to issue a third party notice, the court must give directions as to the further conduct of the proceedings.

Where a notice is issued without leave, the court will fix a date for the pre-trial review. This will be entered on the notice before service. This pre-trial review is the County Court equivalent of the High Court directions' hearing explained above.

16.2.5 Effect of the proceedings

The defendant is in the position of plaintiff against the third party, who is in the position of defendant. Accordingly, similar procedures will apply between them as in an ordinary action, subject to the third party directions that are ordered. The action between them will be tried in the ordinary way, either at the trial of the main action (usually after the hearing of the main action) or separately, depending on what is ordered.

The result of the third party proceedings may depend on what is ordered in the main action but, strictly, they are separate. For example, the third party proceedings may continue even if the main action is settled.

16.3 Contribution between co-defendants

There are procedures which allow for co-defendants to serve notices on each other claiming contribution to, or indemnity for, the damages they have to pay to the plaintiff: *see* RSC O.16 r.8 and CCR O.12 r.5.

However, no notice is needed where two defendants are sued as wrongdoers liable in respect of the same damage. In such a case, the judge automatically has power under the Civil Liability (Contribution) Act 1978 to apportion the damages between them.

It is the practice, however, for a co-defendant through their solicitor to write a letter to the other, warning of their intention to ask the court to make such an apportionment: *see Clayson v Rolls Royce Ltd* (1951).

Furthermore, even in a case covered by that Act, a contribution notice must be served where a co-defendant intends to seek 'discovery' from, or leave to serve 'interrogatories' on, their co-defendant.

Self-assessment questions

1   What is the difference between joinder and consolidation?
2   Is a third party a party in the action between the plaintiff and the defendant?
3   Can a person be a third party *and* a second defendant in the main action?
4   What is the difference between a contribution and an indemnity?
5   Can there be such a thing as a fourth party, fifth party etc?

   (Note: These last three questions may require some research to answer.)

6   Who might become a third party in an action brought by a customer against a supplier of defective goods? What might the plaintiff do on becoming aware of the role of that third party?
7   What must a defendant do in order to commence third party proceedings?
8   What is meant by third party directions?
9   What differences are there between High Court and County Court third party procedure?

Chapter 17

Directions

What are directions? 17.1

After the date of close of pleadings, the court gives directions for the future conduct of the case, ie. the court lays down what future procedural steps are to be taken in the action and a timetable for those steps. At this directions stage, the court also deals with any procedural problems or disputes in the action.

In the High Court 17.1.1

For *personal injury* cases only, there are automatic directions. In other words, court rules lay down an automatic timetable for the procedural steps which will apply in every personal injury case. In all other types of High Court case, there will be an actual directions hearing at which the Master will give directions on the future conduct and timetable of the action.

In the County Court 17.1.2

Automatic directions apply in most cases but certain specified categories of cases require a directions hearing. This is known in the County Court as a *pre-trial review*.

Directions in the High Court (RSC O.25) 17.2

Personal injury cases 17.2.1

In *personal injury* cases only, court rules lay down the following directions, that is, the following procedural timetable must take place in every case (the times stated run from the date of close of pleadings).

Discovery
Discovery, ie. disclosure, of documents must be within 14 days and inspection seven days thereafter. However, where liability is admitted or the action arises out of a road accident, discovery is limited to disclosure by the plaintiff of any documents relating to special damages.

Note

Under this discovery procedure, therefore, the parties must disclose to each other a list of all *factual* documents relevant to the case which they have or have had in their possession or control. The other party can then inspect such documents, unless they are privileged (*see* later detail on discovery in this chapter).

Expert evidence

Where any party intends to rely on expert evidence at the trial, they shall, within 14 weeks, disclose the substance of that evidence to the other parties in the form of a written report which should be agreed if possible.

In other words, the parties must disclose to each other their expert's report relevant to the case, eg. a surveyor's report in a building dispute case, or a medical report in a personal injury case.

Note _____

In a personal injury case, the plaintiff's medical report is served with the statement of claim.

_____

Unless such expert report is agreed, ie. the other party does not dispute its content, parties can call to give oral evidence those experts whose reports have been disclosed. However, the number of witnesses per side is limited to two medical experts and one expert of any other kind (*see* below).

Witness statements

Where any party intends to rely at trial on any other oral evidence, they shall, within 14 weeks, serve on the other parties written statements of all such oral evidence which they intend to adduce.

In other words, the parties must disclose to each other the full details of what their factual witnesses are going to say at trial (*see* below).

Photographs, sketches and police accident report books

Photographs, sketch plans, any police accident report book are receivable in evidence at the trial and should be agreed, if possible.

In other words, the parties should agree the form of any photos or plans relevant to the accident which should be shown to the judge at trial.

Trial centre

The action shall be tried at the trial centre for the place in which the action is proceeding or at such other trial centre as the parties may agree in writing. The 'trial centre' refers to the relevant High Court building, eg. the Royal Courts of Justice in London.

Setting down

'Setting down' is the date of notifying the court that the parties are ready for trial.

The action must be tried by judge alone as a category B case and shall be set down within six months of close of pleadings. Cases are categorised in terms of difficulty.

The court must be notified on setting down of the estimated length of trial. This is so that the court office can arrange timetabling of cases appropriately. Solicitors will often ask experienced barristers for an estimate of how long the trial will take.

Note _____

If any party wants further or different directions from the above in personal injury cases, eg. more than two non-medical experts, they must apply to the court by summons.
_____

Non-personal injury cases   17.2.2

In most non-personal injury cases (except those listed in O.25 r.1), the directions are *not automatic*. Instead, there is a directions hearing, at which a Master gives a timetable for the procedural steps in the action and deals with any procedural problems or disputes.

Summons for directions

The plaintiff applies for this directions hearing by issuing a 'summons for directions' within one month after close of pleadings. This summons is in a standard printed form containing the usual possible directions that the plaintiff could ask for, eg. discovery within 14 days, inspection within seven days.

The plaintiff indicates, by deletion and filling in the gaps, which directions are wanted. The plaintiff can also add in further directions required.

The summons is then issued at court, a hearing date given, and served on the defendant. The defendant must give notice to the plaintiff if any additional directions are required.

The plaintiff will usually ask for a standard timetable similar to the automatic directions in personal injury cases. The defendant in turn will usually agree with this timetable. Consequently, most directions hearings are very brief, the parties agree the required directions by letter ('by consent') and junior members, often articled clerks, of the firms attend a brief hearing where a Master rubber-stamps the agreed directions.

In some cases, there may be dispute over what the directions should be, eg. how many experts should be allowed. In such cases, this will be argued and adjudicated upon at the directions hearing.

Witness statements

As stated above, the directions will usually be similar to the automatic directions in personal injury cases, adapted or added to as appropriate to the case. However, O.38 r.2A provides that:

At the summons for directions ... the court shall direct every party to serve on the other parties, within 14 weeks (or such other period as the court may specify) of the hearing of the summons and on such terms as the court may specify, written statements of the oral evidence which the party intends to adduce on any issue of fact to be decided at the trial.

In other words, it is compulsory for the Master to order exchange of witness statements at the summons for directions.

Disputes

It may also be appropriate to use the directions hearing to deal with any procedural disputes which have arisen. For example, the plaintiff may apply for leave to amend the writ at the directions hearing.

Value of the action

At least one day before the directions hearing, the plaintiff must file at court a statement declaring that the value of the action is £25,000 or more, or explaining why the proceedings are suitable for determination only by the High Court. This is a standard form statement; in its absence, the action will be transferred to the County Court.

Note

Although this is the official rule, the court has issued a practice note stating that in the Queen's Bench Division the statement of value should be handed to the Master at the hearing rather that being lodged at the court the day before.

17.3   Directions in the County Court (CCR O.17)

17.3.1   Automatic directions

Directions in County Court cases are automatic, ie. there is an automatic timetable as in the case of High Court personal injury actions, except for the types of cases listed in O.17 r.11(1) of the County Court rules. Most cases, therefore, have the following automatic directions, as from the date of close of pleadings (14 days after delivery of the defence or, where a counterclaim is served with the defence, 28 days after delivery of the defence).

Discovery

Both parties must make discovery of documents within 28 days and inspection within a further seven days. Where liability is admitted, or in personal injury road accident cases, discovery is limited to disclosure of any documents relating to damages.

Expert evidence and witness statements

Except with the leave of the court, or where all parties agree:

- No expert evidence may be adduced at the trial unless the substance of that evidence has been disclosed to the other parties in the form of a written report within 10 weeks.

- A maximum of two expert witnesses may be called at the trial or, in personal injury cases, a maximum of two medical experts and one other type of expert.

- Any party who intends to place reliance at the trial on any other oral evidence shall, within 10 weeks, serve on the other parties written statements of all such oral evidence which they intend to adduce.

Note

The effect of these rules has been explained in 17.2.1.

Photographs, sketches and police accident report books

Photographs and sketch plans are allowed in evidence at the trial and should be agreed, if possible. In personal injury actions, the contents of any police accident report book shall be receivable in evidence at trial and shall be agreed, if possible.

Fixing a date for trial

Unless a hearing date has already been fixed, the plaintiff must, within six months, ask the court to fix a date. The plaintiff must give an estimate of the length of trial and the number of witnesses (all to be agreed by the parties, if possible). If no request to fix a date is made within 15 months of close of pleadings, the action is automatically struck out by the court.

Note

This is an important rule to be borne in mind by the plaintiff's solicitor.

Any party can apply to the court for further or different directions, eg. an increase in the number of experts allowed.

Pre-trial review   17.3.2

In the cases listed below, automatic directions do not apply and instead, a pre-trial review will take place. This is the equivalent of a High Court summons for directions.

- Those types of cases listed in O.17 r.11(1) CCR, eg. an action for possession of land;

- A case where the defendant has only admitted part of the plaintiff's claim and that is not accepted by the plaintiff;
- Small claims (less than £1,000);
- A case where third party proceedings are issued by the defendant.

At the pre-trial review the District Judge will give directions which are usually agreed by the parties beforehand, as in the High Court. Any procedural disputes may be adjudicated upon at this review.

There is also a rule, equivalent to the High Court rule, requiring the District Judge at the pre-trial review to direct exchange of witness statements within 10 weeks of the pre-trial review.

17.4   Usual practice in relation to directions

In many cases, the parties agree between themselves to extend the time limits allowed by the directions, or do not enforce the time limits on the other side. Frequently, parties only require strict compliance with the directions as a bargaining counter in negotiations to settle the case, or when negotiations have broken down.

If a side has not complied with a time limit, the other side can apply to the court for an 'unless' order, that is, an order that unless the other side carries out a certain procedural step within a specified time limit, that other side's case will be struck out.

17.5   Discovery and inspection (RSC O.24, CCR O.14)

17.5.1   Meaning

Discovery is the process by which each party discloses to the other a list of all documents relevant in any way to the case, which are or have been in the party's possession, custody or power. 'Documents' refers not just to paper writings but to anything on which information is recorded in an intelligible manner, eg. a tape recording or computer database.

The other party is then entitled to inspect the documents listed except those which are privileged from inspection (*see* the manual on *Evidence*). The most common categories of privileged documents are:

- Communications between a party and their solicitor, and instructions and briefs to counsel, counsel's drafts and notes, and advice;
- Communications between a party or their solicitor and

a third party, eg. an expert, if made for the dominant purpose of obtaining advice in respect of existing or anticipated proceedings.

Procedure   17.5.2

High Court

The rules provide for compulsory discovery in writ actions within 14 days after close of pleadings. This is so despite discovery being part of the automatic directions or a usual part of non-automatic directions.

A list of all relevant documents must be prepared in a prescribed form, containing two schedules as follows:

- *Schedule 1, Part 1.* A list of documents which a party has and does not object to producing.
- *Schedule 1, Part 2.* A list of documents which a party has but objects to producing because they are privileged. (Obviously, these documents are not referred to individually in the Schedule but, in general terms, as 'privileged documents'.)
- *Schedule 2.* A list of documents which a party used to have but no longer has. This refers to relevant documents now in someone else's possession; often to the originals of letters sent to the other party.

The other party is then entitled to *inspect* the documents referred to in Schedule 1, Part 1. The discovery list must state a time and place, ie. usually the office of the disclosing party's solicitor, at which those documents can be inspected. The documents must be made available for inspection within seven days after exchange of discovery lists.

The other party then inspects the documents – in a small case, they may be sent copies. A party may by notice require the other side to supply copies of any inspectable documents, if so the copy must be supplied within seven days. The party requiring the copy must undertake to pay reasonable copying charges.

County Court

In cases where the automatic directions apply, discovery (within 28 days after close of pleadings) and inspection (within a further seven days) are part of the automatic directions.

In other cases, discovery is not automatic. An application for an order for discovery must be made to the District Judge, but it will usually be ordered.

The standard form and procedure are similar to that in the High Court. In the County Court, however, there is a prescribed limit on photocopying charges to the other party.

17.5.3   Evidential consequences

A party is deemed to have been served by the other side with a notice requiring them to produce at trial the originals of all documents in their discovery list. If they do not produce the original, the other side can refer to a copy at trial.

> *Note*
>
> This is an exception to the rule that parties can only use original documents as evidence.

The other side is deemed to admit the authenticity of all documents in the discovery list, unless the other side serves notice that they do not.

17.5.4   Inspection of documents referred to in pleadings and affidavits

Where a party's pleading or affidavit refers to any document, the other side can serve a notice requiring production of the document for inspection and the taking of copies.

The party on whom such notice is served must, within four days after service of the notice, give a notice stating a time and place, within seven days, where the document can be inspected.

17.5.5   Non-compliance

In the following cases a party can apply to the court for an order for proper discovery and inspection where the other side has failed to comply with the rules:

- Where a party reasonably believes that the other side is holding back particular documents, that party can apply to the court for an order that the other party:

    - Disclose whether they have particular documents or a class of documents; or

    - That they serve a further and better list; or

    - That they serve an affidavit verifying their list.

- Where a party has failed to comply with the rules on discovery or inspection in any way, the other party can apply to court for an order for compliance, which may be a 'final' or 'unless' order (*see* below).

In both of these cases, the party applies to a Master by summons (High Court) or District Judge by application (County Court) with an affidavit setting out the grounds of their application, eg. why they believe there are other documents being held back.

'Unless' orders

The court can order that unless a party gives the required

discovery within a certain time, their action will be dismissed or defence struck out as the case may be. The usual way of finally obtaining a document is to apply for such an order. However, even when the unless order has not been complied with, the court still has jurisdiction to extend the time for compliance, although this is exercised cautiously: *Samuels v Linzi Dresses Ltd* (1981).

Note

The court is very reluctant to strike out an action or defence for non-compliance with discovery. It will only do so where there is a real risk that the default will render a fair trial impossible or where a document has been deliberately suppressed: *Logicrose Ltd v Southend United Football Club Ltd* (1988), and *Landauer Ltd v Comins & Co* (1991).

Further, or alternatively, the other party can be committed to prison or fined (or, in the case of a company, their assets sequestrated or the person responsible imprisoned) for contempt of court for non-compliance with discovery.

Expert evidence   17.6

Note

See Companion on Evidence for principles on admissibility of expert opinion.

As you have seen, the directions allow for the parties to call expert witnesses to give evidence on matters of expert opinion, eg. doctors in a personal injury case, or engineers in a defective goods case.

However, the automatic directions, or usual directions in non-automatic cases, make it a condition of calling the expert witness that their report on the matter, eg. medical report, be disclosed to the other side before the trial and within a specified time limit. The report itself is not evidence (unless agreed by the other side); it is merely a precondition of the expert giving evidence, so that the other side knows what the expert is going to say and can prepare their cross-examination.

If the other party agrees with what the expert says in the report, the report can be put in evidence, and the expert need not be called. If, as is usual, the other side do not agree with the contents of the report, the expert must be called to give evidence. The expert will then be examined and cross-examined at trial. (The directions will specify how many experts can be called by each side – *see* directions explained earlier.)

Although reports must usually be disclosed simultaneously, in personal injury cases the plaintiff must serve their medical report with their statement/particulars of claim, although updated reports can be served later on in the proceedings. The defendant need not serve their report in reply until the time for disclosure according to the directions, although they may serve their report at an earlier date to force a settlement.

A party need only disclose the report of an expert that they are going to call at trial. Thus, if they instruct an expert who writes a report unfavourable to their case and they decide not to use that expert, they are under no obligation to disclose the report to the other side.

Note

There is nothing to stop the other side interviewing or using that expert if the expert comes to their notice.

In a personal injury case, the defendant is entitled to have the plaintiff examined by the defendant's doctor, and this is usual practice. If the plaintiff refuses, the defendant can apply for the court to order a stay (suspension) of proceedings until the plaintiff agrees to be examined.

However, the plaintiff is entitled to impose reasonable conditions on their agreement to the examination, eg. that the defendant will pay the plaintiff's expenses of attending the examination, that no other person will be present except the plaintiff and the doctor, and that there will be no discussion on liability: *see Starr v NCB* (1977) and *Hall v Avon AHA* (1980).

17.7   Witness statements (RSC O.38 r.2A, CCR O.20 r.12A)

17.7.1   Rules

In both the High Court and County Court it is compulsory for the parties to exchange, within certain time limits, full statements of what their witnesses of *fact* are going to say at trial. This is to allow for preparation, to avoid surprise, and to encourage settlement. The drafting of these statements is an important part of litigation. The following main rules apply:

● Statements must be dated, signed by the witness and include a statement by the witness that the contents are true to the best of their knowledge and belief. The statements must sufficiently identify any documents that they refer to. The statements must be exchanged simultaneously.

- The court may, and usually does, order that the statement stands as evidence in chief. Therefore, there is often nowadays no oral examination in chief. The court reads the statement, and then the case proceeds to oral cross-examination of the witness by the other party's advocate.
- The witness can only give oral evidence of things that they have said in their disclosed statement unless:
  - The court allows otherwise;
  - The other side consents to new matters being raised;
  - New matters have arisen since service of the statement; or
  - Only part of the statement was ordered to be disclosed.
- The ordinary rules of evidence apply to the statement, eg. it cannot include inadmissible opinion evidence.

Format

17.7.2

The statement is drafted by a solicitor or counsel, having interviewed the client at length, in time for the exchange of statements.

The statement should be expressed in the first person and should state:

- The full name of the witness;
- Their place of residence, or if making the statement in their occupational capacity, their work address, their position and the employer's name;
- Their occupation or, if none, their description;
- The fact that the witness is a party to the proceedings or a party's employee, if that is the case.

The statement should read as if the witness was giving evidence in chief in the witness box. It should be full and complete and written in a clear, straightforward narrative form. It should use the style of language of the witness. It should follow the chronological sequence of the events dealt with and should be divided into numbered paragraphs, each paragraph dealing, as far as possible, with a distinct part of the events. Numbers should be expressed in figures (*see* also the first point in 17.7.1 above).

Self-assessment questions

1 What is meant by 'directions'?
2 What is meant by 'automatic directions'?
3 In which cases do automatic directions apply:

(a) in the High Court

(b) in the County Court?

4   When directions are not 'automatic', how are directions decided on and laid down? Answer for both courts.

5   State the High Court and County Court directions in outline.

6   In a case where directions are not automatic, what directions will you usually ask for? How will they be agreed on in practice? What should you do if the other side:

(a) does not agree with a particular direction suggested by you; or

(b) fails to comply with a direction?

7   What is meant by discovery? In which schedule of the discovery list does a party list those documents open to inspection by the other side?

8   Distinguish between discovery and inspection.

9   You are the plaintiff. Are you allowed to inspect the advice given to the defendant by the defendant's counsel?

10 Are you allowed to inspect the advice given to the other side by their counsel?

11 Is your side's expert report produced to the court as evidence at trial?

12 How many experts on either side give evidence at trial?

13 What is the difference between a witness statement and an expert's report?

14 What is the significance of a witness statement?

15 How does High Court procedure differ from County Court procedure in respect of expert reports and witness statements?

Chapter 18

Interlocutory applications

What are interlocutory applications? 18.1

There is a long period – months or even years – between commencement of proceedings and trial. During this period, the steps required by the directions take place and the parties usually try and negotiate a settlement. However, during this period the parties also make various applications to the court for various orders ranging from small procedural applications, eg. applying for amendment of the writ or pleading, or for extension of time for service of a pleading; to more important procedural applications, eg. to join a new party to the action, to strike out the other party's case for non-compliance with a rule; to important substantive applications, eg. for an interim injunction, for interim compensation or for early judgment on the ground that there is no defence to the action.

Collectively, these are known as interlocutory applications.

Procedure for such applications 18.2

Who hears them? 18.2.1

In the High Court, these applications are mostly heard in London by Masters and outside London by District Judges. (Masters and District Judges are, in effect, junior judges who conduct much administrative and pre-trial judicial business.)

However, some High Court interlocutory applications are heard by judges, particularly applications for interlocutory (interim) injunctions, as Masters do not generally have power to hear applications for interlocutory injunctions.

In the County Court, interlocutory applications are heard by District Judges, who are roughly the equivalent of High Court Masters/District Judges.

Note

Do not confuse County Court District Judges with High Court District Judges outside London – although you could be forgiven for doing so!

Where are they held? 18.2.2

Interlocutory applications are mainly held in private rooms in the court building rather than in open court. These private rooms are known as chambers (not to be confused with barristers' chambers).

The hearings are held in private, the lawyers are seated, do not wear wigs or gowns, and solicitors or their clerks may represent their clients 'in chambers'. Those heard in public in open court are usually applications to judges in the Chancery Division of the High Court.

18.2.3   *Ex parte* or *inter partes*

The applications may be made *ex parte*, ie. without the other side being notified of the hearing or being there, or *inter partes*, ie. the other side is notified of the hearing and attends to contest the application.

If made *inter partes*, the application is made by issuing a summons (or 'notice of motion' to a judge in the Chancery Division) in the High Court, or a notice of application in the County Court.

Evidence is generally given in written statements given on oath known as 'affidavits'. At the hearing, the Master/Judge reads the affidavits and listens to the submissions made by the solicitors/counsels for both parties. These hearings are much shorter than trials, ranging from five minutes to approximately two days.

18.3   High Court Masters/District Judges

The High Court has several Masters (or District Judges as they are known in the High Court District Registries outside London). The Masters in London have their own private rooms in the Royal Courts of Justice. Interlocutory applications are heard in these private rooms or in rooms set aside for the hearing of general, short applications.

There is a Senior Master, and one Master sits daily as the 'Practice Master' who will hear short, routine applications on that day, eg. for extension of time for service of a pleading. The individual Masters (and their traits!) become well known to practitioners.

County Court District Judges also have private rooms where they hear applications, and are also well known to practitioners in their locality!

18.4   *Ex parte* applications

These are made where it is not appropriate for another party to attend, eg. an application for leave to issue a third party notice, or where speed or secrecy is essential, eg. emergency and *Mareva* injunctions.

Procedure   18.4.1

In many routine *ex parte* applications, eg. for leave to serve
a writ in various cases or to serve a third party notice, there
is no hearing. The relevant documents are left with the court
for the Master's/Judge's order. In more important *ex parte*
applications, eg. for an injunction, the applicant can go to
court at short notice, having sent the relevant documents to
the court shortly beforehand (*see* Chapter 8, *Emergency
injunctions*).

Inter partes applications   18.5

These are the more usual applications. The other party is
notified of the hearing and attends to contest the application. (Many of these types of applications are dealt with, or
mentioned, during your course.) The following basic procedures apply.

QBD   18.5.1

Step 1. Interlocutory applications are made to a Master/
District Judge or Judge by issuing a summons. The summons is a standard form of document which in theory
'summons' the other party to attend the hearing. The applicant fills in the standard form of summons, stating the order
that is being applied for.

Step 2. The summons is sent or taken to the QBD's Central
Office and is issued by being sealed. The court will insert a
hearing date and time on the summons. A written time
estimate for the hearing should be given to the court so that
a proper date and time can be allocated. An issue fee is paid
in many cases.

Step 3. A copy of the issued summons must be served on the
other side within a certain time; the RSC lay down time
limits depending on the type of application. The hearing
date is referred to in the rules and by practitioners as 'the
return day'.

Step 4. Any affidavit (*see* below) being relied on by a party
must be served on the other side within a certain time before
the hearing. If a side serves their affidavit too late, eg. turns up
with it at the hearing, so that the other side has not had an
opportunity to read and deal with it, the Master may refuse use
of the affidavit or adjourn (postpone) the hearing.

Step 5. The hearing takes place in a private room (chambers) before a Master/District Judge or Judge – in general,
only a Judge, not a Master, can hear an application for an
injunction.

Note _____

The same Master usually hears most summonses in the same action because a named Master is assigned to deal with each action.

Every morning, there is a general list of short applications to be heard by a Master. Shorter applications (roughly five minutes long) are heard between 10.30 am and 12.00 noon – many cases will be timetabled in this period. Slightly longer applications, where barristers represent the client, are timetabled after 12.00 noon.

Any hearing which will last longer than 20 minutes is not timetabled in the general list but is given a special appointment in the Master's private room: *see* RSC O.32 for details.

Step 6. At the hearing, the Master/District Judge/Judge reads the affidavits, listens to the submissions made on either side and makes an order, including who is to pay the costs of the hearing.

Step 7. Generally, the successful party must draft the order and serve it on their opponent.

18.5.2   Chancery Division

Interlocutory applications may be made by summons or by a procedure known as 'a motion'. A motion is where the application is made to a Judge in open court rather than to a Master in chambers. (It is called a motion because, in theory, the court is being 'moved' to make an order.)

Note _____

Applications should not be made by the motion procedure unless there is a sufficient degree of urgency or other good reason, eg. where the claim is for an injunction, as this cannot be granted by a Master.

The summons procedure, in outline, is very similar to that described for the QBD but there are detailed differences in organisation and timetabling. A summons in London is issued at the 'Chancery chambers' office. (You can find details of Chancery procedure in 'Chancery Division Practice Directions' in the *White Book*, Vol. 2.)

18.5.3   County Court

Interlocutory applications are made by 'notice of application' to the District Judge. The procedure is similar in outline to that for the QBD. The application must be served on the opposite party not less than two days before the hearing. (There are rules as to what days are not included in calculating time periods.)

An application is made by using standard form N244. This has the printed words 'I wish to apply for ...'. The applicant fills in the order they require. The form is then served on the other side with notification of the date and time of the hearing.

Affidavits   18.6

An affidavit is a written statement sworn on oath. Evidence at interlocutory hearings is given by affidavit.

You should take a full statement from the client before putting it into the following affidavit form.

Contents and form   18.6.1

An affidavit must be completed as follows.

- The heading of the case (as for pleadings) is shown at the top.
- The top right hand corner of the first page and of the last covering sheet, known as the 'backsheet', must be marked with:

  – The party on whose behalf the affidavit is written;

  – The initials and surname of the person giving the evidence in the affidavit, who is known as 'the deponent';

  – The number of the affidavit in relation to the deponent, ie. is it their first, second, third etc, affidavit in the action?

  – The date on which it is sworn (see below);

  – In the County Court, the date on which it is 'filed' in (given to the) court. For example, 'first defendant: J A Smith; second: 4.3.94'.

- The deponent must then state their name, address, occupation or (if none) description. If they are a party, they must state which party: 'plaintiff', 'defendant' or 'third party'.

  If giving evidence in an occupational capacity, eg. director of a company or solicitor to a party, they must state their capacity or position, and the business name and address.

- The affidavit must then state 'I make oath and say as follows' before setting out the evidence.

- Their evidence is then set out in numbered consecutive paragraphs, telling the story as if giving oral evidence. The affidavit should be written in a clear and thorough form, telling the narrative in a way favourable to the client. It should not contain inadmissible evidence, eg. opinion evidence.

Affidavits often contain arguments in favour of the order being requested, and often end by 'respectfully' asking the court to make the order sought.

- In interlocutory applications, affidavits can contain hearsay. The deponent can state that 'I am informed by ... (name) ... that ... (giving facts told to them by somebody else) ... I believe this to be true.'

  The affidavit usually begins by stating that the facts stated are within the deponent's personal knowledge, except where expressly stated otherwise. Where there are statements of information from others or statements of 'belief' as to the truth, the affidavit must give the sources and grounds of the information or belief.

- The deponent can refer to exhibits, ie. documents, photographs, in the affidavit in the following manner: 'There is now produced and shown to me, marked JS1, a letter dated ...'. The exhibits accompany the affidavit in numbered bundles with covering front sheets. 'JS1' above refers to the initials of the deponent and the number of the exhibit referred to in the affidavit.

  Where more than one similar document is referred to, eg. correspondence, all the documents, eg. letters, are tied together as one exhibit. The deponent may refer to court documents, eg. pleadings or the writ. These are not formally exhibited.

- In certain interlocutory applications, the rules require that the affidavit *must* contain specific statements. For example, on an application for 'summary judgment' on the basis that there is no defence (*see* Chapter 19), the affidavit of the applicant must state 'I believe that there is no defence to this action.'

- Where the deponent is giving the evidence on behalf of someone, eg. as a party's solicitor, or as a company director, the deponent should state 'I am duly authorised by ... (for example, the plaintiff) ... to make this affidavit.'

- The affidavit ends with formal words as to where it was sworn ('the jurat') and on which party's behalf it is filed. A covering 'backsheet' with formal details is added. The affidavit is typed on formal parchment paper and the pages are tied together with green ribbon.

  The exhibits are tied to formal front sheets with green ribbon.

Swearing and service   18.6.2

Once the affidavit is ready, the solicitor takes the deponent
and the affidavit to any nearby firm – it can be any firm other
than that acting for the party on whose behalf the affidavit
is sworn – for the swearing and signing by the deponent.
The sum of £3.50, plus £1.00 for every exhibit, is paid to the
solicitor who hears the oath. *That* solicitor signs the jurat.
The affidavit may also be sworn in front of a judge or court
official, in which case no fee is payable.

The deponent must swear the following oath that the
affidavit contents are true, while holding the holy book of
their religion: 'I swear by ... that this is my name and
signature and that the contents of this my affidavit are true.'

Note

If the deponent objects to swearing a religious oath, they
instead state 'I do solemnly, sincerely and truly declare and
affirm that ...'.

A copy of the affidavit is then served on the other side and
filed in the court within time limits prescribed by the rules
depending on the type of application.

Note

There is a detailed practice direction on the proper form for High
Court affidavits (*see* 1983 1 WLR 922 and notes to RSC O.41).

Payment of costs   18.7

If a party wins an interlocutory hearing they do not necessarily recover from the other side the costs of preparing for
and attending that hearing. The decision is up to the discretion of the Master/Judge who hears the application and will
depend on such factors as who has won, the nature and
merits of the application and the conduct of the parties.

There are several possible orders that the Master/Judge
can make as to costs, the most common being:

- *Costs in the cause.* This order means that whoever loses
  the whole case at the end will have to pay the other side's
  costs of this application.
- *Costs in any event.* The party in whose favour this order
  is made can recover from the other side their costs of this
  application regardless of which party eventually wins
  the whole case.
- *Costs reserved.* Whoever loses the whole case at the end

will have to pay the other side's costs of this application, unless the court at trial orders otherwise.

The party in whose favour a costs order is made cannot recover all the costs they have incurred in relation to the application, only an amount as ordered and taxed on the standard or indemnity basis, or an amount assessed by the court. The amount recoverable is further limited in County Court cases by the appropriate scale. (*See* Chapter 3, *Costs*.)

Further, the costs are not payable by the other side until the end of the whole case unless the Master/Judge orders that they be 'taxed and paid forthwith'.

A party cannot recover from the other side the fees of their barrister attending the application unless the court has 'certified' their attendance as proper, ie. that it was appropriate to use counsel. At the end of the hearing, counsel asks for a 'certificate for counsel'.

In a case where a party is legally aided and an interlocutory costs order is made against them, the court has power to direct that such costs be set off against (deducted from) any damages awarded to the legally aided party at the end of the case: *Lockley v National Blood Transfusion Service* (1992).

18.8   Appealing against interlocutory decisions

A party may appeal against an interlocutory decision as follows:

- An appeal against a decision of a *Master/District Judge of the High Court* is to a High Court judge. Notice of appeal must be drafted and issued within five days after the order appealed against. The notice must then be served on the other party at least two clear days before the appeal hearing.

- An appeal against a decision by a *County Court District Judge* is to a Circuit Judge, ie. a County Court judge. Notice of appeal must be filed at court and served within five days after the order appealed against.

- An appeal against a decision of a *High Court or Circuit Judge* is to the Court of Appeal. Leave to appeal is usually required however.

Self-assessment questions

1   What is an 'interlocutory application'?

2   Who judges an interlocutory application? Where do they take place? How is evidence given?

3 How do you commence interlocutory proceedings? Answer for both courts.

4 What is the difference between a summons and a motion?

5 What is a 'deponent'?

6 Explain the difference between an *ex parte* hearing and an *inter partes* hearing?

7 What is the difference between the term 'costs follow the event' and the term 'costs in any event'?

8 What is a 'certificate for counsel'?

Chapter 19

Summary judgment

Meaning and scope

It may be the case that the defendant has absolutely no defence to the action, eg. has no reason not to pay a debt. If this is so, it would be unjust if the plaintiff had to wait a long time for their money merely because of the long time gap (due to the court's workload) between commencement of proceedings and trial.

In such cases there is a procedure by which the plaintiff can obtain early, speedy (summary) judgment from a Master/District Judge without waiting for a full trial, as long as the plaintiff can prove (on affidavit evidence) that there is no defence. The procedure is governed by RSC O.14 and CCR O.9 r.14.

Summary judgment can be applied for in all actions *begun by writ* (subject to the first exception below). It *cannot* be applied for in claims for:

- Libel, slander, malicious prosecution and false imprisonment; or in

- County Court claims for possession of land or where title to land is in question.

Note

Applications in the Chancery Division for summary judgment for specific performance or rescission of contracts relating to land are governed not by O.14 but by a similar procedure in O.86.

Grounds

The plaintiff can obtain summary judgment by showing, on affidavit evidence, that there is no defence to the claim. The defendant can avoid summary judgment by satisfying the Master/District Judge, on affidavit evidence, that:

- There is a triable issue in the case; or

- There ought for some other reason to be a trial.

As to the first ground, the defendant must show, not that they have a good defence, but that there is some *arguable* defence which should be heard at trial: *see* notes to O.14, *White Book*. As to the second, an example might be where the facts require close investigation and cross-examination of witnesses in open court.

19.3   High Court

19.3.1   Procedure

1   The plaintiff can apply for summary judgment after the statement of claim has been served and the defendant has given notice of intention to defend, ie. even before the defence is served.

The service of a summary judgment application automatically extends the time for service of the defence until 14 days after the hearing or such other time as is ordered (assuming the application fails).

2   The plaintiff applies to the Master/District Judge by summons supported by affidavit. The affidavit must verify the facts on which the claim is based and state that, in the deponent's belief, there is no defence (except as to the amount of damages if the claim is for unliquidated damages).

The affidavit must therefore set out the facts and show there is no defence. Often, in a simple claim, the affidavit merely refers to the facts set out in the statement of claim, in the following manner:

The defendant owes the sum of £ ... for (state nature of debt, what it was for, invoice or bill details). The particulars of the said claim appear in the statement of claim in this action.

The affidavit must also state 'I believe that there is no defence to the claim'.

The affidavit may contain hearsay and statements of belief (stating sources and grounds).

3   The summons and a copy of the affidavit must be served on the defendant not less than *ten* clear days before the hearing date. (In practice, the court is unlikely to have a hearing date until a few months' time.)

4   The defendant must serve their affidavit in reply at least *three* days before the hearing date. The defendant's affidavit should deal with the plaintiff's claim and affidavit, state clearly what the defence is and the facts relied on in support of the defence.

5   The plaintiff may then serve a further affidavit in reply.

Note

The more affidavits there are, the more likely it is the Master will be satisfied there is a triable issue.

Sometimes, affidavits are served very late, often just before the hearing. Here the hearing may be adjourned (postponed), with the late server having to pay the other side's wasted costs.

Possible orders

The Master will read the affidavits and listen to submissions made by both sides; one of the following orders will then be made.

Judgment for the plaintiff

This will be ordered where the defendant does not satisfy the Master that there is an issue which ought to be tried or that there ought, for some other reason, to be a trial. The defendant will be ordered to pay costs, to be taxed.

> *Note*
>
> In a debt claim, the plaintiff will be awarded a prescribed amount of 'fixed costs'.

If the claim is for unliquidated damages, the judgment will usually be on liability with the amount of damages to be assessed at a later hearing.

Unconditional leave to defend

This will be ordered where the defendant satisfies the Master that there is an issue which ought to be tried or that there ought, for some other reason, to be a trial. The usual order for costs is 'costs in the cause'. The action continues.

Conditional leave to defend

Where the Master doubts the *bona fides* of the defendant, or is almost certain that the defence raised is a sham, leave may only be given on condition that all or part of the sum claimed is paid into the court bank account by the defendant, as security pending the trial.

> *Note*
>
> This will not be ordered if the defendant really cannot afford to pay the money: *MV Yorke Motors (a firm) v Edwards* (1982).

The usual costs order is 'costs in the cause'.

Dismissal of the summons

This will be ordered where the plaintiff knew that the application would fail, and leave to defend would be given, so that the summons has been a waste of time and money.

The plaintiff will be ordered to pay the defendant's costs incurred by the summons.

Directions for trial

If the Master gives leave to defend, the Master must, at the end of the hearing, give directions as to the future timetable for the action, eg. defence within 14 days etc, as if the hearing is a summons for directions.

The case may be transferred to a County Court unless the plaintiff files at court a standard form statement declaring that the value of the action is £25,000 or more, or explaining why the proceedings are suitable for determination only by the High Court.

19.3.3   Effect of counterclaim by defendant

It may be the case that the defendant has a counterclaim in response to the plaintiff's claim, eg. the plaintiff is suing for payment for work done, and the defendant claims the work is defective and claims damages; or the defendant might have a completely separate counterclaim relating to some other dispute between the parties.

If the plaintiff claims summary judgment in such circumstances, the Master could make one of the following orders.

Defence of set off

If the counterclaim operates at law or in equity as a defence (the defence of legal or equitable 'set off'), then there is a defence to the claim and unconditional leave to defend will be given.

At law, for example, mutual debts can be set off against each other, or a claim for defective goods operates as a defence to a claim for payment for the goods: s.53(1)(c), Sale of Goods Act 1979.

In equity, one claim can be set off against another where the two claims arise out of the same transaction and are so strongly connected that it would be unjust to enforce one without taking account of the other, eg. in a claim for payment for defective work: *Hanak v Green* (1958).

Counterclaim

If the counterclaim does not operate as a defence, the court has a discretion to give judgment on the claim but subject to a stay of execution pending trial of the counterclaim. Whether a stay will be granted depends on the strength of connection between the claims, the strength of the counterclaim, and the parties' financial circumstances: *see* notes to O.14, *White Book*.

Claim for dishonoured cheque, other bill of exchange or promissory note

If the claim for summary judgment is in respect of a dishonoured cheque (or other dishonoured bill of exchange or promissory note), then, even if the defendant has a counterclaim for the defective work or goods for which the cheque was given, no stay will be granted unless:

- The cheque was obtained by fraudulent or negligent misrepresentation; or

- There was a total failure of consideration given in return for the cheque: *James Lamont & Co Ltd v Hylands Ltd* (1950).

.3.4 Appeals

A party can appeal against an O.14 decision to a Judge in chambers who will rehear the case afresh.

The appeal against a Master's decision must be brought within *five* days after the decision complained of, by notice of appeal served on the other side at least *two* clear days before the hearing.

Note _____

In the case of appeal against a District Judge's decision, the time limits are *seven* and *three* days respectively.

.3.5 Summary judgment on a point of law

The court also has power to give summary judgment on the basis of a pure question of law or construction of a document where the facts are not in dispute: *see* RSC O.14A.

.4 County Court procedure

The County Court procedure and grounds for obtaining summary judgment are very similar to the High Court, with the following exceptions:

- The plaintiff can only apply for summary judgment *after* a purported defence has been served.

- Application for summary judgment is made by *notice of application*, supported by affidavit, to the District Judge. The notice must be served on the defendant not less than *seven* days before the hearing.

- There is no equivalent to the High Court O.14A (summary judgment on a point of law or construction).

- There is a *right of appeal* to the Circuit Judge; notice of appeal must be served within 14 days after an order allowing judgment, or within *five* days after an order giving leave to defend.

Self-assessment questions

1 How and when do you make an application for summary judgment? Answer for both courts.

2 Is an application for summary judgment appropriate in the following alternative cases, and what order would be likely in each case on such an application?

(a) The plaintiff, a builder, sues for work done. The

defendant landowner refuses to pay, showing evidence that the work was defective.

(b) The plaintiff sues the defendant on a personal guarantee for a debt. The defendant, an experienced business person, states vaguely in their affidavit that the guarantee was obtained by undue influence or by a promise that the guarantee would never in practice be enforced.

(c) The plaintiff sues on a short written contract. The only issue is the meaning of two clauses in the contract.

(d) The plaintiff sues for nervous shock suffered after witnessing an accident. She has clear medical evidence of having suffered nervous shock.

(e) The plaintiff sues for an injunction to prevent clear interference with a right of way.

(f) The plaintiff landlord sues the tenant for rent arrears; the tenant counterclaims for the landlord's breach of repairing covenants.

(g) In (f) the tenant counterclaims for damages for libel on account of something the landlord published about the tenant.

(h) P enters into an agency agreement with D under which D is to distribute P's goods and P is to sell the goods to D by individual contracts. By consent, the parties then terminate the first agency agreement and enter into a second. P then terminates the second agreement and sues D for money due under contracts made pursuant to the first agreement. D counterclaims for damages for repudiation of the second agreement.

3   Why should a plaintiff be advised not to make an application for summary judgment where it is not appropriate?

4   You are defending an application for summary judgment. In what ways can the affidavit be drafted and presented so as to give your client the best possible chance of resisting the application?

5   If a High Court master gives leave to defend, what further orders will be made at the end of the hearing?

Chapter 20

Interlocutory injunctions

Context and meaning

An important remedy often claimed in litigation is an injunction. For example, if a business tenant is locked out of their warehouse by the landlord, the tenant may sue for an injunction to stop the landlord from locking out the tenant. If the case were to proceed to trial, the court would consider whether to grant an injunction by:

- First, deciding whether a legal wrong had been committed by the landlord (in our example, breach of covenant or a tort); and

- Second, deciding whether the equitable remedy of an injunction was appropriate according to the substantive law principles on injunctions.

Note

In this chapter we refer to the ordinary equitable principles used at trial in deciding whether to grant an injunction as 'final injunction' principles.

However, due to the court's workload, there is in practice a long time gap between commencement of proceedings and trial. In most cases, the plaintiff will want the injunction very quickly; in the above example, the tenant will want to be let back in fairly quickly and will not want to wait months or years until a trial. In an urgent case, the plaintiff can therefore apply for an emergency *ex parte* injunction (*see* Chapter 8), even before proceedings are commenced.

In less urgent cases, the plaintiff can apply for an *interlocutory injunction*, ie. the court awards an interim injunction to last approximately from commencement of proceedings until trial. In that way, our tenant can obtain an order preventing them from being locked out until trial, when the court can make a full and final decision on whether a permanent (final) injunction should be granted.

However, in deciding whether to grant an interlocutory injunction, the court does not use the 'final injunction' principles it uses in deciding whether to grant an injunction at trial. Instead, the court uses different 'interlocutory injunction' principles, necessary because the court does not at this stage have time for a full trial on all the issues and evidence.

> *Note*
>
> Interlocutory injunctions are regulated by RSC O.29 and CCR O.13, r.6.

20.2   Principles

20.2.1   The *American Cyanamid* principles

In deciding whether to grant an interlocutory injunction to the plaintiff, the judge applies the following principles set out by the House of Lords in *American Cyanamid v Ethicon Ltd* (1975). (We use our tenant example to illustrate application of the principles.)

The issue

Is there a *serious issue* to be tried?

(We will assume that there is a serious issue for trial, ie. as to whether the tenant is in breach of covenant so that the landlord had the right to forfeit the lease by locking the tenant out.)

The plaintiff's loss

If there is a serious issue to be tried, has the plaintiff shown that damages would not adequately compensate if an interlocutory injunction is not granted at this stage and it is found at final trial that the plaintiff was entitled to an injunction.

Damages would not be adequate where the loss is non-financial, or cannot be properly quantified, or the defendant does not have the means to pay.

(We will assume that it is not possible to quantify the loss to the plaintiff's business in the period up to trial if an interlocutory injunction is wrongly not granted, so that damages would not be an adequate alternative to an injunction.)

The defendant's loss

If the answer to the first two questions is 'yes', the court then asks whether, on the other hand, *damages* would adequately compensate the *defendant* if an interlocutory injunction is granted and it is found at final trial that the plaintiff was not entitled to an injunction.

If the answer is 'yes', an interlocutory injunction will be granted.

(We will assume the answer is 'no', because the defendant had plans to redevelop the warehouse, and the loss from not being able to do so now is unquantifiable, or the plaintiff does not have the means to pay any damages.)

The balance of convenience

If neither side can be compensated by damages, the final question is, *which side will suffer greater hardship* if the interlocutory injunction is or is not granted?

This last principle is known as the 'balance of convenience'. In other words, the court assesses the financial and non-financial loss that the tenant will suffer if they are kept out of the warehouse until trial. The court then compares that with the loss that the landlord will suffer if they have to let the tenant back in until trial. If the tenant will suffer greater loss than the landlord, an interlocutory injunction will be granted. If the landlord will suffer greater loss, an interlocutory injunction will not be granted.

You can see from the above principles that in considering whether to grant an interlocutory injunction, the court does not go into the substantive legal merits of the parties' cases, as it would do at trial.

Note

As a condition of obtaining the injunction, the tenant will be required to undertake to pay damages to the landlord for any financial loss suffered by the landlord as a result of the injunction being granted if it eventually turns out at trial that the plaintiff was not entitled to the injunction.

The alternative approach   20.2.2

However, in certain types of cases, the court does not purely use the *American Cyanamid* balance of convenience test; instead, different approaches are taken.

Where the injunction will end the matter

If the interlocutory hearing will in practice be the end of the matter because, by the time of a final trial, an injunction will no longer be wanted, eg. the injunction is required for a short time period or to deal with a short term matter, the court will take into account the relative strengths of both sides' cases in deciding whether to grant an interlocutory injunction, since this will in effect be the final trial of the matter: *see Cambridge Nutrition v BBC* (1990) and *Lansing Linde Ltd v Kerr* (1991).

Example

In *Cambridge Nutrition v BBC* (1990), the plaintiff claimed an injunction to prevent transmission of a programme. The programme was of such short-term topicality that if an *interlocutory* injunction had been granted the BBC would never have shown the programme. This meant that the grant of an

> interlocutory injunction would be the final decision in practice and there would not be a final trial years later. For this reason, the Court of Appeal looked at the relative substantive strengths of the parties' cases in deciding whether or not to grant the interlocutory injunction and, using substantive final injunction principles on broadcasting, eg. the right to free speech and the public interest in the programme, refused to grant an interlocutory injunction.

Where the balance of convenience is equal

If the balance of convenience is equal, the court may take into account the relative strengths of both sides' cases, but 'only where it is apparent on the facts disclosed by evidence as to which there is no credible dispute that the strength of one party's case is disproportionate to that of the other party': *per* Lord Diplock in *American Cyanamid*.

Plaintiff's claim will fail at trial/no arguable defence

If it is obvious that the plaintiff's claim will fail at trial, an interlocutory injunction will not be granted: *Re Lord Cable* (1977).

Conversely, there is authority that an interlocutory injunction will be granted regardless of the balance of convenience test where there is no arguable substantive defence to the claim: *Patel v W H Smith (Eziot) Ltd* (1987).

Broadcasting, libel actions/employment contracts

There is case law laying down special principles in relation to libel actions and actions for breach of a restrictive covenant in an employment contract.

Mandatory injunctions

The Cyanamid guidelines do not apply to mandatory injunctions, ie. one requiring a positive act. A mandatory injunction will only be granted at an interlocutory stage when the case is unusually strong and clear.

20.3   Procedure for application in the High Court

Application is made to a judge. A Master does not have power to grant an injunction.

20.3.1   Queen's Bench Division

The application is made by *summons and affidavit* to a Judge in chambers at any time after issue of the writ. The plaintiff usually issues a writ claiming the injunction (setting out precisely the terms of the injunction required) and, with the writ, serves a summons claiming an interlocutory injunc-

tion in the same terms as the final injunction. The support-
ing affidavit should explain the claim and the grounds for
the interlocutory injunction.

The summons must be served at least *two* clear days
before the hearing. The application is heard in a private
room in the High Court, by the Judge designated on that
day to hear interlocutory injunction applications.

Chancery Division   20.3.2

The application is by 'motion' to a judge in open court and not
by summons, as in the Queen's Bench Division. The applicant
issues a 'notice of motion' and serves this, together with an
affidavit, *two* clear days before the hearing. Again, the notice
of motion is usually served with the writ.

In practice, the court often does not have time to hear the
application on the appointed day and has to postpone
('stand over') the hearing until another day. If the defendant will not undertake to preserve the *status quo* until the
hearing, the plaintiff will have to apply *ex parte* there and
then for a temporary injunction until the hearing. As the
defendant is there to contest this, this is known as an
'opposed *ex parte* motion'.

Note

Whether proceedings are issued in the Queen's Bench Division
or in the Chancery Division depends on the nature of the case,
the experience of the lawyers, the speed of hearing in the
respective divisions and the need for privacy (QBD injunction
applications are heard in private, Chancery Division
applications in public).

Procedure in the County Court   20.4

A District Judge generally only has jurisdiction to hear an
application for an injunction when the value of the action
does not exceed £5,000. Otherwise, application is made to a
Circuit Judge.

The application is made by notice of application (*see*
Form N244) after issue of the summons commencing the
action.

The notice and affidavit should be served not less than
two days before the hearing. The application is usually
heard in open court.

A proposed draft order should be prepared and given to
the Judge.

20.5   Steps in the procedure after issue and service of application

The following headings apply in all courts and divisions.

20.5.1   Hearing

At the hearing, the Judge reads the affidavits, listens to submissions and decides whether to grant an interlocutory injunction according to the principles explained above. The injunction will usually be ordered to last until trial or further order.

A party may apply at any time for the variation or discharge of the injunction.

20.5.2   *Ex parte* injunctions

In the ordinary case of an interlocutory injunction the writ/summons is issued, the interlocutory application is served at the same time or shortly thereafter and a hearing follows fairly quickly; the injunction will therefore apply from shortly after commencement of proceedings until trial.

However, in an urgent case, no notice of the application is given to the other side and the application may even be made before the writ/summons is issued (*see* Chapter 8). In such a case, the emergency injunction is only granted for a few days (an interim injunction) after which both sides must come to court for an *inter partes* hearing as to whether the injunction should continue until trial or further order, on the principles explained above.

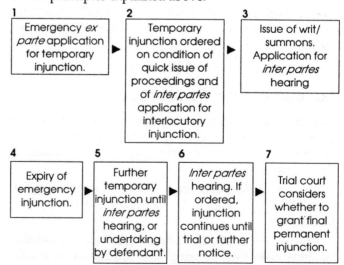

If *ex parte* urgent injunction is not needed, only 3, 6 and 7 apply, as explained in this chapter. *See* Chapter 8 for emergency injunctions.

Fig 20.1 Procedure for obtaining an injunction

The plaintiff, during the period of the temporary emergency injunction, must apply for a full *inter partes* interlocutory injunction hearing. As the hearing date will usually not be until some time after the expiry of the emergency injunction, the plaintiff may apply for a further temporary injunction to cover the gap until the *inter partes* hearing (this further temporary application may be an opposed *ex parte* application). More usually, the defendant will undertake to preserve the *status quo* until the *inter partes* hearing.

Figure 20.1 shows these procedures in a flow chart.

Undertaking as to damages   20.5.3

As a condition of the grant of an interlocutory injunction, the plaintiff will be required to undertake to pay damages to the defendant in respect of any loss suffered by the defendant as a result of the injunction being granted, in the event of the court deciding at trial that the plaintiff was never entitled to an injunction.

> *Note*
>
> In *Allen v Jambo Holdings Ltd* (1980), the plaintiff was held to be entitled to an interlocutory injunction even though their undertaking in damages was of limited value because they were legally aided.

The plaintiff should consider whether they could afford to meet the undertaking in damages, in deciding whether to seek an interlocutory injunction.

> *Note*
>
> For cases on whether the plaintiff *must* apply for an interlocutory injunction and, therefore, must give an undertaking in damages, see *Blue Town Investments Ltd v Higgs & Hill plc* (1990) and *Oxy Electric Ltd v Zainuddin* (1990).

Costs of application for interlocutory injunction   20.5.4

The judge has a discretion as to who pays the costs of the application. However, if the injunction is granted, the normal order is costs in the cause. If the injunction is refused, the plaintiff may be ordered to pay the defendant's costs in any event, but the order may be costs in the cause if the 'balance of convenience' (*see* above) is close.

Undertaking in lieu of injunction   20.5.5

Often, instead of the court ordering an injunction, the defendant gives an undertaking (promise) to the court in the same terms as if an injunction had been granted, eg. the defendant undertakes to refrain from specified acts. The defendant will give this undertaking as part of a settlement, in return for the plaintiff not proceeding with the injunction application, or will give it for a period pending the hearing of the application.

The defendant's undertaking is recorded in a formal order in the County Court (*see* form N117 and CCR O.29 r.1 and r.1A) and it is equivalent to an injunction, with the same effects (*see* below) in the event of breach. The *plaintiff* will often be required to give an undertaking to pay damages (*see* above) in return, this is known as a 'cross-undertaking'.

20.5.6   **Drafting and service of an injunction**

The judge writes ('endorses') a note of their decision on the summons/application. In the Queens Bench Division, the plaintiff drafts ('draws up') a formal injunction order and takes it (with a copy for filing) to the central office/District registry. In the Chancery Division and County Court, the court itself drafts the formal order.

The court then issues the order, and the plaintiff serves the order. The order contains a penal notice, warning the defendant of the effects of non-compliance with the order, in the following terms:

- High Court penal notice to individual defendant: 'If you, the within named X disobey this order, you may be held to be in contempt of court and liable to imprisonment'.

- High Court penal notice to corporate defendant: 'If you, the within named Xy Ltd disobey this order, you may be held to be in contempt of court and liable to sequestration of your assets'.

- High Court penal notice, where plaintiff will seek to enforce judgment against director or other officer of a company: 'If Xy Ltd disobey this order, you, X (a director or officer of the said Xy Ltd) may be held in contempt of court and liable to imprisonment'.

- County Court penal notice (*see* form N16 for general form of injunction) to individual: 'If you do not obey this order you will be guilty of contempt of court and you may be sent to prison'. Penal notices to corporate defendants will be worded accordingly, as in the High Court.

The plaintiff must serve the order personally on an individual defendant. Where the defendant is a company, and the plaintiff intends to enforce the judgment against a director or other officer of the company, the order must be served personally on that director or other officer.

Effect of breach of injunction (RSC O.45 rr.5 and 7; CCR O.29)

20.5.7

If the defendant breaches the injunction, the defendant can be committed to prison or fined for contempt of court. If the defendant is a company, in the High Court the plaintiff can apply for the seizure of the defendant's assets by writ of sequestration (*see* procedure in RSC O.46 r.5) or in either the High Court or the County Court the company can be fined. Further or alternatively, in the High Court only, a director or other company officer could be committed to prison (or have their assets sequestrated).

Note

The High Court committal procedure is set out in RSC O.52, the County Court procedure is set out in CCR O.29.

In practice, a committal order is often suspended on the defendant undertaking to comply with the injunction.

Note

The above rules apply also to breach of an undertaking given in lieu of an injunction. (*See Hussain v Hussain* (1986) for practice on enforcing an undertaking).

Self-assessment questions

1 Why does a plaintiff apply for an interlocutory injunction? For how long does an interlocutory injunction last?

2 You act for Superfoods plc, who wish to build a huge supermarket on farmland they have recently purchased. Farmer Giles, who owns a nearby milk distribution and farm produce business, is resisting the development. He claims it will infringe the prescriptive right of way that his delivery lorries have over the land.

(a) Is farmer Giles likely to obtain an emergency or interlocutory injunction to prevent the development?

(b) Is any consideration likely to prevent farmer Giles from seeking an injunction?

(c) Would it be appropriate for your client to seek an injunction? If so, would you first apply for an emergency or an interlocutory injunction?

(d) How would you apply for the interlocutory injunction?

(e) What principles *in this case* would the court look at to decide whether to grant your application should you decide to apply for an interlocutory injunction?

Chapter 21

Security for costs, striking out, dismissal and discontinuance of actions

Security for costs (RSC O.23; CCR O.13 r.8)   21.1

Meaning   21.1.1

A defendant can apply for an order that a plaintiff give security for the defendant's costs of the action, ie. that the plaintiff give some financial guarantee that if the plaintiff loses the case, the money will be available to pay the defendant's costs. This usually takes the form of the plaintiff *paying money into court*, or *giving a bond*. This is a very useful tactic for a defendant, either to protect their position or to force a settlement.

The action can be dismissed if the plaintiff fails to comply with an order to give security.

> *Note*
>
> A plaintiff cannot apply for security for costs against a defendant.

Grounds   21.1.2

A defendant can only claim security against the following *categories of plaintiffs*.

1 *Residence* The plaintiff is ordinarily *resident out of the jurisdiction* (High Court) or *out of England and Wales* (County Court).

2 *Nominal plaintiff* The plaintiff is a *nominal plaintiff* suing for the benefit of some other person, eg. the plaintiff assigned the benefit of the action but is lending their name to the proceedings, and there is reason to believe the plaintiff will be unable to pay the defendant's costs if ordered to do so (High Court ground only).

3 *Address* The plaintiff's *address is not stated*, or is *incorrectly stated*, in the writ, or the plaintiff has *changed their address* during the course of the proceedings with a view to evading the consequences of the proceedings (High Court ground only). In these cases, if the court thinks it just (or 'reasonable' in the County Court) to do so having regard to all the circumstances of the case, the court may order the plaintiff to give such security for the defendant's costs as it thinks just.

4 *Limited company* Where the plaintiff is a *limited company*, if it appears by credible testimony that there is reason to believe that the company will be unable to pay the defendant's costs, the court may require sufficient security to be given for those costs and may stay all proceedings until the security is given: s.726(1), Companies Act 1985.

Note

This is the most important ground in practice. A defendant can make effective tactical use of the right to apply for security for costs where the plaintiff is an impecunious company.

21.1.3   The court's discretion

Even if one of the above grounds is satisfied, the court has a discretion whether or not to order security for costs. The court will take into account, among other things:

- The plaintiff's prospects of success;
- Admissions by the defendant;
- Open offers of settlement and payments into court;
- Whether a security order would force the plaintiff to abandon a reasonable claim: *see Trident International Freight Services Ltd v Manchester Ship Canal Co* (1990) and *Aquila Design (GRB) Products Ltd v Cornhill Insurance plc* (1988). *See* also the principles set out by Denning MR in *Sir Lindsay Parkinson Ltd v Triplan Ltd* (1973) and notes in *White Book* to RSC O.23.

21.1.4   Procedure

Application is made by summons/application to a Master/District Judge, together with an affidavit. Where the defendant relies on the impecunious company ground, their affidavit must show evidence of the *inability of the plaintiff company to pay* the defendant's costs and must provide an *estimate of the defendant's likely costs* in the action. A *draft bill of likely costs* should be exhibited.

21.1.5   Order for security for costs

If security is ordered, the court will fix the *amount* of security (roughly the likely future amount of the defendant's costs, perhaps with a discount), the *mode* of giving security (usually by payment into court or by a bond with sureties) and the *time* within which the security must be given. The order will usually provide that proceedings shall be stayed until the security is given.

The court has power to dismiss the action where it is satisfied that:

- The action is not being pursued with *due diligence*; and
- There is *no reasonable prospect* that the security will be paid; and
- The *time limit* for the giving of security has been disregarded: *Speedup Holdings Ltd v Gough & Co (Handly) Ltd* (1986).

Striking out and dismissal   21.2

The plaintiff's action or the defendant's defence can be struck out or dismissed – they therefore lose the case – in certain circumstances.

Failure to comply with an 'unless order'   21.2.1
(RSC O.3 r.5, CCR O.13 r.4)

If a party fails to comply with any procedural rule or order, eg. to serve a pleading or to disclose documents, the other party can apply to the Master/District Judge for an 'unless' order, ie. that unless they comply with the rule or order within a certain time, their action/defence (as the case may be) will be struck out.

The court has a *discretion* whether to make an 'unless' order.

If the party against whom the order is made *is present* when it is made, the form of the order should be: 'unless by (eg. 2 pm on Friday 1 February 1994) the defendant (eg. serves their list of documents) the defence will be struck out and judgment entered for the plaintiff with costs.'

If the party against whom the order is made *is not present*, the form is: 'unless within (eg. 14) days of service of this order the defendant etc (as above)'. (*See* practice direction 1986 1 WLR 948.)

Even if an 'unless' order is not complied with, the court still has a discretion to further extend the time for compliance with the order, although this discretion should be exercised cautiously and on stringent terms as to payment of costs or bringing money into court or the like: *Samuels v Linzi Dresses Ltd* (1981).

However, the party's case will not be struck out if the failure to comply was not intentional but due to extraneous circumstances: *see Grand Metropolitan Nominee (No 2) Co Ltd v Evans* (1992) and *In re Jokai Tea Holdings Ltd* (1992).

21.2.2   Want of prosecution (RSC O.25 r.1 notes)

In some cases, the plaintiff literally takes years to proceed with steps in the case. For example, there are personal injury cases where the plaintiff has still not brought the case to trial six or seven years after commencing proceedings. In such cases, the defendant can apply to a Master/District Judge for the case to be struck out for want of prosecution, ie. for taking too long to proceed with the case.

In order to strike the case out for want of prosecution, the defendant must show:

- Inordinate and inexcusable *delay* by the plaintiff ('inordinate' means materially longer than the time usually regarded by the profession and the courts as an acceptable period); and

- That this has caused *prejudice* to the defendant, eg. witnesses' memories have faded, witnesses have died or disappeared, or the case has been hanging over the defendant for too long. (*See* notes to RSC O.25 r.1 for full principles and cases.)

Example

In *Biss v Lambeth HA* (1978), a medical negligence claim was struck out where 11.5 years after the alleged negligence the case had still not been taken further than the order for directions stage.

Note

In any event, in the High Court, where a year or more has passed since the last step in the action, the party who desires to proceed with the action must give to every other party not less than one month's notice of their intention to proceed.

21.2.3   County Court automatic striking out – CCR O.17 r.11(9)

In cases where the automatic directions apply, ie. most cases, the plaintiff must, within six months of close of pleadings, request the court to fix a trial date. If the request is not made within 15 months of close of pleadings (or nine months after any extended time allowed), the court will automatically strike the action out. This means that there is little need for an application to strike out for want of prosecution in the County Court.

Where 12 months have expired from the date of service of a default summons in the County Court, and there has been no admission, defence or counterclaim delivered, the court will strike out the action if the plaintiff has not entered judgment in default.

Abuse of process of court/no reasonable cause of action (RSC O.18 r.19; CCR O.13 r.5)

A party may apply to strike out the whole or part of the other side's case if that case:

- Discloses *no reasonable cause of action or defence*, as the case may be, eg. the defendant can apply to strike out the plaintiff's case if there is no such cause of action known to the law.

Example _____

In *Hill v Chief Constable of West Yorkshire* (1988), an action by the mother of a 'Yorkshire Ripper' victim against the police for failing to catch him was struck out on the ground that there was no duty of care owed by the police in the circumstances.

Alternatively, the other side's case can be struck out if it:

- Is scandalous, frivolous or vexatious; or
- May prejudice, embarrass or delay the fair trial of the action; or
- Is otherwise an abuse of the process of the court.

The latter three categories generally apply to cases where the allegations are, for example, scandalous and irrelevant, or ridiculous, or totally groundless, or where the matter has already been litigated. (*See* notes to RSC O.18 r.19 for full details.)

Note _____

If a person has habitually and persistently and without reasonable grounds instituted vexatious proceedings or made vexatious applications to court, the Attorney General can apply for an order that the person cannot institute proceedings/ make an application without the leave of the High Court: s.42, Supreme Court Act 1981.

Discontinuance (RSC O.21; CCR O.18)

In the High Court

The plaintiff may discontinue (withdraw) a *writ action* without leave of the court at any time not later than 14 days after service of the defence, and an *originating summons action* may be discontinued without leave at any time not later than 14 days after service of the defendant's affidavit in reply. The plaintiff will have to pay the defendant's costs of the action.

After these time limits, the plaintiff must apply to court for leave to discontinue, which will be given on terms that the plaintiff pay the defendant's costs, and other terms, eg. that a new action is not started.

The plaintiff discontinues by serving notice of discontinuance on the defendant(s).

21.3.2   In the County Court

The plaintiff may discontinue the action at any time before judgment, by giving notice of discontinuance (form N279) to the court and the defendant(s). In contrast to the High Court, leave is *not* required.

The plaintiff will have to pay the defendant's costs of the action, unless the court orders otherwise.

Self-assessment questions

1   You are acting for the defendant. What procedure would you use, and what documents would you prepare, to attempt to end the litigation in the following cases? In each case, are you likely to be successful in your attempt? What factors will the court take into account?

(a) The plaintiff is a small new company, with a current overdraft of £80,000. The company sues your client for £150,000; you raise a doubtful defence. The costs of the case overall are likely to be £30,000 on both sides.

(b) The plaintiff failed to give adequate further and better particulars of their statement of claim. They were given a further 21 days to do so but have failed to comply through carelessness in interpreting the time allowed and also because their expert is taking time to calculate certain of the particulars required.

(c) In 1988, the plaintiff sues in the High Court in respect of damage suffered 5 years before, just within the limitation period. The plaintiffs, in 1993, have still not set the case down for trial. The defendant company is suffering anxiety and loss of financial credit, due to the case hanging over them and appearing in their accounts.

How would your answer differ if the case were in the County Court?

2   Explain the difference between the plaintiff's case:

(a) being weak

(b) disclosing no reasonable cause of action.

Chapter 22

Interim payments (RSC O.29; CCR O.13)

Meaning of interim payments

22.1

It may be the case that the plaintiff would suffer financial hardship if they had to wait months or years until trial to receive damages (in a case where summary judgment is not appropriate). Alternatively, in a personal injury case, the plaintiff may urgently require money for treatment or equipment.

Therefore, there is a procedure by which the plaintiff can claim payment of a certain amount of damages before trial, ie. 'interim payments'.

Grounds for claiming

22.2

Criteria

22.2.1

To be entitled to an interim payment, the plaintiff must establish one of the following:

- That the defendant has *admitted liability*, eg. by letter or pleading, so that only the amount of damages remains to be assessed; or

- That the plaintiff has *already obtained judgment on liability* (in default, or by summary judgment, or at a trial just on liability) with damages to be assessed later; or

- That if the action proceeds to trial, the plaintiff would *obtain substantial damages* against the defendant. This is a difficult ground because the plaintiff must satisfy the Master/District Judge on affidavit evidence before trial, on the balance of probabilities, that the plaintiff will succeed and obtain substantial damages at trial: *see Shearson Lehman Bros Inc v Maclaine Watson & Co Ltd* (1988) and *British and Commonwealth Holdings plc v Quadrex Holdings Inc* (1989).

If one of the above grounds are proved, the court has a *discretion* to award an interim payment.

Personal injury actions

22.2.2

In a personal injury action, the court cannot make an order for an interim payment unless the defendant is:

- A *public authority*; or

- *Insured* in respect of the plaintiff's claim; or
- A person whose *means and resources* are such as to enable them to make an interim payment.

Note

A defendant to a road accident claim does not fall within the first two of these categories purely because the Motor Insurers Bureau is obliged to meet any unsatisfied judgment: *Powney v Coxage* (1988).

22.3   Procedure

22.3.1   In the High Court

In the High Court an application for an interim payment may be made at any time after the writ has been served and the time limit for acknowledging service has expired.

The plaintiff applies to the Master/District Judge by summons supported by affidavit. The summons and affidavit must be served not less that 10 clear days before the hearing.

22.3.2   In the County Court

In the County Court, application is to the District Judge by notice of application and affidavit served seven days before the hearing.

22.4   Contents of the affidavit

The affidavit should:

- Verify the *amount* of damages or the debt claimed;
- State the *grounds* of the application;
- *Exhibit* any documentary evidence relied on; and
- If the claim is made under the Fatal Accidents Act 1976, it should contain the particulars in s.2(4).

The affidavit must explain the *cause of action* and the *steps* already taken in the action (referring to the pleadings) and *how* the case falls within a ground for awarding interim payments.

22.4.1   Personal injury actions

In a personal injury action, the affidavit must:

- Exhibit the *medical report(s)*:
- Set out in detail the *special damages*, including past and future loss of earning; and
- Explain why the plaintiff *needs* an interim payment with details of any special needs and hardship.

Other actions 22.4.2

In actions other than for personal injury, the plaintiff is *not* required to satisfy the court of their need for the interim payment or that they would suffer prejudice if denied the interim payment: *Schott Kem Ltd v Bentley* (1990).

The amount 22.5

The court will order interim payment of such amount *as it thinks just*, not exceeding a reasonable proportion of the damages which, in the opinion of the court, are likely to be recovered by the plaintiff after taking into account any contributory negligence and any set-off or counterclaim.

Personal injury actions 22.5.1

In personal injury actions, the court usually orders interim payment of an amount to compensate the plaintiff for lost wages or other financial hardship up to the anticipated date of trial, together with sums needed for special treatment or equipment.

If the plaintiff seeks to recover a greater amount representing some of the general damages they would receive at trial, they will have to show good reasons.

Other actions 22.5.2

In other actions, the amount is *discretionary*, subject to the above rule.

If the defendant's resources are such that an order for interim payment will cause irremediable harm which cannot be made good by eventual repayment, this is a very relevant factor to be taken into account in fixing the amount of a payment: *British and Commonwealth Holdings plc v Quadrex Holdings* (1989).

Where the plaintiff is a *minor* or *mental patient*, the payment is usually limited to sums needed by the next friend for maintenance and expenses of the plaintiff until trial. This sum is paid into court, and the next friend takes the money out whenever it is needed for maintenance or expenses.

Effect on trial and final award of damages 22.6

An interim payment must not be pleaded and the trial judge must not be told about it until all questions of liability and quantum have been settled, otherwise the judge may be prejudiced. The fact that a master decided that the plaintiff would win substantial damages at trial has no influence on the trial, and is not revealed to the trial judge.

If the plaintiff, at trial, is awarded an amount of damages greater than the interim payment, the defendant pays the balance.

If the plaintiff loses at trial, or wins an amount of damages less than the interim payment, the court will order appropriate repayment by the plaintiff.

The court has discretion to award *interest* on the repayment: *Mercers Co v New Hampshire Insurance Co* (1991).

Self-assessment questions

1   What are the grounds for claiming an interim payment?
2   At what stage in the proceedings can you apply for an interim payment?
3   In a personal injury case, what documents must be prepared for such an application and what must be shown in such documents? In principle, how will the court calculate the amount of the interim payment awarded?
4   What risk is the plaintiff taking in receiving an interim payment?

Chapter 23

Further procedures for obtaining evidence and information

Inspection, detention and preservation of property (RSC O.29; CCR O.13 r.7)

It may be relevant to inspect the property which is the subject matter of the action where that property is in the possession of the other party, eg. the plaintiff is suing the defendant in respect of a defective machine, or defective working practice, in the defendant's factory.

In such a case, if a party will not allow inspection, the other party can apply for a court order allowing detention, custody, preservation, photographing or sampling of the property. Further, the court has jurisdiction to allow inspection and videoing of the other party's industrial process where that is necessary to do justice: *Ash v Buxted Poultry Ltd* (1989).

The court may authorise entry onto the other party's land for these purposes.

A party applies for an order by summons/application and affidavit, showing the grounds of their claim.

Interrogatories (RSC O.26; CCR O.14 r.11)

Another useful way of obtaining information or admission from the other side, or of casting doubt on their case, is to serve 'interrogatories' on them.

Interrogatories are formal written questions relating to any facts relevant to the action – the pre-trial equivalent of oral cross-examination at trial. They should not, however, be used as a replacement for cross-examination at trial but to obtain further information about the other side's case in order to prepare your own case properly, particularly where only the other party knows the facts.

Form and examples

After the formal heading of the case, the questions are set out in numbered order. They should be relevant, clear and precise, and drafted so as to prevent the other party escaping from answering helpfully.

Example

1   In *McKenna v Cammell Laird Ship Repairers Ltd* (1989), a claim in respect of industrial deafness, the defendant asked the following:

'6 Has the plaintiff made a claim against any other person in respect of industrial deafness?

7 If the answer to 6 is 'yes', what was the result of that claim? In particular, has the plaintiff received any compensation from such person and, if so, when and in what sum?'

2 In *Model Farm Dairies (Bournemouth) Ltd v Newman* (1943), a claim in respect of sale of infected milk, the plaintiff asked the following:

'During the investigation by officials of the Ministry of Health into the cause of the outbreak of Typhoid Fever at Bournemouth (in 1936), were you not examined and found to be a carrier of the germs of Typhoid Fever?'

3 In *Turner v Goulden* (1873), an action against a valuer for negligence, the footnotes to the case report set out the substantial interrogatories served on the defendant, asking about how he came to his valuation.

There is then a formal ending. The rules require that, at the end, the interrogatories must specify a period of time (not less than 28 days from service of the interrogatories) within which they are to be answered. Further, when the other side is a company or unincorporated body, the ending must specify the officer or member on whom they are to be served.

23.2.2   Interrogatories allowed and prohibited

Interrogatories are only allowed if they are relevant to the facts in issue and are necessary for disposing fairly of the cause or matter, or for saving costs, ie. they help prepare for or clear up issues in the case.

The following types of questions, *inter alia*, will not be allowed:

● *'Fishing'* questions asked for the purpose of building up a case not yet pleaded;

● Questions to obtain an *admission*, which could equally be put to a witness at trial;

Note

It is often difficult to know on which side of the line a question falls. Can it properly be asked before trial to dispose fairly of the case or to save costs?

- Questions where it is plain that *no admission will be obtained*, eg. on the central issue;
- *Oppressive* questions, eg. that impose a huge burden on the other party;
- Questions as to what *evidence* the other party intends to present;
- Questions solely as to the *trustworthiness* of the other party as a witness.

Procedure   23.2.3

Interrogatories may be served on the other side on *two occasions* without leave of the court being necessary. A party must apply to court for an order allowing service of *further* interrogatories.

A party on whom interrogatories are served may, within 14 days of service, apply to the court for their variation or withdrawal. In this way, the receiving party can challenge questions which are not allowable as interrogatories.

Answers should be given by *affidavit*. If the answers are insufficient, the questioning party may request further and better particulars of the answer, or apply for a court order that a further answer be given, by affidavit or oral examination.

If a party *fails to answer*, the other party can apply for an 'unless' order, ie. that the other side's action or defence be struck out unless the interrogatories are answered within a specified time.

Further and better particulars   23.3

Another device for obtaining further information from the other side is to serve a request for further and better particulars of their pleading. (This is covered in Chapter 15.)

Notice to admit facts (RSC O.27 r.2,   23.4
O.62 r.6(7); CCR O.20 r.2)

A good way of forcing the other side to admit certain facts relevant to the case is to serve on them a formal notice requiring them to admit certain facts.

In the *High Court*, the notice must be served within 21 days after the matter is set down for trial. In the *County Court*, the notice must be served not later than 14 days before the date fixed for trial.

The effect of the notice is that if the other side does not admit the facts (within 14 days in the High Court, within 7 days in the County Court), they will have to pay the costs that the other side incurs in successfully proving the facts at trial, irrespective of who wins the case overall.

This procedure may, therefore, induce the other party to admit minor facts in the action.

23.5   Discovery and inspection of documents and property in the possession of non-parties

23.5.1   The general rule

The general rule is that parties have *no right* to compel non-parties to disclose relevant documents in their possession, and no right to compel non-parties to allow inspection of their property. However, there are four important exceptions to this rule.

23.5.2   Exceptions

1 *Personal injury or death cases* – here a party can apply for an order allowing the inspection, photographing, preservation, detention or sampling of property in the possession of a non-party, which property is the subject matter of proceedings or as to which any question arises in the proceedings: s.34(3), Supreme Court Act 1981 and s.53(3), County Courts Act 1984.

A party applies by summons and affidavit, showing how the case falls within the rule: RSC O.29 r.7A; CCR O.13 r.7.

2 *Disclosure of documents in personal injury or death cases* – in such cases a party can apply for an order for disclosure of relevant documents by a non-party: s.34(2), Supreme Court Act 1981 and s.53(2), County Courts Act 1984. A party applies by summons and affidavit, showing how the case falls within the rule: RSC O.24 r.7A; CCR O.13 r.7.

3 *Facilitation of the wrong* – a party can bring an action for discovery against a non-party who facilitated the wrong by the defendant, under the principle in *Norwich Pharmacal Co v Customs and Excise Commissioners* (1974) (*see* Chapter 7).

The action is brought by originating summons/application and affidavit.

4 *Subpoena dues tecum* – non-party can be compelled to attend the trial with relevant documents by a *subpoena dues tecum*, an order to attend as a witness with documents.

This rule does not allow for inspection of the documents before trial.

Self-assessment questions

1   As plaintiff, can you compel the following during the proceedings?

(a) Inspection of the defendant's car in a road accident case, when the car is stored in an independent garage.

(b) Disclosure of the defendant's hospital records by the hospital, in a personal injury case.

(c) Production of hotel records by a hotelier, to show that the defendant to a possession of land case has been staying at a hotel (and is therefore not a resident tenant with security of tenure of a certain house).

2   Explain the difference between:

(a) interrogatories

(b) a notice to admit facts

(c) a request for further and better particulars.

3   Your client, a manufacturer of machinery, has been sued for providing defective machinery in a factory. Your client claims the machinery was not installed correctly, the plaintiff's staff were not trained properly in the installation and use of the machines, and the plaintiffs have a record of incompetent use and installation. What sort of interrogatories could you ask? In what other ways could and would you discover information during the case on the issues of how the defects were caused and what damage and losses ensued? (Think about what you have read in other chapters.)

4   Would the following interrogatories be allowed by the court?

(a) Why did the display collapse? (In a case where a supermarket display fell on top of a customer.)

(b) Is it not true that you were present at the site (where the alleged contract took place)? If not, where were you? Did you make the contract on behalf of an undisclosed principal (where this is suspected)? What is the name of that principal? (In a case of an alleged oral contract.)

(c) What expert evidence have you in your possession to prove your loss of profits? How is your loss calculated?

Chapter 24

Payment into court, Calderbank offers and settlement of actions

Payment into court 24.1

Meaning 24.1.1

Payment into court is a procedure by which the defendant can formally pay into the court office an amount of damages in an *attempt to settle the case.*

If the plaintiff accepts the sum, that will be the end of the case. However, if the plaintiff does *not* accept the sum paid in and, at trial, the plaintiff wins but is not awarded a greater amount of damages than that which was paid into court, the plaintiff will have to pay the defendant's costs of the proceedings from the date of the payment into court onwards, and will also have to bear their own costs from that date.

This is known as a 'failure to beat a payment into court'.

Example

P sues D for negligence, claiming £50,000. Shortly after service of the writ, D pays £20,000 into court. P does not accept this and continues the case. At trial, two years later, D is found to have been negligent but is only ordered to pay £10,000 damages. P is therefore ordered to pay D's legal costs from the date of the payment into court and these could easily amount to £10,000, thereby wiping out the damages.

The theory is that P has wasted everyone's time and money by continuing with the case after the payment into court. In reality, P takes a risk in deciding whether or not to accept the payment because the amount of damages which would be awarded at trial cannot be predicted with accuracy; the plaintiff will depend on competent advice from their solicitor as to the likely outcome of a trial. A payment into court is therefore a very useful, common tactic for a defendant who wishes to settle the case.

The payment into court is not revealed to the trial judge, as this would prejudice the defendant – the payment is not evidence of an admission but merely a formal device for settling cases.

24.1.2   Procedure

High Court

At any time *after service of the writ*, the defendant prepares a standard form of 'request for lodgement' and sends this, with the payment and the sealed writ, to the court. The sealed writ is returned to the defendant with a receipt. The defendant serves a formal notice of payment in (Form 23, Appendix A, *White Book*) on the plaintiff.

The plaintiff must acknowledge receipt of the notice within three days.

County Court

At any time *before judgment*, the defendant sends to the court the payment, a notice or letter stating the case number and indicating that the sum is paid in satisfaction of the claim, and an addressed reply envelope. The court will send a notice of the payment in to the plaintiff (Form N242) and a receipt to the defendant.

Both courts

In both courts, the sum should include interest, and the defendant should state whether a counterclaim or interim payment has been taken into account.

Note the following points:

- The defendant may later increase the sum paid in; on each increase, a new notice is served on the plaintiff.

- The defendant may make a payment into court, or increase, even after the trial has begun.

- Conversely, the defendant may withdraw an unaccepted payment in, but the court's leave will be needed.

Personal injury cases: deduction of benefits

In a personal injury case, where the plaintiff has received *state benefits* in respect of the injury, the Deduction of Benefits procedure applies:

1   The defendant obtains from the DSS a *certificate of benefits paid to the defendant* ('Certificate of Total Benefit'). The amount of benefits paid is deducted by the defendant from the sum paid in.

2   The defendant provides the court with a *certificate detailing the amount deducted*. The sum paid in is then regarded as being increased by the sum deducted.

3   The defendant *pays the amount deducted* to the DSS Compensation Recovery Unit upon the defendant being notified that the payment into court has been paid out to the plaintiff.

Acceptance

Procedure

The plaintiff is allowed 21 days from receipt of notice of
payment in to accept. After 21 days, payment can only be
accepted with the court's leave.

The plaintiff's solicitor will have an important role at
this point in advising their client on whether to accept the
payment into court. They will advise their client on the
likely outcome of a trial and will often obtain an updated
expert's report and counsel's opinion before giving their
advice. Since this will take time, they will often ask the
defendant for an extension of the time allowed for acceptance without leave.

Note

If the plaintiff is legally aided, their solicitor should notify the
Legal Aid Board of a payment in. The legal aid certificate may
be discharged if a reasonable payment is rejected.

The plaintiff accepts by serving a notice of acceptance on the
defendant (and the court, in a county court case).

Leave of the court

A payment can only be accepted with the court's leave
(permission) where the:

- Plaintiff wishes to accept *after 21 days* (or any extended
  time allowed by the defendant). The court is unlikely to
  allow late acceptance where the merits of the case have
  substantially altered in the defendant's favour since the
  payment in, eg. it has since been discovered that the
  plaintiff's medical prognosis is much better than was
  first thought.

- Payment in was made by *one of two defendants*.

- Plaintiff is a *minor* or *mental patient* – in these cases the
  court must be satisfied that the amount paid in is in the
  plaintiff's best interests.

- Action is brought under the Fatal Accidents Act 1976
  and the Law Reform (Miscellaneous Provisions) Act
  1934 together, or where the action is brought under the
  1976 Act alone and more than one person is entitled to
  the money.

The plaintiff applies for leave to accept by summons/
application to a master/district judge.

Effects

Acceptance within 21 days has the following effects:

- The action is *stayed*, ie. stops;
- The plaintiff is entitled to have their *costs* up to the date of notice of acceptance paid by the defendant;
- The plaintiff can obtain *payment out of the money*.

Note _____

Where the plaintiff is legally aided, the money must be paid to the plaintiff's solicitor, so that the solicitor can deal with the money in accordance with the Legal Aid regulations.

24.1.4   Non-acceptance

The action continues if the payment is not accepted. The money remains in court. After 21 days it will be transferred to a deposit account to earn interest for the defendant.

The trial judge will not be told of the payment in until judgment has been given and damages awarded.

Costs consequences

If the plaintiff wins at the trial and the judge awards an amount of damages greater than the amount paid in – the plaintiff 'beats the payment in' – the usual order for costs will follow, ie. the defendant pays the plaintiff's costs.

If, however, the plaintiff wins but is awarded an amount of damages equal to or less than the amount paid in – the plaintiff 'fails to beat the payment in' – the judge will order that:

- The defendant must pay the plaintiff's costs up to the date of receipt by the plaintiff of notice of payment in; and
- The plaintiff must pay the defendant's costs (as well as bearing their own costs) from the date of receipt of notice of payment in onwards. (This is the central point on payment into court; even though the plaintiff has won the case, the plaintiff is liable for substantial costs, which may exceed the amount of damages won.)

Note _____

If the plaintiff wins the trial, the judge will probably order payment out of the money in court to satisfy the judgment, though this may be refused, eg. because of the plaintiff's liability for the defendants costs.

24.1.5   Consequences of failure to beat payment in where plaintiff is legally aided

Even in the case of a failure to beat a payment in, a legally aided plaintiff will only be ordered to pay a *reasonable amount* of the defendant's costs having regard to the parties' means and conduct: s.17, Legal Aid Act 1988. This may only be a small amount, or none at all. However, the court may deal with the situation by reducing the amount of damages payable by the amount of costs owed to the defendant.

Failure to beat a payment in is a common example of where the s.16 legal aid statutory charge will apply. In such a case, the plaintiff wins but does not recover all their costs back from the defendant. Therefore, the Legal Aid Board will recoup from the damages received the legal costs they have paid to the plaintiff's solicitor. In this way, the amount of damages received by a legally aided plaintiff is further reduced.

Calderbank offers   24.2

In cases where the claim is for a remedy other than money, eg. a claim for an injunction, a payment into court cannot apply. Instead, a party may make a 'Calderbank' offer to settle the claim under RSC O.22 r.14; CCR O.11 r.10. This type of offer originates from the case of its first reported use, *Calderbank v Calderbank* (1976).

Procedure and effect   24.2.1

In a case of a claim other than money, a party wishing to settle sends a letter (known as a 'Calderbank letter') to the other party, making an offer, eg. not to do a specified act, in an injunction claim. The letter is expressed to be 'without prejudice save as to costs'.

The effect of this letter is that it is 'without prejudice' as to liability. Hence, in the ordinary way, it is not revealed to the court when the question of liability and remedy is being considered. However, it can be revealed to the court when the court is considering who is to pay the costs of the case and the court may take the offer into account in deciding who is to pay costs.

The court has a discretion as to how the offer will affect liability for costs, but it has been said that if the party to whom the offer was made unreasonably fails to accept the offer, then, unless there are special reasons, the offeror will be entitled to have their costs paid by the other party from the time that the offer should have been accepted: *per* Waller J in *Chrulew v Borm-Reid & Co* (1992).

In other words, a 'Calderbank letter' has a similar effect on costs to a payment into court. However, a 'Calderbank letter' should not be used instead of a payment into court in monetary claims: *Cutts v Head* (1984).

In the County Court, the offer must be filed at court in a sealed envelope.

24.3   Settlement of actions

Most cases are settled before they come to trial. In most cases, the parties, through their solicitors, will make and negotiate offers and counter-offers of settlement throughout the proceedings. Indeed, many disputes are settled by negotiation even before proceedings are issued.

Often, steps in the action, eg. issue of proceedings, asking for discovery, setting down, are only really taken as tactics to force a settlement, or when negotiations have broken down.

24.3.1   A solicitor's authority

You have implied *authority* to settle the case on behalf of your client, as long as you are acting bona fide and not contrary to the express instructions of your client. Further, you have ostensible auth*ority*, as between yourself and the opposing party, to settle a claim: *Waugh v Clifford (H B) and Sons Limited* (1982).

However, you should not make an offer to the other side, or accept or reject an offer from the other side, without your client's instructions. When the other party makes an offer of settlement, you should advise your client on whether or not to accept the offer (looking at the legal and practical merits of the offer, and the costs considerations), but the *final decision* should be left to the client.

24.3.2   Procedures

Once the parties have agreed terms of settlement, there are different ways in which the settlement can be formalised.

Judgment/Order by consent
This is a common method of settlement. The parties draft the agreed terms of settlement in the form of an order, eg. 'by consent, it is ordered that the Defendant do within 21 days pay the sum of ... together with costs to be taxed, if not agreed' (or the amount of costs payable may be specified in the order). They must then place the order before the trial judge or, if before trial, before a judge or master, who must sign their name on the judgment. In effect, it is a court judgment, but one made by consent rather than after a hearing.

In the Queen's Bench Division of the High Court, and in the County Court, there is a procedure by which certain types of consent judgments can be entered purely by administrative procedure at the court office, without the need for signing by a judge or master. This procedure is commonly used. *See* RSC O.42 RSA and CCR O.22 r.7A.

A consent judgment can be enforced in the same way as
an ordinary judgment.

Stay of action

The parties may agree an order that the action be stayed on
the terms contained in the order (being the agreed terms of
settlement) 'Save for the purpose of carrying the said terms
into effect'.

This means that if a party does not comply with the
order, the other party can go back to court to ask for an order
for compliance with the terms of settlement.

'Tomlin' order

This is a special agreed order, commonly used, whereby the
terms of settlement are set out in a schedule attached to the
order. The order provides:

'And, the Plaintiff and Defendant having agreed to the terms set
forth in the schedule hereto, it is ordered that all further proceedings in this action be stayed, except for the purpose of carrying
such terms into effect. Liberty to apply as to carrying such terms
into effect.'

The 'Liberty to apply' sentence means that a party can
return to court to obtain an order for compliance with the
terms of settlement where the other side will not comply.
(Costs liability is dealt with in the body of the order.)

A Tomlin order is used:

- Where the terms of settlement are complex; or
- Do not fit easily within the precise issues in the action; or
- Where the parties wish the terms of settlement to be
  hidden from publicity in a schedule.

However, a Tomlin order is not a money judgment and does
not carry interest under the Judgments Act 1838 or County
Court Act 1984, s.74.

A Tomlin order can be entered by administrative procedure without the signature of a judge or master, under RSC
O.42 R5A and CCR O.22 r.7A.

Less common methods

1   A *consent order* staying all further proceedings upon terms
endorsed on counsels' briefs. (This is difficult to enforce.)

2   *Withdrawal of the action by consent*, in the High Court only
(RSC O.21 r.2(4)). The problem for the plaintiff is that there
is no judgment or ability to restore the action.

3   The court is informed by counsel that the case has been
settled *on the terms endorsed on counsels briefs*. This creates a
contract. The plaintiff would have to sue on the contract to

enforce it. It is, therefore, not as good as a formal judgment or a stay with liberty to apply.

24.3.3   Drafting of settlements

You need to become skilled at drafting settlements, often at speed outside court or in negotiation rooms. (However, counsel often drafts the settlement.) Precedents of settlement orders can be found in *Atkins Court Forms*, Vol 12: 'Compromise and Settlement'.

The terms should be drafted as precisely as possible, to avoid dispute over their meaning. The terms should also deal with the question of who is to pay the costs of the proceedings.

24.3.4   Persons under a disability

Any settlement made on behalf of a person under a disability, ie. a person under 18 years of age or a mental patient, is not valid unless it is approved by the Court. If the Court does approve the payment of money to such a person, the money is not paid to them. It is paid into court and invested, sums being paid out to the person's next friend when needed for their welfare.

For the full procedure in this area, *see* RSC O.80 rr.16–12 (and notes thereto) and CCR O.10 rr.10 and 11.

Self-assessment questions

1   How does a payment into court differ from:

(a) an ordinary offer of compensation in settlement of the claim

(b) a Calderbank offer?

2   If you were acting for the defendant in an action, at what sort of level would you pitch the amount of your payment into court? At what stage of the proceedings would you advise the making of a payment? What factors would you consider in deciding these questions?

3   What is the important role of the plaintiff's solicitor on receiving notification of a payment into court?

4   Explain the nature and effect of a payment into court clearly and concisely to a layperson.

5   Will the plaintiff be able to accept a pre-trial payment into court during the trial?

6   How does a Calderbank offer differ from an ordinary 'without prejudice' offer?

7   Explain the differences, in nature and effect, between:

(a) a judgment by consent

(b) a stay of the action by consent

(c) a Tomlin order

(d) a withdrawal of the action by consent

(e) a settlement on terms endorsed on counsel's briefs.

Which of these methods of settlement would you prefer
to use and in what circumstances might each method be
used?

Chapter 25

Setting the case down for trial (High Court): Requesting a hearing date (County Court) and preparations for trial

Setting the case down for trial: High Court (RSC O.34)

25.1

After a long time period, of months or even years, when the directions have been complied with, negotiations have not been successful and the plaintiff is satisfied that they wish to proceed to a trial, the plaintiff will set down the matter for trial. This is the procedure by which the plaintiff informs the court that the case is ready for trial and lodges certain documents with the court in preparation for the trial. The court then puts the case in the list of cases due for trial, or gives a fixed date for the trial (if a fixed date is asked for).

Time

25.1.1

The automatic directions in personal injury cases provide, and the directions ordered in other cases usually provide, that the plaintiff must set the case down within six months of close of pleadings (personal injury cases) or within six months of the summons for directions (other cases).

In practice, the plaintiff often takes longer than this because the parties frequently do not comply with the directions within the required time limits. In many cases, parties will only seek to enforce the time limits as a negotiating tactic, or when negotiations are not going well, or when they themselves are ready to proceed.

Before setting the case down, the plaintiff should ensure that all the directions have been complied with. If the defendant has not complied with the directions the plaintiff may seek an order that the defence be struck out unless the defendant complies. If the plaintiff has failed to comply, the defendant may seek an order that the action be struck out unless the plaintiff complies, or the defendant may attempt to strike out the action for want of prosecution.

If a year or more has elapsed since the order for directions or since the last interlocutory proceedings in the case, a party desiring to proceed, eg. the plaintiff desiring to set the case down, must give to every other party not less than one month's notice of intention to proceed (RSC O.3 r.6).

25.1.2   Procedure for setting case down

In order to set the case down, the plaintiff must send the following to the centre where the trial will take place, ie. the Royal Courts of Justice or the District Registry:

- The *fee payable* for setting down, currently £30;
- A standard *form of request* that the action be set down;
- Two *bundles* (one for the trial judge, one for the court record) containing copies of:
  - the writ;
  - the pleadings and any further and better particulars;
  - any third party orders, notices and pleadings;
  - in a personal injury case, any disclosed expert reports upon which any party intends to rely;
- Requests or orders for *particulars*, the particulars given, and any *interrogatories* and answers;
- Any *orders* made in the action except any order relating only to time;
- A standard form *statement of the value of the action*, ie. that it is worth £25,000 or more or explaining why it is suitable for trial in the High Court. (In the absence of this form, the case will be transferred to the County Court.)
- A *note* agreed by the parties or, failing agreement, a note by each party giving an estimate of the *length of the trial*, and also a note as to the *court list* in which the action is to be included (*see* below);
- If a party is legally aided, notice of *issue of legal aid* and any notice of amendment of the legal aid certificate;
- In a case to be tried *outside London*, a statement as to the following:
  - whether the order for directions has been complied with;
  - whether experts' reports have been submitted and agreed;
  - how many experts will be called;
  - whether plans and photographs have been agreed;
  - an estimate of the length of trial;
  - names, addresses and phone numbers of solicitors, agents and counsel.

Note

For full administrative details on how the bundles should be prepared and the exact room in the court to which they should be taken or sent, *see* RSC O.34 r.3 and notes in *White Book* thereto. *See* also Practice Direction (Trials Out of London) 1987 1 WLR 1322, printed in notes to O.34 in *White Book*.

Having sent these documents, the plaintiff must notify all other parties within 24 hours that the case has been set down.

At the stage of setting down, the court will consider whether to transfer the case to the County Court: *see* Practice Direction (County Court: Transfer of Actions 1991 1 WLR 643), printed in *White Book* notes to O.34. If the case is transferred from the High Court to the County Court, the relevant procedures are set out in CCR O.16 r.6 and Practice Directions in notes to O.16 r.6 in *Green Book*.

High court listing of case for trial and arrangements for hearing date for trial (RSC O.34)

25.1.3

Allocating a date for trial after the case has been set down is unfortunately a far more complicated matter than the court office simply looking for a convenient date in its diary. The procedure is as follows:

In London

Once the case has been set down, the court will insert the case into the 'general list' of cases. This list is subdivided into the following lists.

1   *Queen's Bench Division*

- The Crown Office list – for cases of judicial review and where the Queen's Bench Division sits as an appeal court;
- The jury list – cases tried with a jury;
- The non-jury list – the most typical category – general litigation cases;
- The short cause list – actions not expected to take longer than 4 hours;
- The commercial list – actions in the Commercial Court;
- The Arbitration list – Arbitration proceedings;
- The Admiralty list – Admiralty cases.

Note

There is no similar listing system for Queen's Bench trials outside London.

2   *Chancery Division*

Actions are divided into the:

- Witness list part 1 – trials estimated to exceed three days – and part 2; and

- Non-witness list – trials not involving oral evidence.

Outside London

There is a setting down list divided into witnesses cases and non-witness cases.

The general list

The case stays in this general list, gradually moving up from the bottom of the list. There is no fixed date for trial, unless applied for. After a time, the action will appear in the 'warned list', a list of the cases that are relatively near to coming on for trial. Depending on the court's workload, the case will gradually rise to the top of the list and be heard.

Solicitors, and barristers' clerks, keep a watch on the progress of the case in the list. They will warn the client and witnesses when the case is coming close to trial.

Eventually, the case will appear in the weekly and then daily lists of cases to be heard in that week or day. This is all a very uncertain process and the time period from setting down to trial is likely to be many months.

Fixed date trials

To avoid this uncertainty, and the possibility of lawyers or witnesses not being available on the date when the case is heard, parties can instead apply for a fixed date for the trial. The disadvantage of this is that you tend to have to wait longer for a fixed date slot than for a slot under the listing system. However, a plaintiff will often apply for a fixed date to ensure the availability of expert witnesses and their chosen barrister.

For full details on listing and fixed dates *see* Queen's Bench Practice Directions 1981 1 WLR 1296 and 1987 1 WLR 1322 (printed in *White Book* notes to O.34) and Chancery Division Practice Directions in volume 2 of *White Book*.

25.2   Fixing a date for trial in the County Court (CCR O.17 r.11(9))

In the County Court, in contrast to the High Court, all cases are given a fixed date for trial. In cases where the automatic directions apply (which is most cases), the plaintiff must, *within six months of close of pleadings*, apply to the court requesting it to fix a hearing date.

When making the request, the plaintiff must file at court a note, which should be agreed with the other side if possible, of the likely length of the trial and the number of witnesses likely to be called.

If *no request* for a hearing date is made within *15 months of close of pleadings*, the court must *automatically* strike out the action and the plaintiff will lose the case.

Note ————————————————————————

In cases where there is a pre-trial review, the court will fix a hearing date at the pre-trial review.

Therefore, in automatic directions cases, the plaintiff's solicitor must be sure to request a hearing date within 15 months of close of pleadings.

Note ————————————————————————

The court can extend the time allowed for requesting a date.

The court office will then arrange a hearing date, which will depend on its workload. There will usually be a wait of several months before the trial. Furthermore, in many courts, even if a trial is listed to take place on a certain day, the court may not have time to hear it on that day or at the time specified.

Note ————————————————————————

County courts tend to list a number of small cases and interlocutory applications to be heard at, eg. 10.30 am. This does not mean they all begin at 10.30. They are taken in order. Often, parties have to wait for several hours, and then the case may not be heard at all.

Preparations for trial   25.3

In the long time period of several months, or years, between setting down/fixing a hearing date and trial, the following steps should be taken or considered by both sides:

1   *Settlement negotiations and proposals*, including payment into court.

2   *Directions* – ensure that the directions have been complied with. Most importantly, ensure there has been *full discovery*, exchange of *experts' reports* and *witness statements*. Consider an *'unless' order* or *dismissal for want of prosecution* against the other side to ensure compliance.

3 *Interlocutory applications* – consider any interlocutory applications which may be appropriate, eg. for summary judgment, interim payments or specific discovery.

4 *Advice from counsel* – it is common practice to instruct counsel to advise on evidence. All relevant documents should be sent to counsel, with instructions for counsel to advise on what evidence is needed, how facts are to be proved, any evidential problems and any evidential procedures which will be necessary.

5 *Service of documents* – consider serving various documents on the other side in order to obtain further information or to deal with evidential matters, eg. a request for further and better particulars, interrogatories, notice to admit facts, notice to produce documents (originals), notice of intention to produce hearsay evidence under the Civil Evidence Act 1968.

6 *Progress of case* – continue to investigate the merits of the case and the evidence and to advise client on the progress of case.

25.4   Shortly before trial

25.4.1   Notification of trial date and attendance

Notify all witnesses of the date for trial, or (in High Court listing case) that trial is likely to take place in the near future. Check their availability and whether they are prepared to attend voluntarily.

Note

A witness can be compelled to attend by serving on them a subpoena (High Court) or witness summons (County Court).

In the *High Court* a writ of *subpoena ad testificandum* (compelling a witness to attend to give oral evidence) or *subpoena dues tecum* (compelling a witness to bring a document to court) is applied for by issuing a *praecipe* (request) to the court. The court will then issue the subpoena which must then be served personally on the witness. All this is within prescribed time limits (*see* RSC O.38 rr.14–18 for details).

In the *County Court*, a witness summons is applied for, issued and served personally (*see* CCR O.20 r.12 for details).

In *both courts*, witnesses are entitled to expenses and allowances for attending. In the High Court, the taxing master decides what amounts are reasonable. In the County Court, the rules set limits to the amounts allowed, but the district judge still has a discretion (*see* CCR O.38 rr.13–15).

In the *High Court* the punishment for non-attendance by a witness is committal to prison, in the *County Court* the witness is fined.

Counsel   25.4.2

Consider whether a conference with counsel is necessary. Often, one or more conferences with counsel are held shortly before the trial to allow for full preparation and advice on the case as between counsel, yourself, client and perhaps expert witnesses.

Strategy, tactics and last minute service of notices and use of evidence can be considered.

Court bundle   25.4.3

High Court (RSC O.34 r.10)

At least 14 days before the date fixed for trial, or within three weeks of the defendant receiving notice of entry of the case into the warned list, the defendant must inform the plaintiff of those documents central to the defendant's case which the defendant wants included in the court bundle.

At least two clear days before the date fixed for trial the plaintiff must lodge at court two bundles, ie. two copies of the court bundle, containing the following:

- *Witness statements* which have been exchanged and *experts' reports* which have been disclosed, together with an indication of whether the contents are agreed by both parties;
- *Documents* which the defendant wishes to have included in the bundle and documents central to the plaintiffs case. ('Documents' refers to correspondence and other relevant documents – a large part of the pre-trial work will involve the parties creating an agreed bundle of documents for use at the trial – these documents will come from the bundles of documents disclosed on discovery.)
- If so directed by the master at the summons for directions, a *summary* of the *issues* involved, a summary of the *law* and *authorities* to be cited and a *chronology* of relevant events.

This court bundle is *very important* – it must be distinguished from the earlier bundle to be produced on setting down the action – and its purpose is to enable the trial judge to read about the case and to read its relevant documents in advance of the trial.

The bundle should be properly paginated and ordered and it should follow the detailed format required for the setting down bundle (*see White Book* O.34, note 34/3/2).

The plaintiff should make multiple copies, eg. four each for all parties. The other party should undertake to pay reasonable photocopying charges.

Preparation of the court bundle is very time-consuming and expensive.

Note

In the Chancery Division, only one bundle is lodged together with a separate bundle of core documents at least two days, but not more than seven days, before the date fixed for trial.

County Court (CCR O.17 r.12)
At least 14 days before the date fixed for the hearing, the defendant must inform the plaintiff of the documents that the defendant wishes to have included in the court bundle.

At least 7 days before the date fixed for the hearing the plaintiff must file at court one copy of a paginated and indexed bundle comprising the documents on which either of the parties intends to rely or which either party wishes to have before the court at the hearing, ie. correspondence and other relevant documents, together with two copies of the following:

- Any requests for particulars and the particulars given, and any answer to interrogatories;
- Witness statements and experts' reports which have been exchanged, together with an indication of whether the contents have been agreed by both parties;
- In a legal aid case, notice of issue of legal aid and any notice of amendment of the certificate.

As in the High Court, multiple copies for both sides should be made.

25.4.4   Exchange of updated statements of special damages in personal injury cases

A practice direction at 1984 1 WLR 1127 requires that in High Court personal injury cases, a schedule of the following must be served on all other parties not later than seven days after the case appears in the warned list.

- Loss of *earnings*;
- Loss of *future earning capacity*;
- *Medical or other expenses* relating to or including the cost of care, attention, accommodation or appliances;
- Loss of *pension rights*.

Not later than seven days after this, the other parties must indicate in writing whether and to what extent each item is agreed and, if not, the reason why not and any counter proposals.

Where there is a fixed date for the hearing, the schedule must be served not later than 28 days before that date and the answer not later than 14 days thereafter.

Failure to comply with these requirements may be taken into account in deciding any question of costs.

There is no practice direction in relation to the County Court, but updated statements of special damages are similarly served before County Court trial in order to facilitate a settlement.

Brief to counsel   25.4.5

Approximately two to three weeks before trial, if instructing counsel to present the case, you should send the brief to counsel. In the majority of cases, you do use counsel to present the case, although this may change as advocacy rights and training given to solicitors increases.

The brief to counsel is the very full set of instructions, instructing counsel to represent the client at trial, containing all relevant documents which they need to present the case in court. You can choose any barrister to present the case, subject to their availability. The barrister chosen will usually be the one who has previously advised on the case. The code of conduct of the Bar of England and Wales sets out rules on when a barrister can refuse a brief: see White Book notes to O.62 A2.

In large, complex cases you should consider using a leading (Queen's) counsel together with a junior counsel, although this requires Legal Aid Board approval in a legal aid case.

Form

There are no official rules on how to set out the brief to counsel, practice varies from office to office. As a general guide, however, a brief should be in the following form.

1 *The heading.* The heading of the case appears at the top, followed by the heading 'Brief to Counsel for the (Plaintiff/Defendant/Third party)'.

2 *List of documents.* Copies (not originals) of the following documents should be enclosed:

- Writ/summons and pleadings (including special damages statements in personal injury cases);
- Discovery lists of documents;
- Disclosed experts' reports;
- Witness statements;

- Agreed court bundle – which will contain all relevant documents, correspondence between the parties prior to and during the case (party and party correspondence) and relevant correspondence between a party and non-parties;
- Agreed photographs/plans and police accident report, where relevant;
- Interrogatories and answers;
- Notices, eg. hearsay notices, notice to admit facts and notice of payment into court;
- Legal aid documents;
- Proofs of evidence of witnesses – in case counsel might wish to make use of evidence not disclosed in witness statements;
- Previous instructions to counsel and advice given by counsel;
- Previous court orders made during the case;
- If helpful to counsel, privileged correspondence between solicitor and client/counsel/third parties.

Note

The brief should not include irrelevant document, eg. old summonses.

The documents should be ordered in as clear and helpful a manner as possible. Generally they are divided into clear sections within lever arch files.

3 *The substance of the case.* You should then in numbered or headed paragraphs:

- Explain and discuss the facts and issues, drawing attention to important points;
- Explain, discuss and draw attention to the pleadings, interrogatories, notices and orders in the action, so far as is important and appropriate;
- Discuss and draw attention to the evidence, dealing with significant evidential issues and procedures and how facts can best be proved;
- Explain your views on liability and quantum of damages or other remedies; (It is often helpful to counsel to draw their attention to the law and to set out your opinion on the case.)
- Advise and instruct as to the position on interest and costs;
- Formally ask counsel to attend the trial, giving place, date and time.

Note _____

The exact layout and style of the brief will depend on the nature of the case and the particular office.

Fee

A day or two after the brief has been delivered, you should negotiate counsel's fee with the clerk in counsel's chambers. (In a legal aid case, the fee is not agreed but is decided on taxation.) In agreeing the fee, it is important to bear in mind that the taxing officer will only allow a reasonable amount to be recovered from the other side.

Note _____

The fee is for preparation and the first day of the trial, an additional refresher fee is paid for each subsequent day of the trial.

Further, once the brief has been delivered to counsel, the fee is payable even if the case is settled. However, in such a case counsel can agree to accept a lesser fee and you have a duty to renegotiate for a lesser fee.

Getting all persons to court   25.4.6

The day before the fixed date for trial, or when the case is listed for the next day, you should inform the client, witnesses and counsel of the time and place of the hearing and ensure their availability. Due to the uncertainty of the listing system, the barrister who has been briefed is sometimes double-booked and another barrister has to be instructed shortly before the trial.

Lodging authorities   25.4.7

It is the practice for solicitors and/or counsel to lodge a list of legal authorities, ie. cases, statutes, with the court just before trial and for counsel on both sides to exchange lists of authorities they intend to rely on.

Self-assessment questions

1 How does High Court 'setting down' differ from requesting a date for trial in the County Court?

2 Why does setting down usually take place so long after the due date for setting down ordered in the directions ? Why is the County Court date for requesting a hearing date taken more seriously?

3 At what various times must bundles of documents be lodged with the court before a High Court trial? Com-

pare the content of the different bundles that must be lodged. How does the time for lodging and the content of the bundles differ in the County Court?

4 What is the difference between the non-jury list and the short cause list? What is the difference between the general list and the warned list?

5 Can you have a fixed date for trial in the High Court? What are the advantages of having a fixed date?

6 What do you think are the most important procedural and practical matters to be undertaken just before trial?

7 What do you do if a witness refuses to attend the trial?

8 Why must updated statements of special damages be exchanged just before High Court trial?

9 How is counsel who is to represent the client in court given instructions and information on the case?

10 How is counsel's fee decided? What is a 'refresher fee'?

Chapter 26

Trial, judgments, costs orders and appeals

Rights of audience   26.1

At the time of writing, all *practising barristers* have a right of audience in the County Court, High Court and Court of Appeal.

Solicitors have full rights of audience in the County Court but do *not* have rights of audience in the High Court or Court of Appeal except for High Court proceedings in chambers.

However, part II of the Courts and Legal Services Act 1990, particularly ss.27 and 28, provides for regulations to be made, allowing solicitors and other authorised persons to appear in all courts. (It is expected that solicitors will soon have rights of audience in all courts.)

Note ───────────────────────────

1 Solicitors clerks have rights of audience in chambers in all courts.

2 Litigants acting in person, ie. litigants presenting the case themselves without a lawyer, have rights of audience in all courts and can bring a 'friend' to sit behind them to take notes and advise them: *R v Leicester City Justices ex parte Barrow* (1991). (3) Lay persons can represent a party in County Court small claims.

Order of proceedings at trial   26.2
(RSC O.33; CCR O.21)

Opening speeches and witnesses   26.2.1

Plaintiff The plaintiff's counsel/solicitor makes an *opening speech*, summarising the facts and issues, and often taking the judge through the pleadings, documents, correspondence and relevant plans and photographs.

The plaintiff then calls their *witnesses*. The witnesses swear an oath or affirmation and are then examined in chief by their own counsel, cross-examined by counsel for the other side, and then re-examined by their own counsel. (*See* Evidence Companion for principles.)

However, the judge may often order that the witness' witness statement should stand as their evidence in chief, so that the proceedings go straight to cross-examination. This will depend on whether the judge and other side want the witness' credibility to be tested by the evidence in chief being given orally.

Note

1 The plaintiff's counsel/solicitor will decide the order in which the witnesses should be called.

2 A barrister must not communicate with a witness whilst the witness is giving evidence, eg. during an evening or weekend break in the giving of evidence by the witness.

Defendant The defendant's counsel/solicitor may then make their *opening submissions* and will call their witnesses in the same way as the plaintiff.

Note

In the County Court they are usually only allowed to make an opening speech or a closing speech, not both.

26.2.2   Closing speeches

The defendant's counsel/solicitor will then make a closing speech, summarising their case and making factual and legal submissions, followed by the plaintiff's counsel/solicitor.

Before the plaintiff's counsel/solicitor has made the closing speech, the judge may indicate that the plaintiff has won by informing them that they need not make a speech.

Note

The judge may vary the order of proceedings and dispense with opening speeches.

26.2.3   Professional conduct

It is a rule of professional conduct that where counsel has been instructed, you are under a duty to attend court or to arrange for the attendance of a responsible representative throughout the proceedings.

The solicitor/representative should look after and advise clients and witnesses, liaise with, help and advise counsel, deal with any problems and take a verbatim note of the proceedings.

Note

In certain circumstances under the Bar Code of conduct, a

barrister may conduct the case without you or your representative being present.

Judgment (RSC O.42; CCR O.22)   26.3

The judge will give judgment immediately or give a re-served judgment, ie. at a later date.

Certificate of judgment   26.3.1

In the Queen's Bench Division, the court clerk known as the 'associate' of, drafts a certificate certifying the judgment given. In London, this certificate, and the pleadings lodged with the court on setting down, are sent to the solicitor for the winning party. In a district registry *outside London*, the winning party must collect the certificate and pleadings from the associate immediately after the hearing.

Drafting the judgment   26.3.2

In the Queen's Bench Division, the winning party's solicitor must draft the formal judgment (*see* forms 39–51, appendix A of *White Book*) and take it, together with the original writ (if they are the plaintiff) and copy pleadings, to the action department for sealing and entry in the records.

In the Chancery Division and County Court, the court itself drafts the judgment.

The judgment cannot be enforced, costs cannot be taxed and money cannot be paid out of court until the judgment has been drawn up.

Payment   26.3.3

High Court judgments are generally payable immediately but the loser can apply for a stay of execution under RSC O.47 r.1, although this only strictly prevents enforcement of the judgment by the 'seizure of goods' method (*see* Chapter 27, para. 27 3.10).

County Court judgments are payable 14 days from the date of judgment unless the court orders otherwise. It has power to order judgments to be paid by instalments, and either the judgment creditor or debtor may apply to the court for an order varying the method of time and payment.

In both courts, the judgment debt must be paid direct to the judgment creditor rather than to the court unless the winner is a minor or mental patient, in which case the money is generally directed to be paid into court and invested.

26.3.4   Interest

Judgment debts carry interest at a prescribed rate (currently 15%) until they are paid.

In the County Court, this only applies to judgments for not less than £5,000. (*See* Judgments Act 1838, s.17 and County Court (interest on judgment debts) Order 1991.)

26.4   Costs orders (RSC O.62; CCR O.38)

After judgment has been given, the winning party's advocate will ask the judge to make an order that the other side pay their costs, usually subject to a payment into court or Calderbank offer and to s.17, Legal Aid Act 1988.

The judge will normally order that the loser must pay the winner's costs ('costs follow the event') on the standard basis, such costs to be taxed if not agreed.

In the County Court, the judge will prescribe the scale on which the costs are to be taxed. In some County Court cases, eg. actions for possession of land, the judge will not order taxation of costs but will assess there and then the exact amount of costs to be paid by the loser.

At this stage, the judge will also make an order in respect of any previous interlocutory application where the costs were 'reserved', ie. the loser of the whole case was to pay the costs of that interlocutory application unless ordered otherwise by the trial judge.

Since all these costs matters are *discretionary*, both sides may make submissions as to any of these matters, eg. the loser may argue that, in the special circumstances of the case, they should not be ordered to pay the winner's costs.

Finally, if a party is legally aided, the judge will order a legal aid taxation of their costs, ie. a taxation as to the amount of costs to be paid by the Legal Aid Board to that party's solicitor.

(*See* Chapters 3 and 28 for details and meanings of the above.)

26.5   Other orders

If there has been a *payment into court*, the judge will be informed of this after judgment. The plaintiff, if they have won, will apply for an order for payment out and directions as to how the interest which has accrued on the money in court should be dealt with.

The loser may wish to apply for leave to appeal against the

judgment in those cases where leave is necessary: *see* below.

The party wishing to appeal may apply for a *stay of execution* (enforcement) of the judgment pending the appeal: *see* RSC O.59 r.13. It was held in *Linotype-Hell Finance Ltd v Baker* (1993) that where a party appealing against a monetary judgment can show that, without a stay of execution, they will be ruined and the appeal has some prospect of success, that is a legitimate ground for granting a stay: see *Linotype-Hell Finance Ltd v Baker* (1993).

However, in *Simonite v Sheffield City Council* (1993), Harman J reasserted the old practice that a stay would only be granted if the loser could show that there was no reasonable probability of recovering the damages and costs in the event that the appeal succeeded.

The principles in this area of stay of execution pending appeal are therefore unclear.

Appeals (RSC O.59)   26.6

Right of appeal to Court of Appeal   26.6.1

A party may appeal to the Court of Appeal against a decision of a High Court judge or a circuit (County Court) judge. Generally, leave to appeal is not required except against:

1   An interlocutory order, as opposed to a final order: s.18(1)(h), Supreme Court Act 1981. (RSC O.59 r.1A, and the notes thereto in the *White Book*, sets out rules as to which orders are interlocutory and which are final.)

> *Note*
>
> However, leave is not needed to appeal against an interlocutory order concerning the liberty of the subject or the grant or refusal of an injunction.

2   An order made with the consent of the parties.

3   A judge's order exercising their discretion as to costs.

Exceptions 2 and 3 are covered by s.18(1)(f), Supreme Court Act 1981.

4   A County Court judgment in a case where the value of the claim is below a certain amount (except where the judgment includes or preserves an injunction, or concerns the upbringing of a child), eg. a tort or contract claim for less than £5,000.

(*See* County Court Appeals order 1991 for full details – printed and explained in *White Book* and *Green Book*.)

Note _____

Section 7, Courts and Legal Services Act 1990 provides for changes in the rules as to when leave is required but this section has not yet come into force.

_____

In the cases of 1 and 4 above, a party can apply to the trial judge and/or the Court of Appeal for leave to appeal. In the cases of 2 and 3, a party can only apply to the trial judge for leave.

26.6.2 Procedure for appealing

Within four weeks of the judgment being sealed, the appellant must issue and serve notice of appeal.

The full details on procedure and principles governing appeals are set out in RSC O.59, and in the *Green Book* notes to s.77, County Courts Act 1984.

26.6.3 Appeal to the House of Lords

By virtue of the Administration of Justice (Appeals) Act 1934, a party can appeal to the House of Lords against a Court of Appeal decision, but *only* with leave of the Court of Appeal or House of Lords, and *only* on a *point of law of general public importance.*

A party may appeal directly from the High Court to the House of Lords (the 'leapfrog' procedure) if the conditions in ss.12 and 13, Administration of Justice Act 1969 are satisfied.

26.6.4 European Courts

A case may be:

- Referred to the European Court of Justice for a decision on a point of European Community law: *see* RSC O.114 and CCR O.19 r.11; or

- Taken to the European Court of Human Rights, using the right of individual petition under Article 25 of the European Convention on Human Rights.

Self-assessment questions

1 In which courts do solicitors have a right to present the case?

2 How many speeches does the defendant's advocate make? What is the difference between examination-in-chief and cross-examination? Why is examination-in-chief not always carried out?

3 Who drafts the court judgment?

4 What matters may be argued about after the judge has
   given judgment?
5 List the cases where leave to appeal is needed.

Chapter 27

Enforcement of judgments

Matters to be considered 27.1

Even if the plaintiff wins the case against the defendant, that is often by no means the end of the matter. The plaintiff must then consider how to get the money from the defendant, or how to get possession of the land, or enforce the injunction etc, as the case may be.

In the case of a *money judgment*, the plaintiff's solicitor must consider, as appropriate, whether:

- The defendant can be found;
- The plaintiff can discover how much money and what assets the defendant has, and their whereabouts;
- The defendant is worth suing (they may not have the money); and
- How the plaintiff can obtain the money from the defendant.

Note _____

After judgment, the winner is referred to as the *judgment creditor*, and the loser as the *judgment debtor*. Those terms will be used in the rest of this chapter.

Discovering the judgment debtor's money and assets 27.2

The creditor can:

- Carry out an *oral examination* of the debtor (*see* below);
- Make an *official company search*, where the debtor is a company;
- Seek a post-judgment *Mareva injunction*, which could include a requirement that the debtor discloses their accounts and assets;
- Employ an *inquiry agent* to investigate;
- Apply for an *order allowing inspection of the debtors bank accounts* under s.7, Bankers' Books Evidence Act 1879.

Oral examination 27.2.1

The most common and useful method of discovering the debtor's assets and their whereabouts is to apply to court

for an order allowing you to orally examine the debtor: RSC
O.48; CCR O.25. This enables the creditor (usually their
lawyer) to cross-examine the debtor as to their debts and
assets in front of a court officer; the debtor is usually
ordered to produce relevant books and documents.

The cross-examination can be extensive and 'of the
severest kind': *see Republic of Costa Rica v Strousberg* (1880).
The debtor will be in contempt of court if they fail to attend
or to answer the questions.

High Court procedure

The creditor applies *ex parte* for an order for oral examination (paying a fee), with an affidavit:

- Showing that they are entitled to enforce the judgment;
- Identifying the judgment by date and serial number;
- Stating the amount remaining unpaid (*see* practice Forms
  98 and 99 in *White Book*, vol 2, part 2); and
- Stating the debtor's last known address and the appropriate County Court venue for the examination (*see*
  below).

The affidavit should be placed before the master/district
judge.

If the order is granted, it should be served personally on
the debtor, or on any company officer where the debtor is a
company. The order will contain a penal notice, warning
the debtor of the consequences of contempt of court, ie.
imprisonment, sequestration of assets or a fine.

The examination will usually be ordered to take place at
the County Court for the area where the debtor resides. The
debtor will be given their expenses of attending (this is
known as 'conduct money').

The examination will be held in front of an officer of the
court.

County Court procedure

The procedure is similar to the High Court procedure
(including payment of a fee) but Form N316 (request for
oral examination) is used, together with a certificate of
interest due in the case of a judgment exceeding £5,000.

The order must be served in the same manner as a
default summons.

Note

In both courts, the creditor will be entitled to their costs of the
examination, if oral examination was justified.

Methods of enforcing the judgment   **27.3**

Post-judgment *Mareva* injunction   **27.3.1**

A *Mareva* injunction may be granted after judgment to help enforcement where there are grounds for believing the debtor intends to dispose of assets in order to avoid execution of the judgment: *Orwell Steel Ltd v Asphalt and Tarmac UK Ltd* (1984), and County Court Remedies Regulations 1991, 3(3)(c)). (*See* Chapter 9 for full details.)

Seizure and sale of the debtor's goods   **27.3.2**

In order to satisfy a money judgment, the creditor can apply for an order that the sheriff (the term for a High Court enforcement officer) or the bailiff (County Court) should seize and sell the debtor's goods in order to satisfy the debt, the costs of the proceedings and the costs of enforcement: RSC O.46 and 47; CCR O.26.

Where the debt is *more than £5,000*, execution by seizure and sale can only be carried out through the *High Court*, where it is *less than £2,000* only through the County Court, and where it is between £2,000 and £5,000, the creditor can choose the court.

Note

The High Court is often preferred because sheriffs are considered more efficient than bailiffs, and interest on a judgment for less than £5,000 can only be claimed in the High Court.

High Court procedure

The creditor must deliver at court:

- A *request* for a writ of execution; (The request is known as a *praecipe* and can be found at practice Form 86, *White Book*, vol 2.)
- The *judgment*;
- Two *copies* of the proposed writ of execution, known as a writ of *fieri facias*, or ('Fi Fa');
- The *court fee*; and
- The *certificate* showing their entitlement to the costs of the action.

The court will then draw up and issue a writ of execution, which is a writ delivered to the under-sheriff directing the sheriff to seize and sell sufficient of the debtor's goods to satisfy the debt and costs.

County Court procedure

The creditor must file at court a request for the issue of a warrant of execution (Form N323) and pay the fee. The court will issue a warrant, directing the bailiffs to seize and sell.

Manner of seizure and sale

The sheriffs or bailiffs go to the debtor's residential or business premises. They cannot force their way into the debtor's house (*Vaughan v McKenzie* (1969)) or break open the front door (*Hodder v Williams* (1895)) but they can break open the front door of business premises: (*Hodder v Williams*).

They cannot seize:

- Such tools, books, vehicles and other items of equipment as are necessary for the debtor's personal use in the debtor's employment, business or vocation;
- Clothing, bedding, furniture, household equipment and provisions which are necessary for the basic domestic needs of the debtor and their family;
- Money, bank notes, bills of exchange, promissory notes, bonds, securities for money;

  (Authorities for the above exceptions are s.138(3A), Supreme Court Act 1981 and s.89, County Courts Act 1984.)

- Goods on hire purchase.

In practice, the sheriffs/bailiffs do not usually take the goods away, but sign a 'walking possession' agreement with the debtor – the goods are left on the premises until sale on condition that the debtor undertakes not to remove the goods or to permit their removal: Form in *White Book*, vol 2, para.1081 and County Court form N42(c).

The goods are then sold, usually by public auction, and the judgment, costs and enforcement fees are satisfied out of the proceeds.

(For more details on sale, see s.138, Supreme Court Act 1981, Sheriffs' fees section in *White Book*, vol 2, and ss.89–102, County Courts Act 1984 .)

Note

As to the effect of the debtor's insolvency on seizure and sale *see* ss. 183, 184 and 346, Insolvency Act 1986.

27.3.3 Garnishee proceedings

Meaning

It may be that the debtor is owed money by a third party. Through garnishee proceedings, the judgment creditor can obtain a court order that the third party should pay the money over to the judgment creditor and not to the judgment debtor: RSC O.49; CCR O.30.

This method of enforcement is most commonly used to obtain money from the debtor's bank account, since the bank technically owes money to the debtor when the debtor's account is in credit.

Therefore, a garnishee order is typically where the debtor's bank or building society (known as 'the garnishee') is ordered to pay money from the debtor's account over to the creditor, to satisfy the judgment.

The creditor will hopefully have discovered what bank accounts the debtor has through oral examination.

Procedure

The judgment creditor applies *ex parte* to the Master/district judge, with an affidavit stating the:

- Name and address of the debtor;
- Amount unpaid; and
- Name, branch and number of the garnishee bank account.

The Master/district judge will then make an order that the garnishee and debtor should attend a further hearing to 'show cause' why a garnishee order should not be made. This first order is known as a 'garnishee order nisi'.

This 'nisi' order must be served personally on the garnishee at least 15 days before the further hearing, and on the debtor at least seven days before the further hearing. (A bank/building society must be served at its registered office but a copy is usually sent to the relevant branch.)

At the further hearing, if the garnishee does not attend or does not dispute the debt owed to the judgment debtor, the court has discretion as to whether to make a final 'garnishee order absolute'.

The court will *not* make a garnishee order absolute if, for example:

- The debt is *disputed*;
- There is *insufficient money* in the account;
- The order would give the creditor an *advantage* over other unsecured creditors: *Rainbow v Moorgate Properties Ltd* (1975); or
- A debtor company has been wound up since the order nisi: *Roberts Petroleum v Bernard Kenny Ltd* (1983). (For the relationship of garnishee proceedings to the debtor's insolvency, *see* ss.183, 184 and 346, Insolvency Act 1986 and notes to RSC O.49.)

The garnishee order will usually cover such sum as is sufficient to cover the judgment debt, and costs.

Note

Banks/building societies usually comply with a garnishee order as a matter of course.

27.3.4   Charging orders

Under the Charging Orders Act 1979, the court has power to impose a charge on:

- The debtor's land;
- Stocks (other than building society stocks) held by the debtor;
- The debtor's beneficial interest under a trust.

The charging order makes the creditor a secured creditor and the creditor can then enforce the charge by obtaining an order for sale of the charged property, the debt being satisfied out of the proceeds of sale.

Procedure

The creditor applies *ex parte* with an affidavit to the Master/district judge (*see* RSC O.49 and CCR O.31 for full affidavit details).

Note

The High Court only has power to impose a charging order where the judgment debt exceeds £5,000.

The Master/district judge will make an order that the debtor and any other person interested should attend a further hearing to 'show cause' why a charging order should not be made. This first order is known as a *charging order nisi*. If the charged asset is *land*, the order nisi should be registered as a caution in the Land Register.

This nisi order is then served on the debtor and certain other persons at least seven days before the further hearing.

At the further hearing, the Master/district judge will decide whether to make a *charging order absolute*, taking into account all the circumstances, particularly the personal circumstances of the debtor and whether any other creditor of the debtor would be likely to be unduly prejudiced by the making of the order: s.1(5), Charging Orders Act 1979. For example, the considerations mentioned above as to the making of a garnishee order absolute apply; further, a charge is unlikely to be imposed on an asset of substantial value in respect of a relatively small debt. (For the effect of insolvency, *see* notes to RSC O.50.)

Note

Between the nisi and absolute stage the Master/district judge may also grant an injunction restraining the debtor from disposing of the charged asset.

Land

If the charged asset is land, the charge should be registered in the Land Registry by a *notice* or *caution*. Where the land is co-owned, the charge will be on the debtor's beneficial share. The creditor can then apply for sale of the legal estate under s.30, LPA 1925: See *Harman v Glencross* (1986), *Austin-Fell v Austin-Fell* (1990), *Midland Bank v Pike* (1988), *Lloyds Bank plc v Byrne* (1991).

Application for sale

Once a charge has been imposed on the debtor's property, the creditor can apply for sale of the property to satisfy the debt out of the proceeds of sale. The creditor applies for sale in the High Court by originating summons (using RSC O.88 procedure) and in the County Court by originating application (using CCR O.31 r.4 procedure).

However, proceedings to enforce sale can only be taken in the County Court where the judgment debt does not exceed £30,000: s.23(c), County Courts Act 1984.

Appointment of a receiver

27.3.5

It may be that the debtor is entitled to income from, for example, the letting of property, or from a trust fund or a business. In such cases, where no other method of enforcement is possible, equity will appoint a responsible person to take the debtor's place, receive the income and use it to satisfy the judgment.

Procedure

The creditor applies for the appointment of a receiver by summons/notice of application with an affidavit: RSC O.51; CCR O.32. The court will consider whether it is just or convenient to appoint a receiver having regard to the amount claimed, the amount likely to be obtained by the receiver and to the probable costs of the receiver's appointment.

The court will appoint a 'responsible person', eg. a solicitor, to be a receiver. The receiver will have to give security for the carrying out of their duties, ie. give a guarantee to pay for any losses caused due to their default. They will be entitled to remuneration for their work.

Attachment of earnings

27.3.6

Where the debtor is in employment, a useful method of enforcement is to apply for an attachment of earnings order under the Attachment of Earnings Act 1971; CCR O.27. This is an order compelling the debtor's employer to make regular deductions from the debtor's earnings and to pay them into court. (The employer may be convicted of an offence and fined for not complying.)

Procedure
The creditor applies by filing at the County Court an application in Form N337, with an affidavit in Form N321. The court office will send to the debtor notice of the application and a statement of means to be filled in by the debtor. The debtor must then return this within eight days.

Note

The *High Court* only has power to make an attachment of earnings order in certain Family Division cases. Even in the case of a High Court judgment, the creditor must apply for such an order to the County Court for the district in which the debtor resides.

Initially, the matter is not decided by a court hearing. The court officer will decide whether to make an attachment of earnings order and the rate and periods of deduction of earnings. If the officer does not have sufficient information to make a decision, or either party objects to the officer's order, there will be a hearing in front of the district judge.

The order is then served on the debtor and employer. The order specifies the normal rate of deduction from earnings, but also a 'protected earnings rate' – a minimum net wage set by the court. The order will provide that deductions must not be made which will reduce the debtor's earnings below this minimum wage.

27.3.7   Imprisonment, fine or sequestration of assets to enforce an injunction

A party who has failed to comply with an injunction (or undertaking given instead) will be in *contempt of court* and can be committed to prison or fined: *see* generally Contempt of Court Act 1981; County Courts (Penalties for Contempt) Act 1983; RSC O.52, CCR O.29.

Note

If the party is a company, a director, or other officer, can be imprisoned or fined.

Further, a party who fails to comply with an injunction can have their assets seized under a writ of sequestration: RSC O.46 r.5, ss.38 and 76, CCA 1984. Four sequestrators are appointed to seize and detain the party's property until the injunction is complied with. The sequestrators will need further court orders in order to be able to, for example, sell or let the property.

Judgments for possession of land or for delivery of goods 27.3.8

Possession of land
In the *High Court*, a judgment for possession of land is enforced by writ of possession: *see* RSC O.45 r.3 (but *see* O.88 in relation to mortgage possession actions and O.113 in relation to eviction of squatters). The sheriff's officers enforce the judgment.

In the *County Court*, possession is enforced by a warrant of possession, executed by the bailiffs: *see* CCR O.26 r.17 (and O.24 in relation to squatters).

> *Note*
>
> A detailed knowledge of housing and landlord and tenant litigation is required in this area.

Delivery of goods
A judgment for delivery of goods is enforced in the *High Court* by writ of delivery (RSC O.45 r.4) and in the *County Court* by warrant of delivery (CCR O.26 r.16).

Insolvency proceedings 27.3.9

As methods of enforcing a judgment
An important weapon in enforcing a judgment is the threat or presentation of a bankruptcy petition against an individual debtor or the threat or presentation of a winding-up petition against a company debtor.

The threat or presentation of the petition may well force the debtor to pay up because of the bad publicity and because, after the presentation of the petition, the debtor cannot dispose of their property without the court's permission: s.284 and 127, Insolvency Act 1986. Further, the winding-up of a company would eventually lead to the company going out of existence.

> *Note*
>
> Although explained here in relation to enforcement of a judgment, bankruptcy and winding-up proceedings can be used *at any time* to recover a debt as an alternative to ordinary litigation.

Personal insolvency
A creditor may present a bankruptcy petition where the debt exceeds £750 and either the creditor has served a

statutory demand (Insolvency Regulations (IR) 6.1–6.5) on the debtor claiming the debt and the demand has not been complied with within three weeks, or enforcement of the judgment by other methods have not satisfied the judgment (ss.264–271, IA). The debtor may challenge the demand: *see* IR 6.4 and 6.5.

In London, the petition is presented at the Bankruptcy Registry of the High Court. Outside London, it is presented at the County Court where the debtor has resided or carried on business longest during the previous six months. The petition procedure is set out at IR 6.6–6.36.

The debtor may prevent bankruptcy by:

- *Paying* the debt;
- Applying for an *interim order*, which prevents further proceedings for 14 days (initially) while a *voluntary arrangement* is put forward in settlement: ss.252–263;
- *Opposing* the petition, eg. on the ground that the debt is not due or can be paid: s.271;
- Offering to *secure* or *compound* for the debt: s.271.

The court may dismiss, stay or adjourn the petition, or make a bankruptcy order. If an order is made, the bankrupt can no longer deal with their property, which is then managed by the official receiver until title to it vests in the trustee in bankruptcy. (The IA contains detailed provisions as to how the bankrupt's estate is to be dealt with.)

Where the debtor is adjudged bankrupt, any disposition of their property by the debtor after presentation of the petition is void, unless made with the consent of the court: s.284. This is an important effect of the petition and may force a debtor to pay up even if the petition is only threatened.

On the other hand, where the debtor is adjudged bankrupt, the creditor is not entitled to retain the benefit of any other method of execution already begun, eg. seizure and sale, garnishee, charging order, appointment of a receiver, unless that execution is completed before the date of the bankruptcy order: s.346, IA. Thus, it may be desirable to pursue these other methods of enforcement rather than commence bankruptcy proceedings because bankruptcy means that all available assets will have to be shared among all the creditors and also used to pay the costs of the insolvency (*see* below).

Corporate insolvency

A company may be wound up by the court if, *inter alia*, it is unable to pay its debts: s.122, IA. It will be deemed unable to pay its debts if the debt exceeds £750:

- The creditor has served a statutory demand (IR 4.4–4.6) on the debtor claiming the debt and the demand has not been complied with within three weeks;
- Other methods of enforcing the judgment have not satisfied the judgment; or
- It is proved that the company is unable to pay its debts; or
- It is proved that the value of the company's assets is less than the amount of its liabilities.

The creditor applies for the winding-up of the company by presenting a winding-up petition. If the company's paid-up share capital does not exceed £120,000, the petition can be issued in the County Court for the district in which the company's registered office is situated: s.117(2). Otherwise, the petition is issued in the Companies Court in the Chancery Division of the High Court, or in one of the Chancery District Registries outside London.

Note

The creditor's solicitor should search the Companies Court central index of petitions to see if a petition has already been issued against the debtor by another creditor.

The procedure for the presentation of the petition is set out in IR 4.7–4.24. Important points are that the petition is advertised before the hearing, and that other creditors or contributories (defined in s.79) can appear at the hearing to support or oppose the petition.

The debtor company often initially challenges the petition by quickly claiming an injunction restraining presentation of the petition or (importantly for the company's reputation) restraining the advertisement of the petition. The company applies for the injunction by originating motion to a judge of the Companies Court. The injunction will be granted if the company:

- Has a prospect of success in defending the petition; and
- Is solvent.

Petitions are heard in open court by the Registrar of the Companies Court in London or by a district judge outside London. Many petitions are heard and are dealt with quickly, particularly if they are unopposed, when a formal winding-up order is quickly made. However, there are often procedural disputes, or an extra creditor or contributor applies to be added to the list of people appearing. In some cases, the hearing is adjourned.

If the petition is *opposed*, the registrar will adjourn the matter for it to be heard by the judge of the Companies Court.

An effect of a winding-up order is that it *renders void any disposition of the company's property* made after the presentation of the petition unless the court orders otherwise: s.127. This, and the advertisement of the petition, may be factors which force the company to pay up when a petition is threatened.

On the other hand, as with the bankruptcy process, where the debtor company is wound up, the creditor is not entitled to retain the benefit of any execution already begun unless the execution was completed before presentation of the petition: ss.183–184. Thus, it may be desirable to pursue these other methods of enforcement rather than to present a winding-up petition.

Once the winding-up order has been made, the winding up is conducted by the liquidator. (This process is outside the scope of the litigation companion but *see* the companion on *Corporate Insolvency*.)

Insolvency process or ordinary litigation?
Although insolvency procedure is discussed above in the context of enforcement of judgments, it is a procedure that can be used on its own as an alternative to suing for a debt by writ or summons. The question is should a creditor claim a debt by suing by writ/summons and then entering judgment in default or claiming summary judgment, or should the creditor claim the debt by issuing a bankruptcy/winding-up petition?

The creditor should consider the following factors:

- The courts prefer a debt, particularly if it is disputed, to be claimed through writ or summons followed by summary judgment, rather than through insolvency proceedings: *see Re a company* (1992) 1 WLR 351.

- The insolvency process is complex and expensive, and gives various chances to the debtor to challenge the proceedings. Further, the insolvency process brings in other creditors who will share in the debtor's assets and the creditor who initiated the process may not recover all their money, or may recover nothing, due to other creditors having priority.

- On the other hand, insolvency is much more of a threat to the debtor than the threat of straightforward summary judgment litigation. The mere threat of insolvency or a statutory demand may force the debtor to pay up.

- The insolvency process enables the creditor to re-open past transactions by the debtor or take misfeasance proceedings against the debtor or its directors.

If the creditor decides to pursue the ordinary litigation route, they should pursue this route quickly if there is a possibility that the debtor owes money to others, who may start insolvency proceedings. Such proceedings would prevent the creditor from continuing with their own action: ss.126, 130, and 285, IA.

The most appropriate method?   27.3.10

This will first depend on what property the debtor has.

Oral examination
It is important to begin with an oral examination.

Seizure of goods
This is usually the first option considered. The problems with this method are that:

- The debtor might not have sufficient seizable goods on the premises;
- There may be disputes about whether goods are owned by the debtor;
- County Court bailiffs are notoriously inefficient; and
- High Court sheriffs are expensive.

Garnishee order
This should be considered next. However, there may not be enough money in the accounts.

Charging order
A charging order, usually on land, is the next possibility. However, there may not be enough value left in the land once prior creditors, eg. mortgagees, have been satisfied, particularly if the land is co-owned. Also, there will be a delay before sale takes place, and in some cases the court may refuse to order sale.

Appointment of a receiver
This can only be used in certain types of cases and when other methods have failed. It is also expensive.

Attachment of earnings order
This is only really appropriate when an individual is in regular employment. It is also a method of last resort, since it is difficult to apply successfully for some other method of execution once the debtor's earnings have been attached.

Insolvency
You have a general survey of this method of enforcement above (*see* 35.3.9) and further detail on this more specialised subject would be outside the scope of this companion (but *see* companions on *Business Law and Practice* and *Corporate Insolvency*).

Note

1 Throughout, the creditor must bear in mind that the costs of the proceedings will be added to by the costs of enforcement, though these costs are generally recoverable. 2 There are particular rules as to how judgments may be enforced against a partnership (*see* RSC O.81 r.5; CCR O.25 r.9)

27.3.11   Enforcement of judgments outside England and Wales and enforcement of foreign judgments in England and Wales

There are statutes and rules of court providing for reciprocal enforcement of judgments between:

- EC countries and between UK countries (Civil Jurisdiction and Judgments Act 1982, RSC O.71, CCR O.35);

- Certain countries under the Administration of Justice Act 1920 and the Foreign Judgments (Reciprocal Enforcement) Act 1933 (RSC O.71, CCR O.35); and

- States within the European Free Trade Association who have ratified the Lugano Convention (Civil Jurisdiction and Judgments Act 1991).

Self-assessment questions

1 Your client has obtained judgment for £10,000 against Mr Smith, the freeholder of 16, The Vale and who works as manager for a company. In what ways could the judgment be enforced, and what factors would you consider? How could you discover what assets Mr Smith has?

2 How would your answer to question 1 differ if the judgment was against a company?

3 What is meant by the following:

(a) a penal notice

(b) conduct money

(c) a writ of 'Fi Fa'

(d) a praecipe

(e) a 'walking possession' agreement?

(f) a sheriff

(g) a garnishee order

(h) a charging order nisi

(i) a writ of sequestration?

4 By what methods do bailiffs usually sell seized goods?

5 If a charging order is imposed on land, does that mean that the land is immediately sold?

6 Is a charging order on land imposed on the legal estate or the beneficial interest(s)?

7 What unusual rules of procedure apply to an attachment of earnings application?

8 What is the sanction for failing to comply with an injunction?

9 Why will the presentation of an insolvency petition often force the debtor to pay up?

10 Which courts hear a petition for:

(a) bankruptcy

(b) winding-up?

11 What is the effect of a bankruptcy or winding-up order on other methods of enforcing the debt?

12 What common court application is made by a debtor or company faced with a petition?

13 Are the costs of enforcement generally recoverable from the debtor?

14 What is the usual non-insolvency process for claiming a debt in the courts?

Chapter 28

Taxation

Meaning

Taxation (a technical term which has no relation to the usual meaning of the word) is the process by which the court decides:

- Exactly how much money, in figures, one party should pay to another under a costs order; or
- Exactly how much your client, or the Legal Aid Board, should pay you in satisfaction of your bill.

As we explained in Chapter 3 (which you should read in conjunction with this chapter), at the end of the case the loser is usually ordered to pay the winner's costs on the standard basis, ie. such of the winner's costs as are reasonable in nature and amount. The judge does not actually specify in figures how much of the winner's costs are to be paid by the loser; the actual amount to be paid is decided, in the event that the parties cannot agree it themselves, at a court hearing called a taxation, which takes place a few months after the trial.

Example

P sues D. P wins. D is ordered to pay P's costs on the standard basis. P's solicitor's bill is £50,000. The parties fail to agree on how much of that sum should be paid by D. They therefore apply for a taxation hearing. At the hearing, the Taxing Master (High Court) or District Judge (County Court) rules that only £30,000 of P's solicitor's bill is reasonable. Therefore, D only has to pay £30,000 to P's solicitor.

The £20,000 balance of the bill has to be paid by P (subject to P challenging the bill on taxation on the indemnity basis).

Taxation is also the process by which the court decides how much the Legal Aid Board must pay to the assisted party's solicitor for their work done on the case, and the process by which the court decides exactly how much a privately paying client should pay to their solicitor for work done where the client challenges their solicitor's bill.

Taxation as between party and party and as between each party and their solicitor (or as between the Legal Aid Board and solicitor) is usually decided at the same hearing. However, different bases of taxation apply (*see* 28.2).

Note _____

In practice, parties often agree on the amount to be paid under a costs order in order to avoid the expense and delay of taxation. Further, it is uncommon for a party to challenge their own solicitor's bill by taxation. However, it is normal for there to be a taxation of the amount to be paid by the Legal Aid Board to the assisted person's solicitor, although there are exceptions to this (*see* Chapter 4).

28.2   The basis of taxation

The court may tax costs, ie. decide how much should be paid, either on the standard basis or on the indemnity basis.

28.2.1   Standard or indemnity basis

If the court uses the *standard basis*, it will order the payment of such costs as are reasonable in nature and amount. Any doubt as to reasonableness will be resolved in favour of the *paying* party.

If the court uses the *indemnity basis*, it will order the payment of *all* costs except insofar as they are of an unreasonable amount or have been unreasonably incurred. Any doubt as to reasonableness is resolved in favour of the *receiving* party.

The effect is that more costs will be payable if the indemnity basis is used than if the standard basis is used.

28.2.2   Which basis?

As between the parties, the loser will usually be ordered to pay the winner on the *standard* basis. The indemnity basis is only used in some cases, eg. where the loser has conducted the litigation in a morally reprehensible manner.

The Legal Aid Board will pay the assisted party's solicitor on the *standard* basis. The usual result of this and the previous point is that the amount paid out by the Legal Aid Board and recovered from the other side will be a similar amount, although there maybe some short fall because the other side may not have to pay for certain matters relating to legal aid procedure.

A bill as between solicitor and client will be taxed on the *indemnity* basis. This means there is usually a shortfall between the amount of costs a client has to pay to their solicitor (say £60,000) and the amount recovered from the other side which is taxed on the standard basis, not on the indemnity basis (say £40,000).

County Court scales 28.3

In the County Court, the amount of costs to be paid by one side to another is not governed just by the basis of taxation but also by the appropriate *scale* of costs. There is an ascending scale of maximum amounts of costs allowable on taxation which depends on the item of work done and the amount of damages claimed in the action. There are three scales.

- Lower scale: £25–£100
- Scale 1: £100–£3,000
- Scale 2: Above £3,000

The sums indicated are the amounts recovered if the plaintiff wins, or the amount claimed if the defendant wins.

Example

Assume the plaintiff wins £2,000 in damages. The defendant will usually be ordered to pay the plaintiff's costs on the standard basis and under Scale 1. Under Scale 1, using present figures, the plaintiff can, for example, only recover from the other side up to £31.50 in respect of the costs of preparing, issuing and serving proceedings. Other figures apply to other items of work.

Thus, on taxation the District Judge will decide what is a reasonable sum, up to a maximum of £31.50, for the defendant to pay to the plaintiff in respect of the plaintiff's costs of preparing, issuing and serving proceedings.

Note

Under Scale 2, there are no maximum amounts set. As in the High Court, the amount of costs recoverable in Scale 2 claims is in the District Judge's discretion, subject to the basis used.

An outline of the taxation process 28.4

Assume D has been ordered to pay P's costs on the standard basis. P's solicitors bill is £50,000. P and D cannot agree how much of that is reasonable so the matter goes to taxation. P's solicitor prepares a detailed formal bill supported by the relevant case files and other documents. On the bill, P sets out all the work done on the case in chronological order. Alongside this are columns setting out the amount of profit costs, expenses and VAT claimed for each item of work.

The taxation consists of the court deciding whether each piece of work:

- Was actually carried out;
- Was reasonable in nature and duration; and

- Whether the amount claimed is reasonable.

The court will tax off, ie. cross out or reduce, any item of work or amount claimed which it decides is unreasonable.

28.5   Taxation procedure (RSC O.62 rr.29–35; CCR O.38 rr.20–24)

The plaintiff's solicitor draws up a detailed bill of their costs. (This is discussed in more detail below.)

High Court cases in London are taxed at the Supreme Court Taxing Office by a Taxing Master or Taxing Officer. High Court cases outside London, and County Court cases, are taxed by the District Judge or a Taxing Officer.

Within three months after the judgment (in the case of taxation between parties), the party requiring taxation must lodge their bill at court with all necessary documents as listed in the rules, for example, the:

- Judgment;
- Legal aid certificates;
- Counsel's fee notes;
- Pleadings;
- Attendance notes;
- Medical reports.

A copy of the bill must be served on every other party. In the County Court, the copies of the bill are filed in court, and the court serves them on the other parties.

In the *High Court*, the Taxing Officer gives to all parties not less than 14 days notice of the date of the taxation hearing. In the *County Court*, the District Judge will provisionally tax the bill without a hearing, although the parties will be given an opportunity to give notice that they require a hearing. After a provisional taxation, the District Judge will issue a certificate stating the amount they propose to allow and requiring a party to notify the Court within 14 days if they require a hearing in order to object to the provisional taxation. (Provisional taxation is possible in the High Court.)

At the *taxation hearing*, or provisional taxation, the Taxing Master/District Judge will decide the amount of costs that can be recovered. The *inter partes* and legal aid taxations will be decided together.

After the taxation a certificate of the costs allowed is issued by the Court. In a legal aid case a special summary of the costs allowed must be endorsed on the bill.

A party dissatisfied with a taxation may request a review by the taxing office. There is provision for further review by a circuit or High Court judge.

In a legal-aid case, once the certificate of costs allowed has been received, the solicitor for the legally aided party completes CLA16, which is the report on the case and the claim for costs from the Legal Aid Board. When the other side sends a cheque in payment of the costs, the solicitor sends this on, in reimbursement, to the Legal Aid Board.

Presenting a formal bill for taxation 28.6

Drafting bills 28.6.1

Court rules and practice directions require the bill to be set out in a certain formal manner. The drafting of the bill is a specialist skill, requiring long experience. Indeed, there are specialist firms of legal costs experts who do nothing but draft bills for taxation and represent parties at taxation hearings; solicitors may employ these experts to draft the bill. Alternatively, many large firms have their own in-house costs experts. Thus, you cannot be expected to have detailed knowledge of taxation procedure and how to draft a bill although you should be aware of the general layout of a bill for taxation.

Form 28.6.2

The bill should commence with a succinct narrative of the entire case. This should be followed by a statement showing the status and expense rates of the fee-earners who did the work.

The bill should then set out in chronological order, with dates, all the work done on the case, under the following headings:

Item 1: Interlocutory hearings

Item 2: Conferences with counsel

Item 3: Attendance at trial

Item 4: Preparation of case throughout

Item 5: The work done for taxation itself.

Note

The costs of the taxation process itself should be borne in mind as it will significantly increase the costs of the proceedings

Under each item a claim can be made in respect of:

- The direct cost of the work, which depends on the amount needed to cover salary and overheads;
- Care and conduct – a sum allowing for a profit element

and to cover imponderables such as general supervision of subordinate staff;

● Travelling and waiting time.

Note

Amounts are allowed for each letter and phone call.

The chronological list of work done appears in the middle of the bill. On the right hand side are three columns showing the profit costs, disbursements, ie. expenses such as counsel's fees and court fees, and VAT.

On the left hand side is a column for items 'taxed off' by the taxing Master/district judge. In this column the Master/Judge indicates any reduction/disallowance that they make.

If a legal aid taxation is being carried out as well as an *inter partes* taxation, ie. the court is deciding how much the Legal Aid Board should pay to the assisted party's solicitor as well as how much that party should recover from the other party, the bill will contain *six* columns on the right hand side instead of three. This is because the columns are duplicated in respect of profit costs, disbursements and VAT. The court must decide the amounts claimable separately for the legal aid taxation and the *inter partes* taxation.

Some items of work, eg. legal aid enquiries, may be payable by the Legal Aid Board but not recoverable from the other side.

28.7   Deciding on the amount recoverable

Assume there is an item of work headed 'attending meeting with client (4 hours)' for which the solicitor is claiming £100 an hour. The Master/Judge may decide the meeting was unnecessary or unreasonably long or the rate of £100 an hour is unreasonably high. The Master/Judge will reduce the amount claimed to what they consider to be a reasonable amount. They will indicate the reduction in the left hand column of the bill.

The other side attends the hearing to make as many objections as possible to the amounts and items claimed.

The amounts recoverable on taxation are a matter of *discretion* for the Master/Judge, depending on what is reasonable. The Master/Judge will have regard to, for example, the:

● Complexity of the item of work;

● Skill and labour involved;

● Level of responsibility of the person who carried out the work;